FIFTH EDITION

2A

GRAMMAR *in* CONTEXT

SANDRA N. ELBAUM

The cover photo shows the
San Francisco-Oakland Bay
Bridge over San Francisco Bay
in California.

HEINLE
CENGAGE Learning™

Australia • Brazil • Japan • Korea • Mexico • Singapore • Spain • United Kingdom • United States

Grammar in Context 2A, Fifth Edition
Student Book
Sandra N. Elbaum

Publisher: Sherrise Roehr

Acquisitions Editor: Tom Jefferies

Development Editor: Sarah Sandoski

Technology Development Manager:
  Debie Mirtle

Director of Global Marketing: Ian Martin

Director of US Marketing: Jim McDonough

Product Marketing Manager: Katie Kelley

Marketing Manager: Caitlin Driscoll

Content Project Manager: Andrea Bobotas

Senior Print Buyer: Susan Spencer

Project Manager: Chrystie Hopkins

Production Services: Nesbitt Graphics, Inc.

Interior Design and Cover Design:
  Muse Group, Inc.

© 2010 Sandra N. Elbaum

Library of Congress Control Number: 2009936998

ISBN 13: 978-1-4240-8090-8

ISBN 10: 1-4240-8090-8

Heinle

20 Channel Center Street

Boston, Massachusetts 02210

USA

Cengage Learning is a leading provider of customized learning solutions with office locations around the globe, including Singapore, the United Kingdom, Australia, Mexico, Brazil, and Japan. Locate our local office at international.cengage.com/region

Cengage Learning products are represented in Canada by Nelson Education, Ltd.

Visit Heinle online at **elt.heinle.com**

Visit our corporate website at **www.cengage.com**

Printed in China.
4 5 6 7 8 9 10 — 13

Contents

Lesson 3

Grammar Context

Lesson 4

Grammar Context

Lesson 5

Lesson 6

Lesson 9

Lesson 10

Grammar Context

Lesson 11

Grammar Context

Lesson 12

Lesson 13

Lesson 14

Appendices

Index

Acknowledgments

Many thanks to Dennis Hogan, Sherrise Roehr, and Tom Jefferies from Heinle Cengage for their ongoing support of the *Grammar in Context* series. I would especially like to thank my development editor, Sarah Sandoski, for her patience, sensitivity, keen eye to detail, and invaluable suggestions.

And many thanks to my students at Truman College, who have increased my understanding of my own language and taught me to see life from another point of view. By sharing their observations, questions, and life stories, they have enriched my life enormously.

This new edition is dedicated to the millions of displaced people in the world. The U.S. is the new home to many refugees, who survived unspeakable hardships in Burundi, Rwanda, Sudan, Burma, Bhutan, and other countries. Their resiliency in starting a new life and learning a new language is a tribute to the human spirit.—*Sandra N. Elbaum*

Heinle would like to thank the following people for their contributions:

Elizabeth A. Adler-Coleman
Sunrise Mountain High
  School
Las Vegas, NV

Dorothy Avondstondt
Miami Dade College
Miami, FL

Judith A. G. Benka
Normandale Community
  College
Bloomington, MN

Carol Brutza
Gateway Community
  College
New Haven, CT

Lyn Buchheit
Community College of
  Philadelphia
Philadelphia, PA

Charlotte M. Calobrisi
Northern Virginia
  Community College
Annandale, VA

Gabriela Cambiasso
Harold Washington College
Chicago, IL

Jeanette Clement
Duquesne University
Pittsburgh, PA

Allis Cole
Shoreline Community
  College
Shoreline, WA

Fanshen DiGiovanni
Glendale Community
  College
Glendale, CA

Antoinette B. d'Oronzio
Hillsborough Community
  College-Dale Mabry
  Campus
Tampa, FL

Rhonda J. Farley
Cosumnes River College
Sacramento, CA

Jennifer Farnell
University of Connecticut
  American Language
  Program
Stamford, CT

Gail Fernandez
Bergen Community College
Paramus, NJ

Irasema Fernandez
Miami Dade College
Miami, FL

Abigail-Marie Fiattarone
Mesa Community College
Mesa, AZ

John Gamber
American River College
Sacramento, CA

Marcia Gethin-Jones
University of Connecticut
  American Language
  Program
Storrs, CT

Kimlee Buttacavoli Grant
The Leona Group, LLC
Phoenix, AZ

Shelly Hedstrom
Palm Beach Community
  College
Lake Worth, FL

Linda Holden
College of Lake County
Grayslake, IL

Sandra Kawamura
Sacramento City College
Sacramento, CA

Bill Keniston
Normandale Community
  College
Bloomington, MN

Michael Larsen
American River College
Sacramento, CA

Bea C. Lawn
Gavilan College
Gilroy, CA

Rob Lee
Pasadena City College
Pasadena, CA

Oranit Limmaneeprasert
American River College
Sacramento, CA

Linda Louie
Highline Community
  College
Des Moines, WA

Melanie A. Majeski
Naugatuck Valley
  Community College
Waterbury, CT

Maria Marin
De Anza College
Cupertino, CA

Michael I. Massey
Hillsborough Community
  College-Ybor City Campus
Tampa, FL

Marlo McClurg-Mackinnon
Cosumnes River College
Sacramento, CA

Michelle Naumann
Elgin Community College
Elgin, IL

Debbie Ockey
Fresno, CA

Lesa Perry
University of Nebraska at
  Omaha
Omaha, NE

Herbert Pierson
St. John's University
New York City, NY

Dina Poggi
De Anza College
Cupertino, CA

Steven Rashba
University of Bridgeport
Bridgeport, CT

Mark Rau
American River College
Sacramento, CA

Maria Spelleri
State College of Florida
  Manatee-Sarasota
Venice, FL

Eva Teagarden
Yuba College
Marysville, CA

Colin S. Ward
Lone Star College-North
  Harris
Houston, TX

Nico Wiersema
Texas A&M International
  University
Laredo, TX

Susan Wilson
San Jose City College
San Jose, CA

A word from the author

My parents immigrated to the U.S. from Poland and learned English as a second language. Born in the U.S., I often had the task as a child to explain the intricacies of the English language. It is no wonder that I became an English language teacher.

When I started teaching over forty years ago, grammar textbooks used a series of unrelated sentences with no context. I knew instinctively that there was something wrong with this technique. It ignored the fact that language is a tool for communication, and it missed an opportunity to spark the student's curiosity. As I gained teaching experience, I noticed that when I used interesting stories that illustrated the grammar, students became more motivated, understood the grammar better, and used it more effectively.

In 1986, I published the first edition of *Grammar in Context* and have continued to search for topics that teach grammar in contexts that are relevant to students' lives. The contexts I've chosen each tell a story: practical ones about technology (social networking and e-books), interesting people (Tiger Woods), and events that made history (the election of President Barack Obama). Whether the task is a fill-in grammar exercise, a listening activity, an editing exercise, an interactive conversation activity, or free writing, the context is reinforced throughout the lesson.

I hope you enjoy the new edition of *Grammar in Context*!

Sandra N. Elbaum

In memory of
Roberto Garrido Alfaro

Welcome to *Grammar in Context*,
Fifth Edition

Grammar in Context presents grammar in interesting contexts that are relevant to students' lives and then recycles the language and context throughout every activity. Learners gain knowledge and skills in both the grammar structures and topic areas.

The new fifth edition of *Grammar in Context* engages learners with updated readings, clear and manageable grammar explanations, and a new full-color design.

New To This Edition!

Full-color design makes grammar more visually contextualized and even easier to study and teach from.

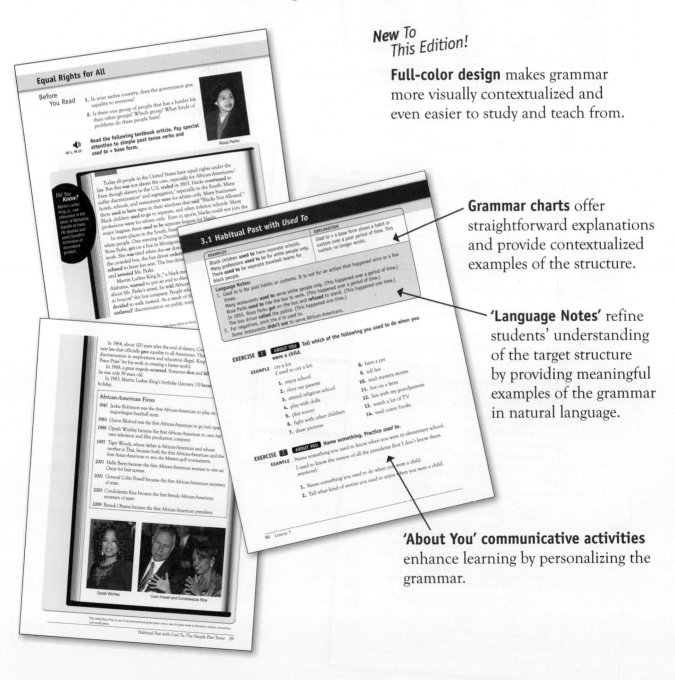

Grammar charts offer straightforward explanations and provide contextualized examples of the structure.

'Language Notes' refine students' understanding of the target structure by providing meaningful examples of the grammar in natural language.

'About You' communicative activities enhance learning by personalizing the grammar.

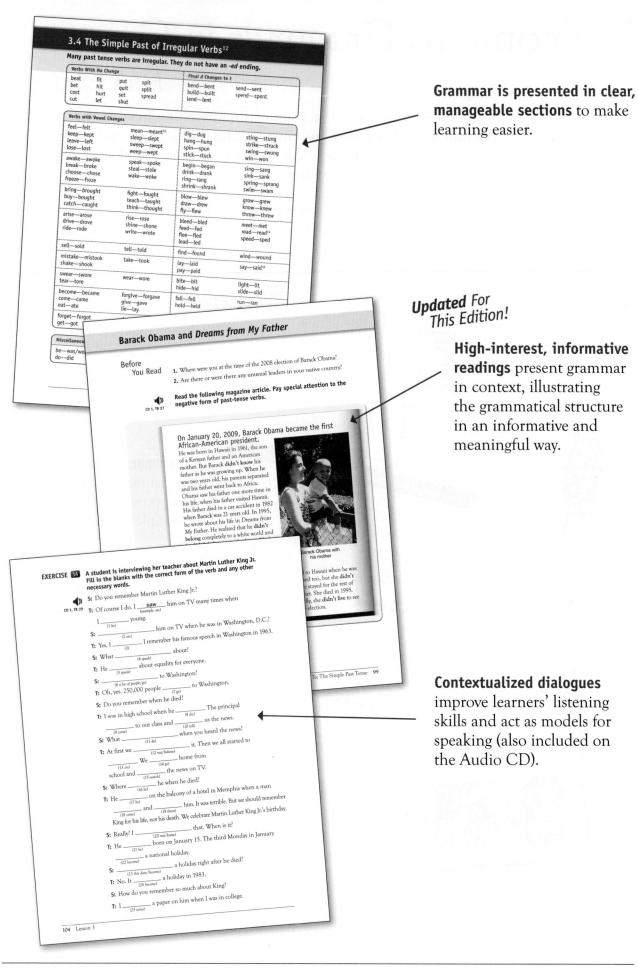

3.4 The Simple Past of Irregular Verbs[12]

Many past tense verbs are irregular. They do not have an -ed ending.

Verbs With No Change				Final *d* Changes to *t*	
beat	fit	put	spit	bend—bent	
bet	hit	quit	split	build—built	send—sent
cost	hurt	set	spread	lend—lent	spend—spent
cut	let	shut			

Verbs with Vowel Changes			
feel—felt	mean—meant[13]	dig—dug	sting—stung
keep—kept	sleep—slept	hang—hung	strike—struck
leave—left	sweep—swept	spin—spun	swing—swung
lose—lost	weep—wept	stick—stuck	win—won
awake—awoke	speak—spoke	begin—began	sing—sang
break—broke	steal—stole	drink—drank	sink—sank
choose—chose	wake—woke	ring—rang	spring—sprang
freeze—froze		shrink—shrank	swim—swam
bring—brought	fight—fought	blow—blew	grow—grew
buy—bought	teach—taught	draw—drew	know—knew
catch—caught	think—thought	fly—flew	throw—threw
arise—arose	rise—rose	bleed—bled	meet—met
drive—drove	shine—shone	feed—fed	read—read[14]
ride—rode	write—wrote	flee—fled	speed—sped
		lead—led	
sell—sold	tell—told	find—found	
mistake—mistook	take—took	lay—laid	wind—wound
shake—shook		pay—paid	say—said[15]
swear—swore	wear—wore	bite—bit	
tear—tore		hide—hid	light—lit
become—became	forgive—forgave	fall—fell	slide—slid
come—came	give—gave	hold—held	run—ran
eat—ate	lie—lay		
forget—forgot			
get—got			

Miscellaneou...	
be—was/we...	
do—did	

Barack Obama and *Dreams from My Father*

Before You Read
1. Where were you at the time of the 2008 election of Barack Obama?
2. Are there or were there any unusual leaders in your native country?

🔊 CD 1, TR 27 **Read the following magazine article. Pay special attention to the negative form of past-tense verbs.**

On January 20, 2009, Barack Obama became the first African-American president.
He was born in Hawaii in 1961, the son of a Kenyan father and an American mother. But Barack **didn't know** his father as he was growing up. When he was two years old, his parents separated and his father went back to Africa. Obama saw his father one more time in his life, when his father visited Hawaii. His father died in a car accident in 1982 when Barack was 21 years old. In 1995, he wrote about his life in *Dreams from My Father*. He realized that he **didn't belong** completely to a white world and

Barack Obama with his mother

...to Hawaii when he was ...ed too, but she **didn't** ...e stayed for the rest of ...et. She died in 1995. ...ly, she **didn't live** to see ...election.

...To; The Simple Past Tense 99

EXERCISE 14 **A student is interviewing her teacher about Martin Luther King Jr. Fill in the blanks with the correct form of the verb and any other necessary words.**

🔊 CD 1, TR 29

S: Do you remember Martin Luther King Jr.?

T: Of course I do. I _____**saw**_____ (example: see) him on TV many times when

I _____ (1 be) young.

S: _____ (2 see) him on TV when he was in Washington, D.C.?

T: Yes, I _____ (3) I remember his famous speech in Washington in 1963.

S: What _____ (4 speak) about?

T: He _____ (5 speak) about equality for everyone.

S: _____ (6 a lot of people/go) to Washington?

T: Oh, yes. 250,000 people _____ (7 go) to Washington.

S: Do you remember when he died?

T: I was in high school when he _____ (8 die). The principal

_____ (9 come) to our class and _____ (10 tell) us the news.

S: What _____ (11 do) when you heard the news?

T: At first we _____ (12 not/believe) it. Then we all started to

_____ (13 cry). We _____ (14 go) home from

school and _____ (15 watch) the news on TV.

S: Where _____ (16 be) he when he died?

T: He _____ (17 be) on the balcony of a hotel in Memphis when a man

_____ (18 come) and _____ (19 shoot) him. It was terrible. But we should remember

King for his life, not his death. We celebrate Martin Luther King Jr.'s birthday.

S: Really? I _____ (20 not/know) that. When is it?

T: He _____ (21 be) born on January 15. The third Monday in January

_____ (22 become) a national holiday.

S: _____ (23 this date/become) a holiday right after he died!

T: No. It _____ (24 become) a holiday in 1983.

S: How do you remember so much about King?

T: I _____ (25 write) a paper on him when I was in college.

104 Lesson 3

Grammar is presented in clear, manageable sections to make learning easier.

Updated *For This Edition!*

High-interest, informative readings present grammar in context, illustrating the grammatical structure in an informative and meaningful way.

Contextualized dialogues improve learners' listening skills and act as models for speaking (also included on the Audio CD).

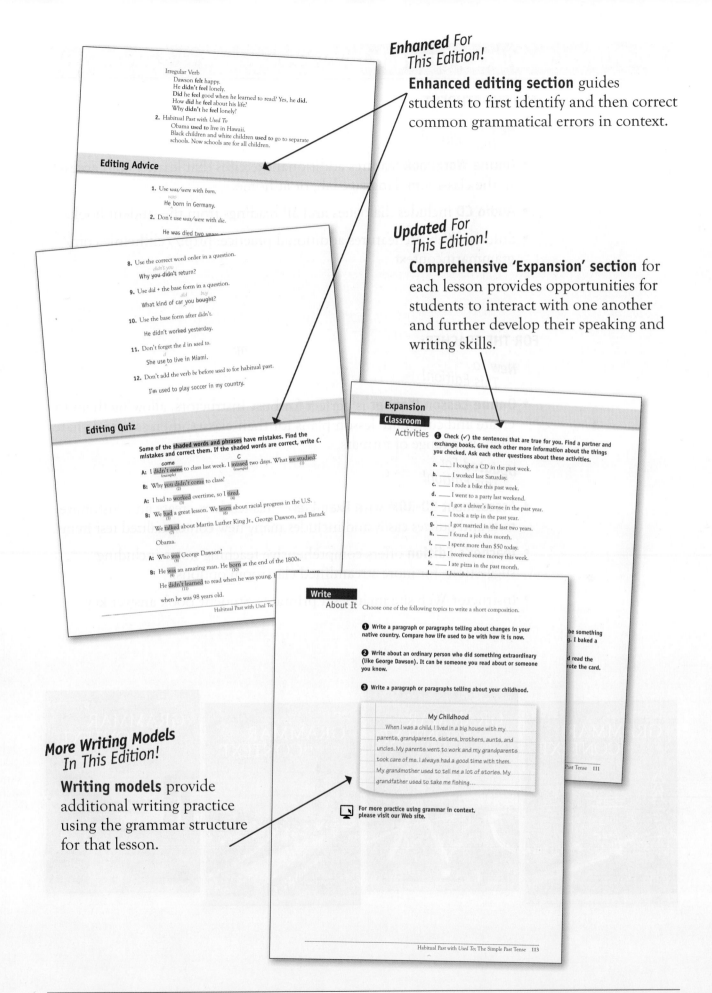

Enhanced For This Edition!

Enhanced editing section guides students to first identify and then correct common grammatical errors in context.

Updated For This Edition!

Comprehensive 'Expansion' section for each lesson provides opportunities for students to interact with one another and further develop their speaking and writing skills.

More Writing Models In This Edition!

Writing models provide additional writing practice using the grammar structure for that lesson.

Irregular Verb
Dawson **felt** happy.
He **didn't feel** lonely.
Did he **feel** good when he learned to read? Yes, he **did**.
How **did** he **feel** about his life?
Why **didn't** he **feel** lonely?

2. Habitual Past with *Used To*
Obama **used to** live in Hawaii.
Black children and white children **used to** go to separate schools. Now schools are for all children.

Editing Advice

1. Use *was/were* with *born*.
was
He born in Germany.

2. Don't use *was/were* with *die*.
He was died two years...

8. Use the correct word order in a question.
didn't you
Why you didn't return?

9. Use *did* + the base form in a question.
did buy
What kind of car you bought?

10. Use the base form after *didn't*.
He didn't worked yesterday.

11. Don't forget the *d* in *used to*.
d
She use to live in Miami.

12. Don't add the verb *be* before *used to* for habitual past.
I'm used to play soccer in my country.

Editing Quiz

Some of the shaded words and phrases have mistakes. Find the mistakes and correct them. If the shaded words are correct, write C.

come   C
A: I didn't came to class last week. I missed two days. What we studied?
     (example)   (example)   (1)

B: Why you didn't come to class?
          (2)

A: I had to worked overtime, so I tired.
            (3)   (4)

B: We had a great lesson. We learn about racial progress in the U.S.
        (5)   (6)
We talked about Martin Luther King Jr., George Dawson, and Barack
      (7)
Obama.

A: Who was George Dawson?
        (8)

B: He was an amazing man. He born at the end of the 1800s.
        (9)   (10)
He didn't learned to read when he was young. ...
       (11)
when he was 98 years old.

Habitual Past with *Used To*;

Expansion

Classroom
Activities ❶ Check (✓) the sentences that are true for you. Find a partner and exchange books. Give each other more information about the things you checked. Ask each other questions about these activities.

a. ____ I bought a CD in the past week.
b. ____ I worked last Saturday.
c. ____ I rode a bike this past week.
d. ____ I went to a party last weekend.
e. ____ I got a driver's license in the past year.
f. ____ I took a trip in the past year.
g. ____ I got married in the last two years.
h. ____ I found a job this month.
i. ____ I spent more than $50 today.
j. ____ I received some money this week.
k. ____ I ate pizza in the past month.

Write
About It Choose one of the following topics to write a short composition.

❶ Write a paragraph or paragraphs telling about changes in your native country. Compare how life used to be with how it is now.

❷ Write about an ordinary person who did something extraordinary (like George Dawson). It can be someone you read about or someone you know.

❸ Write a paragraph or paragraphs telling about your childhood.

My Childhood
When I was a child, I lived in a big house with my parents, grandparents, sisters, brothers, aunts, and uncles. My parents went to work and my grandparents took care of me. I always had a good time with them. My grandmother used to tell me a lot of stories. My grandfather used to take me fishing...

For more practice using grammar in context, please visit our Web site.

Past Tense   111

Habitual Past with *Used To*; The Simple Past Tense   113

Additional resources for each level

FOR THE STUDENT:

New To This Edition!

- **Online Workbook** features additional exercises that learners can access in the classroom, language lab, or at home.

- **Audio CD** includes dialogues and all readings from the student book.

- Student Web site features additional practice: http://elt.heinle.com/grammarincontext.

FOR THE TEACHER:

New To This Edition!

- **Online Lesson Planner** is perfect for busy instructors, allowing them to create and customize lesson plans for their classes, then save and share them in a range of formats.

Updated For This Edition!

- **Assessment CD-ROM with Exam*View*®** lets teachers create and customize tests and quizzes easily and includes many new contextualized test items.

- **Teacher's Edition** offers comprehensive teaching notes including suggestions for more streamlined classroom options.

- Instructor Web site includes a printable Student Book answer key.

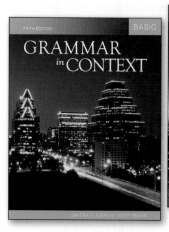
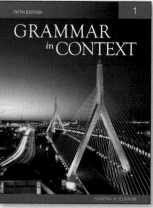

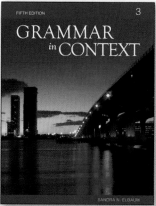

Grammar
The Simple Present Tense

Frequency Words

Context
Pets and Other Animals

Americans and Their Pets

1. Do you like animals?

2. Do you have a pet?

CD 1, TR 01

Read the following magazine article. Pay special attention to the verb *be* and other verbs in the simple present tense.

Most Americans love pets. About 63 percent of Americans **live** with one or more animals. About 39 percent of households **have** at least one dog. Thirty-four percent of households **own** at least one cat.

Americans **think** of their pets as part of the family. Americans **spend** approximately $5 billion a year on holiday presents for their pets. Almost half of all pet owners **talk** to their pets on occasion. Many pet owners **sleep** with their dogs or cats. Many people **travel** with their pets. (It **costs** between $25 and $150 to fly with a pet.) Some hotels **allow** guests to bring their pets.

Americans **pay** a lot of money to keep pets. They **spend** about $43.2 billion a year in vet[1] bills. There **are** schools, toys, hotels, restaurants, clothes, perfumes, and cemeteries for pets. There **are** magazines for pet owners. There **are** hundreds of Web sites for pet owners.

Pets **are** a lot of fun. They **are** affectionate[2] too. People who **are** lonely **get** a lot of love from their animals. Medical research **shows** that contact with a dog or a cat can lower a person's blood pressure.

Pets **need** a lot of attention. Before you **buy** a pet, it **is** important to answer these questions:

- **Are** you patient?
- **Are** you home a lot?
- If you **have** children, **are** they responsible?
- **Are** pets allowed where you live?
- **Do** you **have** money for medical bills for your pet?

Unfortunately, some people **don't realize** that pets **need** a lot of care. Some people **see** a cute puppy or kitten, **buy** it, and later **abandon**[3] it because they **don't want** to take care of it. It **is** important to understand that a pet **is** a long-term responsibility.

[1]Vet is short for *veterinarian*. This is an animal doctor.
[2]*Affectionate* means loving.
[3]*To abandon* means to leave something. When people abandon a pet, they leave it on the street.

1.1 *Be*—Forms and Uses

Forms

EXAMPLES			EXPLANATION
Subject	**Form of *Be***	**Complement**	
I	**am**	home a lot.	Use *am* with *I*.
My father	**is**	patient.	Use *is* with *he, she, it, this, that,* and singular subjects (for example, *cat*).
He	**is**	intelligent.	
She	**is**	lonely.	
The cat	**is**	happy.	
That	**is**	a friendly cat.	
We	**are**	responsible.	Use *are* with *we, you, they, these, those,* and plural subjects (*pets, cats,* etc.).
You	**are**	home a lot.	
Pets	**are**	fun.	
Those	**are**	cute kittens.	

Uses

EXAMPLES	USES
I **am** patient. The pet shop **is** located on the corner. The children **are** excited about the puppy.	With a description (adjective) **Note:** Some words that end in *-ed* are adjectives: *tired, married, worried, interested, bored, excited, crowded, located.*
This **is** a Labrador. A Labrador **is** a big dog.	With a classification or definition of the subject
My dog **is** in the yard.	With a location
My husband **is** from Guatemala.	With a place of origin
It **is** cold outside. The dog **is** cold.	With weather and physical reaction to the weather (*hot, cold, warm*)
My dog **is** three (years old).	With age
The cat **is** hungry. I **am** afraid of dogs.	With physical or emotional states: *hungry, thirsty, afraid*
There **are** toys for dogs. There **is** a dog restaurant near my house.	With *there*
It **is** ten o'clock now.	With time
It **is** warm today.	With weather
Language Note: *Be cold* means to feel a low temperature. *Have a cold* shows an illness. Please bring me my sweater. *I'm cold.* I'm sick. *I have a cold.*	

EXERCISE **1** **Fill in the blanks with the correct form of _be_.**

EXAMPLE My dog ____is____ very small.

1. You take care of your dog. You ____are____ responsible.

2. Pet ownership ____is____ a big responsibility.

3. My cat ____is____ soft.

4. Dogs ____are____ great pets because they ____are____ affectionate.
   They ____are____ also good protection for a house.

5. My dog ____is____ a member of my family.

6. Some cats ____are____ very affectionate. Other cats ____are____ very
   independent.

7. It ____is____ fun to own a pet.

8. Kittens and puppies ____are____ cute.

9. We ____are____ ready to get a pet.

10. Some people ____are____ lonely.

11. My kitten ____is____ very sweet.

12. The dog ____is____ cold.

1.2 Contractions with *Be*

A *contraction* combines two words. We can make a contraction with *be*. We put an apostrophe (') in place of the missing letter.

EXAMPLES	EXPLANATION
I am **I'm** responsible. You are **You're** patient. She is **She's** happy. He is **He's** kind. It is **It's** necessary to walk a dog. We are **We're** busy. They are **They're** cute.	We can make a contraction with the subject pronoun (*I*, *you*, *she*, etc.) and *am*, *is*, or *are*.
There is **There's** a cat hotel near my house. That is **That's** a friendly cat.	We can make a contraction with *there is*. We can make a contraction with *that is*.
My **grandmother's** lonely. Your **dog's** cute.	We can make a contraction with most nouns and *is*.
A fo<u>x</u> **is** a relative of a dog. A mou<u>se</u> **is** a small animal. Thi<u>s</u> **is** a cute cat.	We don't make a contraction with *is* if the noun ends in *s*, *se*, *ce*, *ge*, *ze*, *sh*, *ch*, or *x*.
Pet **products are** expensive. **Dogs are** popular pets. **There are** hotels for pets.	In writing, don't make a contraction with a plural noun and *are* or with *there are*.
The owner **is not** home now. She **isn't** home during the day. You **are not** ready for a pet. You **aren't** patient.	To make a negative with *be*, put *not* after a form of *be*. The negative contractions are *isn't* and *aren't*. There is no contraction for *am not*.

EXERCISE **2**   Which of the sentences in Exercise 1 can use a contraction?

EXERCISE **3**   Fill in the first blank with the correct form of *be*. Then fill in the second blank with a negative form. Use contractions wherever possible.

EXAMPLE   Today<u>'s</u> my daughter's birthday. It <u>isn't</u> a holiday.

1. My daughter and I <u>are</u> at the pet shop. We <u>are</u> at home.

2. My husband <u>is</u> at work now. He <u>is</u> with me.

3. I <u>am</u> patient. My husband <u>is</u> patient.

4. This puppy <u>is</u> for my daughter. It <u>is</u> for my son.

5. My daughter <u>is</u> responsible. My son <u>is</u> responsible.

(continued)

6. Dogs __are__ good for protection. Cats __are__ good for protection.

7. My daughter __is__ excited. She __is__ bored.

8. I __am__ afraid of big dogs. I __am__ afraid of small dogs.

9. This __is__ a Chihuahua. It __is__ a big dog.

EXERCISE **4** **Fill in the blanks.**

EXAMPLE My dog __'s__ hungry. He wants to eat.

1. My cat __'s__ near the window.

2. My aunt __'s not__ married. Her dog __is__ her favorite
(not)

companion.

3. In the U.S., there __are__ cemeteries for pets.

4. Some cats __are__ very affectionate.

5. The dog __is__ thirsty. Put water in his dish.

6. This __is__ a kitten. It __is__ only two weeks __dog__.

7. Don't leave your dog in the car. __It's__ hot today.

8. My dog __is__ cold in the winter. She needs a sweater.

9. My vet's office _____ located about two miles from my house.

10. __This__ is a picture of my dog.

11. I __am__ worried about my dog because she __is__ sick.

12. Your son __is not__ responsible because he __is__ only four
(not)

years __old__.

Dog Walkers

Before You Read

1. Do working people have problems taking care of their pets?

2. Are some animals easier to take care of than others?

CD 1, TR 02

Read the following conversation. Pay special attention to questions with the verb _be_.

A: Your dog is beautiful. What kind of a dog **is it**?

B: It's a Dalmatian.

A: How old **is he**?

B: It's a _she_. She's two years old.

A: What's **her name**?

B: Her name is Missy.

A: **Are we** neighbors? **Are you** new in the neighborhood?

B: I don't live here. Missy isn't my dog. I'm a dog walker.

A: A dog walker? What's **that**?

B: I walk other people's dogs when they're at work or on vacation.

A: **Are you** a friend of the family?

B: No. I'm from an agency.

A: What agency **are you** from?

B: It's a professional dog-walking service.

A: **Are you** serious?

B: Of course I'm serious.

A: **Is the pay** good?

B: It's OK. But I love my job for other reasons. My "customers" are always happy to see me. Also, I'm outside all day.

A: Cool! **Are the owners** happy too?

(continued)

B: Yes, they are. When they go to work, they're worried that their dogs can be lonely or bored. Some people even leave the TV on for their pets. But when they use a dog-walking service, they are happy because their dogs are happy too.

A: **Are there** jobs at your agency?

B: Yes, there are. **Are you** interested in becoming a dog walker too?

A: Yes. It sounds like fun.

B: Here's my card. The agency's phone number is on the card.

A: Thanks!

1.3 Questions with *Be*

Compare statement word order and word order in *yes/no* questions.

STATEMENT WORD ORDER	YES/NO QUESTION	SHORT ANSWER	EXPLANATION
I am responsible.	**Am I** responsible with pets?	Yes, you are.	In a *yes/no* question, we put *am*, *is*, *are* before the subject.
You are a dog walker.	**Are you** a friend of the family?	No, I'm not.	
The owner is busy.	**Is the owner** at home?	No, she isn't.	We usually answer a *yes/no* question with a short answer. A short answer contains a pronoun (*he*, *it*, *we*, *they*, etc.).
The pay is important.	**Is the pay** good?	No, it isn't.	
The dog is a female.	**Is the dog** young?	Yes, she is.	
It is a big dog.	**Is it** a Labrador?	No, it isn't.	
We are new here.	**Are we** neighbors?	No, we aren't.	
The owners are at work.	**Are the owners** happy?	Yes, they are.	
They are out.	**Are they** at work?	Yes, they are.	We don't use a contraction for a short *yes* answer. We usually use a contraction for a short *no* answer.
There are interesting jobs.	**Are there** jobs at your agency?	Yes, there are.	
That is a cute dog.	**Is that** your dog?	No, it isn't.	
It isn't a big dog.	**Isn't it** a puppy?	No, it isn't.	

Pronunciation Note: We usually end a *yes/no* question with rising intonation. Listen to your teacher pronounce the questions above.

Compare statement word order and word order in *wh-* questions.

STATEMENT WORD ORDER	*Wh-* QUESTION	EXPLANATION
I am lost. **You are** from an agency. **That is** a nice dog. **The dog is** old. **That is** a strange pet. **Her name is** long. **You are** here. **There are** a lot of dog walkers.	Where **am I**? What agency **are you** from? What kind of dog **is that**? How old **is the dog**? What **is that**? What **is her name**? Why **are you** here? How many dog walkers **are there**?	We put *am*, *is*, and *are* before the subject.
The owner isn't home. The dogs **aren't bored**. **You aren't** at work.	Why **isn't the owner** at home? Why **aren't the dogs** bored? Why **aren't you** at work?	Notice the word order in negative *wh-* questions.

Language Notes:
1. Most question words can contract with *is*. (Exceptions: *which is; how much is*)
   Who's that?
   What's a Dalmatian?
   Where's your cat?
   Which is bigger, a collie or a Labrador?
2. Study these common questions and answers with *be*.
   What's your name? My name is Linda.
   What time is it? It's 4:32.
   What color is the dog? It's tan.
   What kind of dog is this? It's a Labrador.
   What's a Dalmatian? It's a dog.
   What's this? It's a leash.
   How are you? I'm fine.
   How's the weather? It's sunny and warm.
   How old is your daughter? She's 10 (years old).[4]
   How tall are you? I'm five feet, three inches tall (or 5'3").[5]
   Where are you from? I'm from Mexico.
   What's wrong? I'm sick.

leash

EXERCISE **5** **ABOUT YOU** **Interview another student.**

EXAMPLE
A: Are you interested in a pet?
B: Yes, I am.

1. Are you home a lot? *No, I'm not*

2. Are there children in your house? *No, There're not*

3. Are they responsible? *No, They're not*

4. Are pets allowed where you live? *No, They're not*

5. Are you allergic to cats? *yes, I am*

[4]It is not polite to ask an American adult about his or her age.
[5]For conversion to the metric system, see Appendix D.

The Simple Present Tense; Frequency Words **9**

EXERCISE 6 **ABOUT YOU** Interview another student.

EXAMPLE   **A:** Is this class hard for you?
B: No, it isn't.

1. Are you an immigrant? _yes, I am_
2. Is the teacher from your native country? _No, she's not_
3. Is your country in North America? _No, It isn't_
4. Is your hometown cold at this time of year? _yes, It is_
5. Are we from the same country? _No, I'm not_
6. Are there other students from your country in this class? _yes, They are_
7. Is the school located near your house? _yes, It is_

EXERCISE 7 **One student reads a question. Another student answers.**

1. What pets are good for children? _cats dogs_
2. What kind of pets are popular in your native country (or with people in your native culture)? _Hameser_
3. What's your favorite animal in the zoo? _lion_
4. What's a popular name for dogs in your native culture? _wolf_
5. When's a good time to get a pet?
6. What's a better pet—a dog or a cat? _dog_

EXERCISE 8 **Fill in the blanks to complete this conversation. Use contractions wherever possible.**

🔊
CD 1, TR 03

A: _____Is this_____ your dog?
     (example)
B: Yes, it _____.
          (1)
A: He _____ beautiful.
          (2)
B: Thanks. But it's a "she."
A: _____ friendly?
       (3)
B: Yes, she _____.
            (4)
A: What kind of dog _____?
                       (5)
B: She _____ a collie.
          (6)
A: What _____?
           (7)
B: Her name is Samantha.

A collie

A: _____(8)?

B: She _____(9) three years old now.

A: _____(10) hard to take care of a dog?

B: Not for me. I _____(11) home a lot. And when

I _____(12 not) home, my brother or parents

_____(13) home.

A: I love dogs, but I _____(14 not) home very much, so that's

a problem.

B: Why _____(15) a lot?

A: Because I'm a nurse. I work eight hours a day. I want to get a dog for

my grandmother.

B: Why?

A: Because _____(16) lonely.

B: Why _____(17) lonely?

A: Because nobody _____(18) home all day.

We _____(19) all at work.

B: I think it _____(20) a good idea for your grandmother

to have a dog.

EXERCISE 9 **Fill in the blanks in the following cell phone conversation.**

CD 1, TR 04

A: Hello?

B: Hi. This ___**is**___(example) Betty.

A: Hi, Betty. How _____(1)?

B: I'm fine. How _____(2)?

A: I'm fine. But the cat _____(3) sick.

I _____(4 not) home now.

I _____(5) at the animal hospital.

B: _____(6) wrong?

(continued)

The Simple Present Tense; Frequency Words **11**

A: Fluffy _____ hungry or thirsty.
     (7 not)

He _____ tired all the time.
   (8)

B: _____ so hot today. Maybe the heat
      (9)

_____ the problem.
(10)

A: I don't think so. The house _____ air-conditioned.
                                  (11)

B: _____?
      (12)

A: He _____ only four years _____.
         (13)   (14)

B: _____ alone?
      (15)

A: No, I'm not.

B: _____ with you?
      (16)

A: My daughter _____ with me.
                   (17)

We _____ in the waiting room.
   (18)

B: Why _____ at school?
          (19)

A: She _____ on spring break now. I think
          (20)

the doctor _____ ready to see us now.
           (21)

EXERCISE 10 **Fill in the blanks in the following conversation.**

🔊

CD 1, TR 05

A: Look at the dog. What kind of dog ___is it___?
                                        (example)

B: I think it ___is___ a mutt.
                  (1)

A: What ___is___ a mutt?
           (2)

B: It ___is___ a mixed breed dog. Look, it ___is___
         (3)   (4)

so friendly with those children.

A: My daughter's birthday is next week. She wants a dog. But dogs

___are___ so expensive.
(5)

B: A purebred[6] dog, like a Labrador, is expensive, but a mutt

___is___ so expensive. In fact, there ___are___ animal shelters
(6 not)   (7)

that can give you a dog for free or for a very low price.

A: What ___is___ an animal shelter?
           (8)

---

[6]A *purebred* dog is one breed only. It is not mixed with other breeds.

B: It's an organization that takes unwanted
pets and tries to find homes for them.

A: But _____ healthy?
(9)

B: Yes, they are. The shelter's doctors check
an animal's health before giving it to a
family.

A: Why _____ so many unwanted pets?
(10)

B: There are unwanted pets because some people get a pet and then
realize it _____ too much trouble to take care of it.
(11)

A: That _____ terrible.
(12)

B: Yes, it is. What about your daughter? _____ responsible?
(13)

A: Yes, she _____.
(14)

B: How old _____?
(15)

A: She _____ ten years old.
(16)

B: My son has a dog. But he _____ responsible. He says it's *his* dog,
(17 not)
but I _____ the one who feeds it and takes it out three times a day.
(18)

A: Why _____ responsible?
(19)

B: He says he _____ too busy with school and sports.
(20)
I _____ busy too. But I find time to take care of the dog.
(21)
What about you? _____ home a lot?
(22)

A: No, I _____. My work day _____ very long. And my
(23)   (24)
daughter _____ at school all day.
(25)

B: Then you should find a dog-walking service.

A: _____ expensive?
(26)

B: Yes, it _____. But _____ the only way to have a happy dog.
(27)   (28)

A: Maybe a fish would be a better pet!

Guide Dogs

Before You Read

1. Do you think most dogs are intelligent? Are some dogs more intelligent than others?

2. Do you ever see blind[7] people walking with dogs?

 Read the following magazine article. Pay special attention to simple present tense verbs.

CD 1, TR 06

Most dogs have an easy life in the U.S. They eat, play, get attention from their owners, and sleep. But some dogs work hard. They are called guide dogs. Guide dogs help blind people move from place to place safely.

Guide dogs and their owners are a team. Guide dogs don't lead the owners, and their owners don't completely control the guide dogs. They work together. The guide dogs don't know where the owners want to go, so they follow the owners' instructions. The owners can't see the obstacles[8] along the way, so the dogs make decisions for the safety of the owners. Guide dogs stop at all curbs and intersections before crossing a street. They don't see color, so they don't know if the light is red or green. The owners decide if it is time to cross the street by listening to the sound of traffic. The dogs help the owners get on a bus or train. They learn to obey many verbal commands.

Most guide dogs are golden retrievers, Labrador retrievers, or German shepherds. These three breeds are very intelligent, obedient,[9] and friendly. A guide dog needs to work without distraction in noisy places, bad weather, crowds of people, and difficult situations. When you see a guide dog, it is important that you recognize that the dog needs to concentrate on its job. Don't pet or talk to the dog. Guiding is very complicated, and it requires a dog's full attention.

Guide dog training lasts about five months. Only about 72 percent of dogs that enter the training program "graduate." Those that graduate bring their owners valuable help and love. In other dog training programs, trainers use

food as a reward. In guide dog training, the trainer does not use food. He or she uses physical and verbal affection. This is because a guide dog sometimes takes the owner to a restaurant. It must lie patiently at the owner's feet without wanting to eat.

Guide dogs like to play too, but only after the work is finished. How do dogs know when their work is finished? When the harness is on, they know they have to work. When it is off, they can play. Like all dogs, they love to play.

---

[7]A *blind* person cannot see.
[8]An *obstacle* is something that blocks your way. An obstacle creates an unsafe situation.
[9]An *obedient* animal is one that obeys.

1.4 The Simple Present Tense—Affirmative Statements

Form

A simple present tense verb has two forms: the base form and the -s form.[10]

EXAMPLES			EXPLANATION
Subject	**Base Form**	**Complement**	We use the base form when the subject is *I*, *you*, *we*, *they*, or a plural noun.
I			
You			
We	**work**	hard.	
They			
Guide dogs			
Subject	**-s Form**	**Complement**	We use the -s form when the subject is *he*, *she*, *it*, or a singular noun.
He			
She			
It	**works**	hard.	
The dog			
My family **has** three cats.			We use the -s form with *family*, *everyone*, *everybody*, *no one*, *nobody*, and *nothing*.
Everyone in the shelter **likes** animals.			
No one **wants** the new kittens.			
I **have** a pet dog. My friend **has** a guide dog.			*Have* is an irregular verb.
			have ⟶ has

Use

EXAMPLES	USES
Dogs **give** people love. Guide dogs **help** people. Most dogs **have** an easy life. Americans **love** pets.	With general truths, to show that something is consistently true
Many pet owners **sleep** with their dogs or cats. Some pet owners **buy** presents for their pets. Owners **walk** dogs on a leash.	With customs
He **walks** his dog three times a day. He **feeds** his cat every morning and every night.	To show regular activity (a habit) or repeated action
I **come** from Bosnia. He **comes** from Pakistan.	To show place of origin

[10]For the spelling of the -s form, see Appendix A.

EXERCISE 11 Fill in the blanks with the base form or the -s form.

EXAMPLES Americans __love__ pets.
(love)

My son __loves__ his new kitten.
(love)

1. Most dogs __has__ an easy life.
(have)

2. My dog __sleep__ all day.
(sleep)

3. Guide dogs __learns__ to obey many commands.
(learn)

4. A guide dog __makes__ safety decisions.
(make)

5. Trainers __works__ with a dog for five months.
(work)

6. Most guide dogs __graduate__ from the training program.
(graduate)

7. My girlfriend __gives__ her dog a present on his birthday.
(give)

8. People __gets__ affection from animals.
(get)

9. Everyone __needs__ affection.
(need)

10. It __costs__ a lot of money to have a pet.
(cost)

11. Some pet owners __talk__ to their pets on the phone.
(talk)

12. My daughter __wants__ a puppy for her birthday.
(want)

13. My neighbor's dog __bark__ all the time.
(bark)

14. Some people __travels__ with their dogs.
(travel)

15. Thirty-nine percent of Americans __has__ at least one dog.
(have)

16. My brother __has__ three dogs.
(have)

17. Dogs __protect__ their owners.
(protect)

18. My family __has__ animals.
(love)

19. Nobody __knows__ the dog's age.
(know)

20. Everybody __thinks__ that puppies and kittens are cute.
(think)

1.5 Negative Statements with the Simple Present Tense

EXAMPLES	EXPLANATION
The owner **knows** the destination. The dog **doesn't know** the destination. The dog **stops** at a curb. It **doesn't stop** because of a red light.	Use *doesn't* + the base form with *he, she, it,* or a singular noun. **Compare:** knows ——→ doesn't **know** stops ——→ doesn't **stop** *Doesn't* is the contraction for *does not*.
Some trainers **use** food to reward a dog. Guide dog trainers **don't use** food. Guide dogs **work** when the harness is on. They **don't work** when the harness is off. You **have** a cat. You **don't have** a dog.	Use *don't* + the base form with *I, you,* *we, they,* or a plural noun. **Compare:** use ——→ don't **use** work ——→ don't **work** *Don't* is the contraction for *do not*.

Usage Note: American English and British English use different grammar to form the negative
of *have*.
Compare:
    American: He *doesn't have* a dog.
      British: He *hasn't* a dog. OR He *hasn't got* a dog.

EXERCISE **12** **Fill in the blanks with the negative form of the underlined verb.**

EXAMPLE   A guide dog <u>needs</u> a lot of training. A pet dog _____*doesn't need*_____ a lot
of training.

1. Most dogs <u>play</u> a lot. Guide dogs ___*don't play*___ a lot.

2. Obedience trainers <u>use</u> food to teach dogs. Guide dog trainers
   ___*don't use*___ food.

3. A guide dog <u>works</u> hard. A pet dog ___*doesn't work*___ hard.

4. People <u>see</u> colors. Dogs ___*don't see*___ colors.

5. A guide dog <u>goes</u> on public transportation. A pet dog
   ___*doesn't go*___ on public transportation.

6. My cats <u>eat</u> special food. They ___*don't eat*___ food from
   our table.

7. My cats <u>like</u> fish. They ___*don't likes*___ chicken.

8. One cat <u>sleeps</u> on my bed. She ___*doesn't sleep*___ alone.

9. My landlord <u>allows</u> cats. He ___*doesn't allow*___ dogs.

10. My cats <u>need</u> attention. They ___*don't need*___ a lot of my time.

11. We <u>have</u> cats. We ___*don't have*___ fish.

12. I <u>like</u> cats. My sister ___*don't like*___ cats.

Search and Rescue Dogs

1. Besides helping blind people, do you know of any other ways that dogs work?

2. Do dogs have some qualities that humans don't have?

CD 1, TR 07

Read the following conversation. Pay special attention to questions with the simple present tense.

A: There's a program on TV tonight about search and rescue dogs. **Do** you **want** to watch it with me?

B: I know about guide dogs. But I don't know anything about search and rescue dogs. What **does** "search" **mean**? What **does** "rescue" **mean**?

A: Search means "look for." Rescue means "to help someone in a dangerous situation." These dogs are called SAR dogs.

B: What **do** these dogs **do**?

A: When there is a disaster, like an earthquake or a flood, they help the workers find missing people. They save people's lives.

B: How **do** they **do** that?

A: They have a great sense of smell. They can find things that people can't.

B: **Do** they **need** a lot of training?

A: I think they need at least one year of training.

B: What kind of dogs **do** they **use** as SAR dogs?

A: They usually use large, strong dogs. Labrador retrievers or golden retrievers are often SAR dogs. Let's watch the program together tonight.

B: What time **does** it **begin**?

A: At 9 P.M.

B: **Does** your dog **want** to watch the program with us?

A: My dog is a lazy, spoiled Chihuahua. She just wants to eat, play, and sleep.

1.6 Questions with the Simple Present Tense

Compare statements and *yes/no* questions.

Do	Subject	Verb	Complement	Short Answer	Explanation
	Guide dogs	need	training.		For *yes/no* questions with *I*, *we*, *you*, *they*, or a plural noun, use:
Do	rescue dogs	need	training?	Yes, they do.	
	You	like	dogs.		*Do* + subject + base form + complement
Do	you	like	cats?	No, I don't.	

Does	Subject	Verb	Complement	Short Answer	Explanation
	Jamie	trains	rescue dogs.		For *yes/no* questions with *he*, *she*, *it*, or a singular subject, use:
Does	Jamie	train	guide dogs?	No, she doesn't.	
	My dog	plays	a lot.		*Does* + subject + base form + complement
Does	a rescue dog	play	a lot?	No, it doesn't.	

Compare statements and *wh-* questions.

Wh- Word	*do*	Subject	Verb	Complement	Explanation
		Rescue dogs	need	training.	For *wh-* questions with *I*, *we*, *you*, *they*, or a plural noun, use:
How much training	do	they	need?		
		You	prefer	cats.	*Wh-* word + *do* + subject + base form + complement
Why	do	you	prefer	cats?	

Wh- Word	*does*	Subject	Verb	Complement	Explanation
		The program	begins	soon.	For *wh-* questions with *he*, *she*, *it*, or a singular noun, use:
What time	does	the program	begin?		
		My dog	sleeps	a lot.	*Wh-* word + *does* + subject + base form + complement
Where	does	your dog	sleep?		

Compare negative statements and questions.

Why	*don't/doesn't*	Subject	Verb	Complement
		I	don't like	cats.
Why	don't	you	like	cats?
		My dog	doesn't sleep	in his bed.
Why	doesn't	he	sleep	in his bed?

Language Note: Compare questions with *be* to other simple present tense questions:
Is the dog cold? Yes, it **is**.
Does the dog **have** a sweater? Yes, it **does**.
Where **is** your dog?
What kind of dog **do** you **have**?

EXERCISE 13 **Fill in the blanks to complete this conversation.**

CD 1, TR 08

A: Do you ___like___ animals?
              (example)

B: Yes, I _____. In fact, I love animals very much. I especially like dogs.
         (1)

A: _____ you have a dog?
  (2)

B: No, I _____.
      (3)

A: If you love dogs, why _____ a dog?
                      (4 not/have)

B: Because my landlord _____ dogs.
                     (5 not/permit)

A: _____ he permit cats?
   (6)

B: Yes, he _____.
       (7)

A: _____ a cat?
   (8 have)

B: Yes, I do. But I _____ to find a new home for my cat.
             (9 need)

_____ you know anyone who wants a cat?
  (10)

A: Why _____ your cat?
      (11 not/want)

B: I'm getting married in three months, and my girlfriend

_____ to live with cats.
  (12 not/want)

A: Why _____ to live with cats? Doesn't she
      (13 not/want)

_____ them?
 (14 like)

B: She _____ them, but she's allergic to them. When she
   (15 like)

_____ over, she _____ and _____.
 (16 come)   (17 sneeze)   (18 cough)

She _____ to come over any more.
   (19 not/want)

A: That's a big problem.

EXERCISE 14 **ABOUT YOU** **Part 1: Use the words below to interview a student with a dog.**

EXAMPLES your dog/big

A: Is your dog big?
B: Yes, she is.

your dog/sleep a lot (how many hours)

A: Does your dog sleep a lot?
B: Yes, she does.
A: How many hours does she sleep?
B: She sleeps about 15 hours a day.

1. how old/your dog
2. what/your dog's name
3. it/a male or a female
4. what/your dog/eat
5. how often/you/take your dog out
6. your dog/do tricks (what kind)
7. your dog/have toys (what kind)
8. your dog/friendly
9. your dog/bark a lot
10. why/you/like dogs

Part 2: Use the words below to interview a student with a cat.

1. how old/your cat *are* ?
2. what/your cat's name *are*
3. it/a male or a female *is*
4. *DO* your cat/catch mice
5. *DO* your cat/friendly
6. *Does* your cat/sit on your lap a lot
7. *Does* your cat/have toys (what kind)
8. why/you/like cats *are*

1.7 *Wh-* Questions with a Preposition

EXAMPLES	EXPLANATION

What does she talk **about**?
  She talks about her cats.
What does your cat sleep **on**?
  She sleeps on a pillow.
	In conversation, most people put the preposition at the end of the *wh-* question.

Formal: With whom does the dog sleep? **Informal: Who** does the dog sleep **with**?	Putting the preposition before a question word is very formal. When the preposition comes at the beginning, we use *whom*, not *who*.

Where do you **come from**?
  I come from Mexico.
Where **are** you **from**?
  I'm from Mexico.
	For place of origin, you can use *be from* or *come from*.

What time does the program begin? It begins **at** 9 P.M.	Omit *at* in a question about time.

EXERCISE **15** **ABOUT YOU** Ask a *yes/no* question using the words given. Then use the words in parentheses ( ) to ask a *wh-* question whenever possible. Another student will answer.

EXAMPLE   you/eat in the cafeteria (with whom) OR (who . . . with)

A: Do you eat in the cafeteria?
B: Yes, I do.
A: Who do you eat with? OR With whom do you eat?
B: I eat with my friends.

Do **1.** you/live alone (with whom) OR (who . . . with) *with whom do you live? who do you live with?*

Do **2.** you/go to bed early (what time) *do you go to bed?*

wDo **3.** your teacher/come to class on time (what time) *do*

Do **4.** your teacher/come from this city (where . . . from)

Do **5.** you/practice English outside of class (with whom) OR (who . . . with)

Do **6.** you/think about your future (what else) *what else does think about . . . .*

Do **7.** you/complain about English grammar (what else) *does complain . . . .*

8. you/listen to the radio (what station)

9. your teacher/talk about spelling (what else)

10. you/interested in animals (what animals)

11. you/come from Mexico (where)

12. you/go to sleep before midnight (what time)

EXERCISE **16** **Circle the correct words to complete this conversation.**

CD 1, TR 09

A: We're late. Hurry. The train is ready to leave.

B: Let's go . . . (on the train) . . . Why (*that dog is*/(*is that dog*) on the train?
                                             (example)
    (*Are*/*Do*) they allow dogs on trains?
    (1)

A: That's not an ordinary dog. That's a guide dog.

B: What's a guide dog?

A: It's a dog that helps people with disabilities.

B: How (*do they help*/*they help*) people?
                 (2)

A: They (*help*/*helps*) blind people move from place to place, on foot and
          (3)
    by public transportation.

B: (*Are*/*Do*) they need special training?
    (4)

A: Yes, they (*are*/*do*).
(5)

B: Where (*do*/*are*) they get their training?
(6)

A: They get their training at special schools.

B: Are they only for blind people?

A: No. Guide dogs help people with other disabilities too. There are guide dogs for the deaf[11] and for people in wheelchairs.

B: Why (*are you*/*you are*) such an expert on guide dogs?
(7)

A: My cousin is blind. He has a guide dog.

B: Let's play with the dog.

A: No. (*It's not*/*It doesn't*) good to distract a guide dog. A guide dog
(8)
(*need*/*needs*) to concentrate.
(9)

B: When (*are*/*do*) they play?
(10)

A: They (*play*/*plays*) when the owner (*takes*/*take*) off the dog's harness.
(11)   (12)

B: What (*do*/*does*) they eat?
(13)

A: They eat the same thing other dogs eat.

B: It's amazing what a dog can do.

1.8 Questions About Meaning, Spelling, Cost, and Time

Wh- Word	*Do*/ *Does*	Subject	Verb (Base Form)	Complement	Explanation
What	does	"kitten"	mean?		*Mean, spell, say,* and *cost* are verbs and should be in the verb position of a question. Use the base form in the question.
How	do	you	spell	"kitten"?	
How	do	you	say	"kitten" in Spanish?	
How much	does	a kitten	cost?		
How long	does	it	take	to train a dog?	We use the verb *take* with time. The subject is *it*.

[11]A *deaf* person cannot hear.

EXERCISE 17 Fill in the blanks to complete the conversation.

CD 1, TR 10

A: _____Do you have_____ a pet?
  (example)

B: Yes. I have a new kitten.

A: I don't know the word "kitten." What _____? (1)

B: Kitten means "baby cat."

A: Oh. What's his name?

B: Romeo.

A: How _____? (2)

B: R-O-M-E-O.

A: Where _____? (3)

B: He sleeps with me, of course. _____ any pets? (4)

A: Yes, I do.

B: What kind of pet _____? (5)

A: I have a bird that talks. I don't know the word in English.

How _____ "loro" in English? (6)

B: Parrot. So you have a parrot. What _____? (7)

A: His name is Chico.

B: How old _____? (8)

A: He's almost 20 years old.

B: Wow! How long _____? (9)

A: They live a long time. Some live up to 80 years.

B: Are parrots expensive? How much _____? (10)

A: It depends on what kind you get. But they usually cost between $175 and $1,000.

B: _____ parrots affectionate? (11)

A: Oh, yes. They're very affectionate. Chico sits on my shoulder all the time.

B: What _____? (12)

A: He eats fruit, vegetables, rice, nuts, and seeds.

B: _____? (13)

A: Yes. He talks a lot.

B: What _____(14)_____?

A: He says, "Good-bye," "Hello," "I love you," and many more things.
He speaks Spanish and English.

B: Maybe he speaks English better than we do!

EXERCISE 18 **Fill in the blanks to complete the conversation.**

🔊
CD 1, TR 11

A: I know you love dogs. _____Do you have_____ a dog now?
                          (example)

B: No, I _____(1)_____. But I have two cats. I don't have time
for a dog.

A: Why _____(2)_____ time for a dog?

B: Because I'm not at home very much.

A: Why _____(3)_____?

B: Because I work eight hours a day, and at night, I take classes. Dogs
need a lot of attention. I _____(4)_____ have enough time
right now.

A: What about your cats? _____(5)_____ need attention too?

B: Not as much as dogs. What about you? _____(6)_____ any pets?

A: I have several tropical fish.[12]

B: _____(7)_____ expensive?

A: Some of them are very expensive.

B: How much _____(8)_____?

A: Some of them cost more than $100.

B: Wow! That's a lot of money for a boring pet.

A: Fish _____(9)_____ boring. It _____(10)_____ fun to
look at them. And when I go to work, they _____(11)_____ get
lonely, like dogs and cats.

B: Yes, but they _____(12)_____ affectionate like dogs and cats.

[12]*Fish can be singular or plural. In this case, fish is plural.*

(continued)

A: They _____ make noise like dogs do, so neighbors never
            (13)
complain about fish.

B: How many fish _____?
                            (14)

A: I have about 14 or 15. My favorite is my Oranda.

B: How _____ "Oranda"?
                    (15)

A: O-R-A-N-D-A. It's a kind of a goldfish. When you have time, come and
see my fish tank.

Marianne and Sparky

Before You Read

1. Do people in your native culture treat pets the same way Americans do?

2. What kinds of animals or pets do people prefer in your native culture?

CD 1, TR 12

Read the following e-mail from Elena in the U.S. to her friend Sofia in Russia. Pay special attention to frequency words.

● ● ●

To: sofia1980@e*mail.com

Subject: American pets

Dear Sofia,

I want to tell you about one aspect of American life that seems strange to me—how Americans treat their pets. I have a new American friend, Marianne. She lives alone, but she has a dog, Sparky. Marianne treats him like a child. She **always** carries a picture of Sparky in her wallet. She **often** buys toys for him, especially on his birthday. She **often** calls him on the telephone when she's not home and talks into the answering machine. Sparky **always** sleeps in bed with her.

When she goes to work, she uses a dog-walking service. **Twice a day**, someone comes to her house to play with Sparky and take him for a walk. She says that he gets lonely if he's home alone all day. She **always** leaves the TV on when she goes to work to keep Sparky entertained.

Once a month, she takes him to a dog groomer. The groomer gives him a bath and cuts and paints his nails. When she travels, she usually takes him with her, but sometimes she puts him in a kennel[13] or pet hotel. All of these dog services cost a lot of money. But Marianne doesn't care. Nothing is too expensive when it comes to Sparky.

There's a small beach near her house that is just for dogs and their owners. She takes Sparky there whenever the weather is nice so that he can play with other dogs. While the dogs play together, the dog owners talk to each other. She always cleans up after her dog.

In winter, she always puts a coat on Sparky. In fact, Sparky has about four different winter coats. Whenever it rains, Sparky wears his bright yellow raincoat.

Sometimes I think American dogs live better than most people in the world.

Your good friend,

Elena

1.9 Simple Present Tense with Frequency Words

EXAMPLES	EXPLANATION
Marianne **often** calls her dog on the phone. Sparky **always** sleeps in bed with her. When she travels, she **usually** takes Sparky with her.	We use the simple present tense with frequency words to show a regular activity. Frequency words are: *always, usually, often, sometimes, rarely, seldom, hardly ever,* and *never.*
Whenever the weather is nice, she takes her dog to the beach. Sparky wears a raincoat **whenever** it rains.	*Whenever* shows a regular activity. It means "any time."
Once a month, she takes her dog to a groomer. Someone comes to her house to walk the dog **twice a day**.	Expressions that show frequency are: • every day (week, month, year) • every other day (week, month, year) • once (twice, etc.) a day (week, month, year) • from time to time • once in a while

Frequency Words	always	100%
	usually/generally	↑
	often/frequently	
	sometimes/occasionally	
	rarely/seldom/hardly ever	↓
	never/not ever	0%

[13]A *kennel* is a place where pets are kept while their owners are away.

EXERCISE 19 Fill in the blanks with an appropriate verb. Answers may vary.

EXAMPLE Marianne always ___puts___ a coat on Sparky when the weather is cold.

1. Elena sometimes _____ a letter to her friend Sofia.
2. Marianne _____ always worried about her dog.
3. The dog _____ always happy to see Marianne when she comes home.
4. Marianne often _____ toys for her dog.
5. The TV _____ always on when Marianne is at work.
6. Sparky always _____ in bed with Marianne.
7. Marianne usually _____ with her dog when she goes on vacation.

EXERCISE 20 **ABOUT YOU** Fill in the blanks with an appropriate frequency word.

EXAMPLE I ___rarely___ use a public telephone.

1. I _____ say, "How are you?" when I meet a friend.
2. I'm _____ confused about American customs.
3. I _____ smile when I pass someone I know.
4. I _____ shake hands when I get together with a friend.
5. Americans _____ ask me, "What country are you from?"
6. I _____ celebrate my birthday in a restaurant.
7. I _____ buy birthday presents for my good friends.
8. If I invite a friend to a restaurant, I _____ pay for both of us.
9. I _____ take my cell phone with me.
10. I _____ eat in fast-food restaurants.
11. I _____ leave my computer on overnight.

EXERCISE 21 **ABOUT YOU** Fill in the blanks with an appropriate frequency word. You may find a partner and compare your answers.

EXAMPLE People in my native culture ___rarely___ have cats in the house.

1. Dogs in my native culture _____ sleep with their owners.
2. Dogs in my native culture are _____ part of the family.
3. Cats in my native culture are _____ part of the family.
4. People in my native culture _____ feed pet food to cats and dogs.
5. People in my native culture _____ travel with their pets.

EXERCISE **22** In the sentences in Exercise 21, notice if the frequency word comes before or after the verb. Write *B* for *before* or *A* for *after*.

EXAMPLE People in my native culture ___*rarely*___ have cats in the house. **B**

1.10 Position of Frequency Words and Expressions

EXAMPLES	EXPLANATION
Verb Sparky *is* **always** happy to see Marianne. **Verb** The TV *is* **always** on in the day. **Verb** Marianne *is* **rarely** home during the day.	The frequency word comes **after** the verb *be*.
Verb Marianne **often** *calls* Sparky on the phone. **Verb** She **usually** *travels* with Sparky. **Verb** She **always** *carries* a picture of Sparky.	The frequency word comes **before** other verbs.
Sometimes she puts Sparky in a kennel. **Usually** she feeds Sparky dog food. **Often** Elena writes to her friend about American customs.	*Sometimes, usually,* and *often* can come at the beginning of the sentence too. Do not put *always, never, rarely,* and *seldom* before the subject. 　*Wrong: Always* she carries a picture of her dog.
Once a month, she travels. She travels **once a month**. **Every week**, she goes to the beach. She goes to the beach **every week**.	A frequency expression can come at the beginning or at the end of a sentence. When it comes at the beginning of the sentence, we sometimes separate it from the sentence with a comma.

EXERCISE **23** Rewrite the sentence, adding the word in ( ).

EXAMPLE Marianne carries a picture of Sparky. (always)

Marianne always carries a picture of Sparky.

1. She talks to Sparky on the telephone. (often)

   She often talks to sparky on the telephone.

2. She puts Sparky in a pet hotel. (sometimes)

   Sometimes she puts sparky in a pet hotel.

(continued)

3. She takes her dog on vacation. (usually)

Usually she takes her dog on vacation.

4. She's with her dog. (always)

She is always with her dog.

5. Sparky goes out in the rain without a coat. (never)

Sparky never goes out in the rain without a coat.

EXERCISE 24 **ABOUT YOU** Add a frequency word to each sentence to make a true statement about yourself.

EXAMPLE I drink coffee at night.
I never drink coffee at night.

1. I talk to my neighbors.

2. I study in the public library.

3. I'm busy on Saturdays.

4. I receive e-mail from my friends.

5. I call my family in my native country.

6. I travel in the summer.

7. I speak English at home with my family.

8. I eat meat for dinner.

9. I go out of town.

10. I study in the library.

11. I eat cereal for breakfast.

12. I bring my dictionary to class.

EXERCISE 25 **ABOUT YOU** Add a verb (phrase) to make a true statement about yourself.

EXAMPLE I/usually

I usually **drink coffee in the morning.** OR

I'm usually **afraid to go out at night.**

1. I/rarely/on Sunday

2. I/usually/on the weekend

3. I/hardly ever

_____

4. I/sometimes/at night

_____

5. my family/sometimes

_____

6. my family/rarely

_____

1.11 Questions with *Ever*

We use *ever* in a question when we want an answer that has a frequency word.

Do/Does	Subject	*Ever*	Verb	Complement	Short Answer
Do Does	you the teacher	**ever** **ever**	sleep bring	with your cat? her dog to school?	Yes, I **sometimes** do. No, she **never** does.

Be	Subject	*Ever*		Complement	Short Answer
Are Is	dogs Marianne	**ever** **ever**		unhappy? home during the day?	Yes, they **sometimes** are. No, she **never** is.

Language Notes:
1. In a short answer, the frequency word comes between the subject and the verb.
2. The verb after *never* is affirmative.
   Does your cat ever drink milk?
   No, she never **does**.

EXERCISE 26 **Answer the questions with a short answer and the frequency word in parentheses ( ).**

EXAMPLE Do dogs ever bark? (sometimes)
Yes, they sometimes do.

1. Does Marianne ever sleep with her dog? (always)

2. Does Marianne ever travel? (often)

3. Do fish ever make noise? (never)   *No, They never do*

4. Do birds ever make noise? (always)

5. Do parrots ever live for more than 20 years? (usually)

6. Do dogs ever live for more than 20 years? (rarely)

7. Are parrots ever affectionate? (sometimes)

8. Are cats ever lazy? (usually)   *yes they usually are*

EXERCISE 27 **ABOUT YOU** Fill in the blanks with a frequency word to make a true statement about yourself. Then ask a question with *ever*. Another student will answer.

EXAMPLE   I ___rarely___ eat breakfast in a restaurant.

   A: Do you ever eat breakfast in a restaurant?
   B: No, I never do.

1. I _____ sleep with the light on.
2. I _____ watch TV in the morning.
3. I _____ cry during a sad movie.
4. I _____ dream in English.
5. I _____ take off my shoes when I enter my house.
6. I _____ wear a watch.
7. I _____ use cologne or perfume.
8. I _____ fall asleep with the TV on.
9. I _____ carry an MP3 player.
10. I _____ discuss politics with my friends.
11. I _____ wear sandals in warm weather.
12. I'm _____ friendly with my neighbors.

1.12 Questions with *How Often* and Answers with Frequency Expressions

EXAMPLES	EXPLANATION

How often do you take your dog out?
   I take her out **three times a day**.
How often does Marianne travel?
   She travels **every other month**.
How often do you take your cat to the doctor?
   I take my cat to the doctor **twice a year**.
	We use *how often* when we want to know about the frequency of an activity.

EXERCISE 28   **ABOUT YOU** Ask a question with "*How often do you . . . ?*" and the words given. Another student will answer.

EXAMPLE   eat in a restaurant

> **A:** How often do you eat in a restaurant?
> **B:** I eat in a restaurant once a week.

1. check your e-mail
2. shop for groceries
3. exercise
4. get a haircut
5. use your dictionary
6. use public transportation
7. use the Internet
8. go to the dentist
9. watch the news on TV
10. go to the teacher's office

Summary of Lesson 1

1. Observe the simple present tense with the verb *be*.

   Your dog **is** beautiful.
   It **isn't** big.
   Is it a collie? No, it **isn't**.
   What kind of dog **is** it?

   You **are** young.
   You **aren't** ready for a dog.
   Are you responsible? Yes, I **am**.
   Why **aren't** you ready for a dog?

2. Observe the simple present tense with other verbs.

Base Form	-s Form
My friends **have** a dog.	She **likes** birds.
They **don't have** a cat.	She **doesn't like** cats.
Do they **have** a bird?	**Does** she **like** small birds?
No, they **don't**.	Yes, she **does**.
What kind of dog **do** they **have**?	Why **does** she **like** birds?
Why **don't** they **have** a cat?	Why **doesn't** she **like** cats?

3. Frequency words:

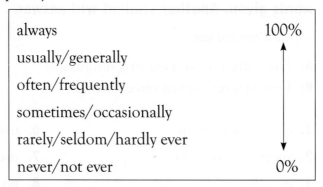

always	100%
usually/generally	
often/frequently	
sometimes/occasionally	
rarely/seldom/hardly ever	
never/not ever	0%

4. Questions with frequency words:

Does he **ever** take his dog to the park? Yes, he often does.
How often does he feed his dog? Twice a day.

Editing Advice

1. Don't use *have* with age. Don't use *years* without *old*.

My daughter ~~has~~ *is* 10 years *old*.

2. Don't use *have* with *hungry, thirsty, hot, cold,* or *afraid*.

Please open the window. I ~~have~~ *am* hot.

3. Don't forget the verb *be*. Remember that some words that end in *-ed* are adjectives, not verbs.

The college *is* located downtown.

I *am* very tired.

4. Use the correct word order in questions.

Why ~~you are~~ *are you* late?

Why ~~your sister doesn't~~ *doesn't your sister* drive?

5. Don't use *be* with another present tense verb.

I~~'m~~ come from Poland.

We~~'re~~ have a new computer.

6. Use the *-s* form when the subject is *he, she, it, everyone,* or *family.*

My father live in New York. [*s*]

Everyone know the answer. [*s*]

My family live in Egypt. [*s*]

7. Use *doesn't* when the subject is *he, she, it,* or *family.*

He ~~don't~~ have a car. [*doesn't*]

My family ~~don't~~ live here. [*doesn't*]

8. Use the base form after *does.*

He doesn't speaks English.

Where does he lives?

9. Don't forget to use *do* or *does* and the base form in the question.

Where your father works? [*does*]

10. Use normal question formation for *spell, mean, cost,* and *take.*

What ~~means "custom"~~? [*does "custom" mean*]

How spell "responsible"? [*do you*]

How much ~~costs~~ the newspaper? [*does*] [*cost*]

How long it takes to do the exercise? [*does*]

11. Use the correct word order with frequency words.

He ~~goes sometimes~~ to the zoo. [*sometimes goes*]

~~Never I~~ eat in a restaurant. [*I never*]

I ~~never am~~ late to class. [*am never*]

12. Don't put a frequency phrase between the subject and the verb.

She ~~all the time~~ talks on the phone. [*all the time*]

Editing Quiz

Some of the shaded words and phrases have mistakes. Find the mistakes and correct them. If the shaded words are correct, write _C_.

       _C_

A: Is that your dog?
   (example)

B: Yes. His name is Buddy.

     _do_

A: How you spell "Buddy"?
    (example)

B: B-U-D-D-Y. He's a therapy dog.

A: What a therapy dog does?
       _(1)_

B: He make sick people feel better. We're often go to hospitals to visit sick
    _(2)_   _(3)_

people. He's sits on their laps and they pet him.
     _(4)_   _(5)_

A: How that makes sick people feel better?
      _(6)_

B: They feel happy when they're with a nice dog. Everyone love
    _(7)_   _(8)_

Buddy—the patients, the nurses, the doctors. He's very popular.

Patients smile usually when they're with Buddy.
     _(9)_

A: How does a dog becomes a therapy dog?
      _(10)_

B: Not every dog is good for this job. First we has to answer a few
                           _(11)_

questions like these:

- Does he like people? (Buddy loves people.)
    _(12)_   _(13)_

- Does he has a calm personality? (Buddy doesn't barks.)
    _(14)_   _(15)_

- Is the dog at least one year old? (Buddy has six years.)
                     _(16)_

Then the dog needs training. And he have to pass a test.
      _(17)_   _(18)_

A: What kind of test does he have to pass?
         _(19)_

B: He has to come when I call him. He has to follow commands, like "sit"

and "stay." And a lot of other things too.

A: How much cost the training?
       _(20)_

B: It costs $10 to register the dog. Then he gets a certificate.
   _(21)_   _(22)_

A: How long it takes to train the dog?
     _(23)_

B: That depend on the dog.
    _(24)_

A: Are the dog owners make money?
(25)

B: No. We work as volunteers.
(26)

A: How often do you visit the hospital with Buddy?
(27)

B: We once a week go to the hospital. The hospital located a few blocks
(28) (29)

from my house. Always I bathe him and brush him before we go.
(30)

If you want more information, go to www.tdi-dog.org.

A: What means TDI?
(31)

B: It means Therapy Dogs International. I have to go now. Buddy needs
(32) (33)

water. He has thirsty.
(34)

A: How you know that?
(35)

B: His tongue is out. That's dog talk for "I thirsty."
(36)

Lesson 1 Test/Review

PART 1 **Fill in the blanks with the affirmative form of the verb in parentheses ( ). Then write the negative form of the verb.**

EXAMPLES Elena _____wants_____ to write about strange American customs.
(want)

She _____doesn't want_____ to write about the weather.

1. Marianne _____ Elena.
(know)

   She _____ Sofia.

2. Marianne _____ a dog.
(have)

   Elena _____ a dog.

3. Elena _____ in the U.S.
(live)

   Sofia _____ in the U.S.

4. Marianne _____ American.
(be)

   Elena _____ American.

(continued)

The Simple Present Tense; Frequency Words **37**

5. You _____ some American customs.
   (understand)

You _____ all American customs.

6. American customs _____ strange for Elena.
   (be)

American customs _____ strange for Marianne.

7. I _____ cats.
   (like)

I _____ dogs.

8. Dogs _____ a lot of attention.
   (need)

Cats _____ as much attention.

9. Almost everyone _____ kittens and puppies.
   (love)

Most people _____ snakes.

PART **2** **Read each statement. Then write a *yes/no* question about the words in parentheses ( ). Write a short answer.**

EXAMPLE Elena lives in the U.S. (Marianne) (yes)

<u>*Does Marianne live in the U.S.? Yes, she does.*</u>

1. Marianne has a dog. (Elena) (no)

_____

2. Elena and Marianne live in the U.S. (Sofia) (no)

_____

3. Elena has an American friend. (Sofia) (no)

_____

4. Elena often writes letters. (you/ever) [Give a true answer about yourself.]

_____

5. You like animals. (you/ever/go to the zoo) [Give a true answer about yourself.]

_____

6. American customs are strange for Elena. (for Marianne) (no)

_____

PART 3

Fill in the blanks to complete the question.

EXAMPLE Dogs like people.

Why _*do dogs like people?*_ _____

1. Marianne sometimes travels with her dog.

   How _____ with her dog?

2. Sofia doesn't understand American customs.

   Why _____ American customs?

3. Elena writes to Sofia once a week.

   How often _____ to Elena?

4. A dog-walking service costs a lot of money.

   How much _____?

5. Elena doesn't have a dog.

   Why _____ a dog?

6. Marianne carries a picture of Sparky in her wallet.

   Why _____ in her wallet?

7. Marianne walks her dog every day.

   How often _____?

8. She takes her dog to the animal hospital.

   How often _____ to the animal hospital?

9. Guide dogs need a lot of training.

   Why _____ a lot of training?

10. Rescue dogs save people's lives.

    How _____ people's lives?

11. A purebred dog costs a lot of money.

    How much _____?

PART **4** **Write a question with the words given.**

EXAMPLE What/a dog/eat

What _does a dog eat?_ _____

1. How/spell/"kitten"

   _____

2. What/ "puppy"/mean

   _____

(continued)

3. How/say/"cat" in Spanish

_____

4. How much/cost/a parrot

_____

5. How long/take/to train a dog

_____

Expansion

Classroom
Activities

❶ Put a check (✓) to indicate which of the following customs are typical customs in the U.S. and which are typical customs in your native culture. Discuss your answers in a small group or with the entire class.

Customs	In the U.S.	In my native culture
People walk their dogs on a leash.	✓	
Dogs have jackets and other clothes.		
Supermarkets sell a lot of pet food.		
Students wear jeans to class.		
Students write in their textbooks.		
People talk a lot about politics.		
Children watch TV a lot.		
Friends get together in coffee houses.		
People eat some foods with their hands.		
People are friendly with their neighbors.		
People say, "How are you?"		
Teenagers text a lot.		
People wear gym shoes.		
People take off their shoes when they enter a house.		
Young adults live separately from their parents.		
People usually leave a tip in a restaurant.		
Students study a foreign language.		

2 Work with a partner or in a small group. Tell if you think each animal is a good pet. Why or why not?

a. a snake

b. a parakeet

c. a rabbit

d. a lizard

e. a turtle

f. a hamster

g. a cat

h. a dog

i. a tropical fish

Talk About It

1 Do you or any of your friends or family members have a pet? Is the pet like a member of the family?

2 The following proverbs mention animals. Discuss the meaning of each proverb. Do you have a similar proverb in your native language?

a. You can't teach an old dog new tricks.

b. When the cat's away, the mice will play.

c. Man's best friend is his dog.

d. Curiosity killed the cat.

e. The dog's bark is worse than his bite.

3 Why do you think pets can improve the lives of sick or elderly people?

4 Do you think some dogs are more intelligent than others? Do you think some dogs have a better temperament than others?

Write

About It

❶ Write about differences in how people treat pets in the U.S. and in another country you know about.

❷ Write about American customs that seem strange to you. Compare these customs to how people behave in your country or native culture.

A Strange American Custom

There is one American custom that seems strange to me. Americans always seem so cheerful. When they meet you, they always smile. When they leave you, they often say, "Have a nice day." In my country, Ukraine, people say hello but don't usually smile...

 For more practice using grammar in context, please visit our Web site.

Grammar
The Present Continuous Tense[1]
Action and Nonaction Verbs
The Future Tense

Context
Getting Older

[1]Some textbooks refer to this tense as the *present progressive tense*.

Retirement Living

Before
You Read

1. What observations do you make about older people in the U.S.?

2. What is the retirement age in other countries? Do older people usually have a good life?

CD 1, TR 13

As the U.S. population ages, many building developers are building homes for people over 55. Read the following conversation between a 62-year-old man, Jack (J), who is taking a tour of a retirement village, and the manager of the retirement village (M). Pay special attention to present continuous tense verbs.

J: I'm **thinking** about moving to this retirement village. Can you give me some information?

M: This is a village for people over 55 years old. The people here are retired, but most are very active. There are different types of housing: single family homes, townhouses,[2] and apartments. For those who need more help, we also have an assisted-living section. Let me give you a tour. This is our fitness center. It has state-of-the-art equipment.[3]

J: What **are** these people **doing**?

M: They're **doing** yoga. And that group over there **is lifting** weights. Another group **is doing** aerobics. Let's move on to the game room. Those people **are playing** chess. And that group **is playing** cards. Now let me take you to the pool area. In this area, people **are swimming** laps.[4]

J: What **are** those people **doing**?

M: Those people **are taking** a water aerobics class. Let's go to the computer room now. That's the computer teacher. He's **teaching** that group how to design Web pages. Jerry, over there, **is putting** all his family pictures

---

[2]A *townhouse* is one of a series of houses attached to each other in a row.
[3]*State-of-the-art* equipment is the latest equipment.
[4]Swimming *laps* means swimming from one end of the pool to the other and back again, over and over.

on his Web site. Marge, in the corner, **is designing** a Web site with her vacation pictures and stories about her interesting trips. She likes to travel all over the world. Now let's look at the dance area.

J: The band **is playing** a great song, and many of the people **are dancing**. This place is beautiful and certainly offers a lot of activities. But I don't know if it's right for me. I don't know how to dance, play chess, or design Web pages.

M: Don't worry. There are instructors here who will help you.

J: **Is** everybody **doing** something?

M: No. My wife is at home now. I think she's **reading** or **watching** TV. Or maybe she's **playing** with our grandchildren.

J: I notice that there are more women than men here.

M: Well, as you know, women live longer than men.

J: I'm a widower, you know. Maybe I can meet a woman here.

M: That's entirely possible. We have a singles group that meets once a week in the game room. Mary Dodge can give you information about the singles group. She's **standing** over there. She's **wearing** blue jeans and a red T-shirt.

J: How much does it cost to live here?

M: That depends on what kind of a house you choose. Come to my office and we'll look at the costs.

The Present Continuous Tense; Action and Nonaction Verbs; the Future Tense   **45**

2.1 Present Continuous Tense

To form the present continuous tense, use a form of *be* (*is, am, are*) + verb *-ing*.[5]

Forms

EXAMPLES	EXPLANATION
Subj. ***Be*** **Verb + *-ing*** **Complement** I am putting my pictures on a Web site. Jack is visiting a retirement village. She is teaching Web design. They **are** **doing** yoga.	I → am He/She/It → is Singular Subject → is } + verb *-ing* We/You/They → are Plural Subject → are
They're playing cards. **Jack's** taking a tour of the retirement village. **He's** asking questions. The **manager's** answering his questions.	We can make a contraction with the subject pronoun and a form of *be*. Most nouns can also contract with *is*.[6]

Jack **isn't** doing yoga.
 Most people **aren't** watching TV.
 I'm not playing tennis.
	To form the negative, put *not* after the verb *am/is/are*.
	 Negative contractions:
	     is not = isn't
	     are not = aren't
	 There is no contraction for *am not*.

Jerry **is designing** a Web site *and* **putting** his family pictures on it.
 They **are playing** cards *and* **laughing**.
 She's **reading** *or* **watching** TV.
	Do not repeat the *be* verb after these connectors:
	     and
	     or

Use

EXAMPLES	EXPLANATION
a. Some people **are dancing** now. b. My wife **is reading** now.	In sentences (a) and (b), we use the present continuous tense to describe an action in progress at this moment.
c. Mary Dodge **is standing** over there. d. She **is wearing** jeans. e. A man **is sitting** in front of a computer.	In sentences (c), (d), and (e), we use the present continuous tense to describe a state or condition, using the following verbs: *sit*, *stand*, *wear*, and *sleep*. We can observe these things now.

[5]For a review of the spelling of the *-ing* form of the verb, see Appendix A.
[6]See Lesson 1, page 5 for exceptions.

EXERCISE **1** **Fill in the blanks with the present continuous form of the verb in parentheses ( ). Use correct spelling.**

EXAMPLE Jack __'s visiting_____ a retirement village.
          (visit)

1. He _____ a tour.
        (take)

2. He _____ at the different activities.
        (look)

3. The manager of the village _____ him information.
                                     (give)

4. Some people _____.
                    (dance)

5. Some people _____ the exercise equipment.
                    (use)

6. One woman _____ weights.
                  (lift)

7. Those people _____ chess.
                     (play)

8. Some people _____.
                    (swim)

9. Jerry _____. He _____
           (not/read)   (put)

   his family pictures on his Web site.

10. The manager's wife is at home. She _____ or
                                          (read)

    _____ TV. She _____ an
         (watch)   (not/take)

    aerobics class.

11. Some people _____ anything.
                     (not/do)

EXERCISE **2** **Fill in the blanks with an affirmative or negative verb to make a true statement about what is happening now.**

EXAMPLES I __'m wearing_____ jeans now.
             (wear)

The teacher ___isn't writing____ on the blackboard now.
                  (write)

1. The sun _____ now.
                (shine)

2. It _____ now.
        (rain)

3. I _____ my answers in my book.
        (write)

(continued)

The Present Continuous Tense; Action and Nonaction Verbs; the Future Tense **47**

4. I _____ a pencil to write this exercise.
(use)

5. We _____ this exercise together.
(do)

6. The teacher _____ the students with this exercise.
(help)

7. The teacher _____ a watch.
(wear)

8. I _____ my dictionary now.
(use)

9. We _____ possessive forms now.
(practice)

10. I _____ jeans.
(wear)

11. The teacher _____.
(stand)

12. I _____ near the door.
(sit)

Life After Retirement

Before You Read

1. Is anyone in your family retired? How does that person keep busy?

2. At what age do you think people should retire?

CD 1, TR 14

Read the following magazine article. Pay special attention to present continuous tense verbs.

The U.S. population **is aging**. More and more Americans **are thinking** about retirement. But today, many people **are retiring** younger and healthier than ever before. People **are living** longer. But they **are not leaving** their jobs to spend their days at the beach or to babysit for their grandchildren. Most older people prefer to keep busy. Many healthy seniors **are starting** new careers. They want to explore new avenues in their lives.

Judy Pearlman is a 62-year-old retired school teacher from Chicago. After 35 years in education, she **is starting** a new career—making dolls. "Now I have time to do what I always dreamed about," she says. "**I'm having** more fun than ever before. **I'm meeting** new people, **traveling** in my new job, and **earning** money all at the same time. And I'm still **getting** my teacher pension. **I'm enjoying** every minute of it. I think this is the best time of my life."

"After 33 years as an accountant, **I'm** now **taking** art classes," says Charles Haskell of Cleveland. "**I'm discovering** a new talent."

Some senior citizens decide not to retire at all. Frank Babbit of Milwaukee is a carpenter. He has his own business and works 50 hours a week. And he**'s** almost 88 years old.

Many older women **are returning** to work after raising their children. "My kids are grown and don't need me now," says Miriam Orland of San Francisco. "So I have time for myself now. **I'm taking** courses at a community college. **I'm thinking** about a career in Web design."

Some retirees **are using** their free time to volunteer. "I retired as an accountant six months ago, and now I volunteer as a math tutor in a public library near my house. I go to the library twice a week to help students who **are having** trouble with math," says Ron Meyers of Miami. "I work in a food pantry and feed the homeless three times a week," says Linda Carlson of Washington, D.C. "It gives me a lot of satisfaction."

Today healthy retirees **are exploring** many options, from relaxing to starting a new business or making a hobby into a new career. How do you see yourself as a retiree?

2.2 Using the Present Continuous for Longer Actions

EXAMPLES	EXPLANATION
Judy **is meeting** new people. She **is getting** her pension and **earning** money from her new job. She is **enjoying** her new career. My grandfather **is planning** to retire soon.	We use the present continuous tense to show a long-term action that is in progress. It may not be happening at this exact moment.
More and more retired Americans **are looking** for a second career. Some older people **are working** because of economic necessity. Americans **are living** longer. Many older women **are returning** to work after their children are grown.	We use the present continuous tense to describe a *trend*. A trend is a behavior that many people in society are doing at this time. It describes a change in behavior from an earlier time.

EXERCISE 3 Fill in the blanks with an appropriate present continuous tense verb. Answers may vary.

EXAMPLE More and more older people _____are working_____ these days.

1. Many people _____ at a younger age.

2. They _____ their time at the beach or babysitting for
   (not)
   their grandchildren.

3. They _____ new careers.

4. People _____ longer and healthier lives.

5. Some people _____ new talents and abilities.

6. Some older women _____ to work after raising a family.

EXERCISE 4 **ABOUT YOU** Write three sentences about being a student. Tell what is happening in your life as a student. You may share your sentences with the class.

EXAMPLES I'm taking five courses this semester.

I'm staying with my sister this semester.

I'm majoring in math.

You may use these verbs:

learn	study
stay	live
plan	take courses
major	improve

1. _____

2. _____

3. _____

EXERCISE 5 **ABOUT YOU** Write three sentences to tell about current changes in your life. Then find a partner and compare your sentences to your partner's.

EXAMPLES
I'm gaining weight.

I'm planning to buy a house.

My English pronunciation is improving.

You may use the following verbs:

plan	get (become)
grow	learn
gain	improve
lose	think about
start	change

1. _____

2. _____

3. _____

EXERCISE 6 Tell if these things are happening at this point in time in the U.S., in the world, or in another country you know about. Discuss your answers.

1. Older people are getting more respect than before.
2. People are living healthier lives.
3. People are living longer.
4. The world is becoming a more dangerous place.
5. The economy is getting better.
6. Medical science is advancing quickly.
7. A lot of people are losing their jobs.
8. People are working harder than before.
9. People are doing more and enjoying less.
10. The cost of a college education is going down.
11. The cost of computers is going down.
12. More and more people are using cell phones.
13. Cars are getting bigger.
14. Kids are growing up faster than before.

2.3 Questions with the Present Continuous Tense

Compare affirmative statements and questions.

Wh- Word	Be	Subject	Be	Verb + -ing	Complement	Short Answer
		Jerry	is	designing	something.	
	Is	he		designing	a house?	No, he **isn't**.
What	is	he		designing?		A Web site.
		They	are	taking	courses at college.	
	Are	they		taking	biology?	No, they **aren't**.
What courses	are	they		taking?		Computer courses.
		He	is	thinking	about a new career.	
	Is	he		thinking	about a career in computers?	No, he **isn't**.

Language Notes:
1. We can leave a preposition at the end of a question.
   What kind of career is he thinking **about**?
2. When the question is "What . . . doing?" we usually answer with a different verb.
   What are they **doing**? They're **taking** an aerobics class.
   What are those people **doing**? They're **playing** chess.

Compare negative statements and questions.

Wh- Word	Be + n't	Subject	Be + n't	Verb + -ing	Complement
		Mary	isn't	dancing.	
Why	isn't	she		dancing?	
		You	aren't	using	the computer.
Why	aren't	you		using	the computer?

EXERCISE 7   Fill in the blanks to make *yes/no* questions about the readings in this lesson.

EXAMPLE   _____Are those men playing_____ checkers?

No, they aren't. Those men are playing chess.

1. _____ this retirement home?

Yes, I am. I'm considering it now that my wife is gone.

2. _____ a Web site? Yes, she is.

Marge is designing a Web site with pictures of her vacations.

3. _____ pictures now? No, she

isn't taking pictures. She's putting her pictures on her Web site.

4. _____ something? No, not

everyone is doing something. Some people are just relaxing.

5. _____ art classes? Yes,

they are. Judy and Charles love art, so they're taking a lot of classes.

6. _____ too many questions?

No, you're not. You can ask as many questions as you want.

EXERCISE **8** **Read each statement. Then write a question using the word(s) in parentheses ( ). An answer is not necessary.**

EXAMPLE Some retirees are discovering new interests. (how)

How are they discovering new interests?
_____

1. Judy is having more fun now. (why)

_____

2. Judy is traveling to many new places. (where)

_____

3. I'm starting a new career. (what kind of career)

_____

4. Some seniors are studying new things. (what)

_____

5. My father is thinking about retirement. (why)

_____

6. My mother is looking for a new career. (what kind)

_____

7. We're not planning to retire. (why)

_____

8. People are living longer nowadays. (why)

_____

9. I'm doing things that interest me. (what kinds of things)

_____

EXERCISE 9   Fill in the blanks to form *yes/no* questions about the reading on pages 44–45. Use the present continuous tense.

CD 1, TR 15

Jack (J) is talking to his neighbor Alan (A).

A: What _____are you doing_____, Jack?
                    (example: you/do)

J: I _____ at some brochures.
            (1 look)

A: What kind of brochures _____?
                                (2 you/look at)

J: They're from a retirement village.

A: So _____ about moving?
            (3 you/think)

J: Yes. I'm thinking about moving into a retirement village.

A: Why?

J: Now that Rose is gone, I feel lonely.

A: But you have a lot of good neighbors here.

J: Most of the people here are young. My neighbors to the north are

never home. Right now they _____. And my
                              (4 work)

neighbors across the street are never home.

A: They're older people. _____ too?
                              (5 work)

J: No. They _____ now. Right now
                  (6 travel)

they _____ a cruise[7] to Alaska.
        (7 take)

A: But I'm here. I _____ my lawn, as usual. And my
                        (8 water)

wife is inside. She _____ on the phone, as usual.
                      (9 talk)

J: I'm sorry I'm complaining so much.

A: You _____. You _____ for
            (10 not/complain)   (11 just/look)

something to do.

J: There's a lot to do. I just don't want to do things alone.

A: But your daughter lives with you.

J: She's in her 20s. She doesn't want to do things with her dad. Right now

she _____ a movie with her friends.
      (12 watch)

A: What movie _____?
                    (13 they/watch)

J: Who knows? Something for young people. Her movies don't interest me.

[7]A *cruise* is a pleasure trip on a large passenger boat.

A: What retirement village _____ to go to?
(14 you/plan)

J: Sun Valley Senior Village seems nice.

A: What about your daughter?

J: She _____ to move in with a friend of hers.
(15 plan)

EXERCISE 10 Fill in the blanks to complete the questions. Use the present continuous tense. Answers may vary.

EXAMPLE

🔊
CD 1, TR 16

A: Why ___is your sister wearing___ sunglasses? It's not sunny.

B: My sister's wearing sunglasses because she wants to look like a movie star.

1. **A:** What _____?

   B: I'm reading an article about older Americans.

   A: _____ the article?

   B: Oh, yes. I'm enjoying it very much.

2. **A:** Where _____ now?

   B: She's going to the park. Grandma always goes to the park on Sundays to jog.

   A: (not) _____ now?

   B: Yes, it's raining. But that doesn't matter. The park has an indoor track.

3. **A:** Martha is on her cell phone. Who _____?

   B: She's talking to her grandfather.

   A: Why _____ on her cell phone?

   Why _____ her home phone?

   B: Because her sister is using the home phone.

4. **Student:** _____?

   Teacher: Yes. Your accent is improving a lot.

   Student: How _____ with my grammar?

   Teacher: You're doing very well.

5. **Wife:** Something smells good. What _____?

   Husband: I'm cooking your favorite dinner—steak and potatoes.

   (A few minutes later)

   Wife: _____ something _____?

   Husband: Uh-oh. The steaks are burning.

   (continued)

6. **A:** The kids are watching TV. What _____?

    B: They're watching cartoons.

    A: Why _____ their homework?

    B: They're not doing their homework because they don't have homework today.

7. **A:** I'm leaving.

    B: Where _____?

    A: I'm going to Grandma's house.

    B: Why _____?

    A: Because you're making too much noise. I have to study. It's quieter at Grandma's house.

8. **Dad:** I'm planning to retire next year.

    Son: You're so young. Why _____?

    Dad: First of all, I'm not so young. I'm almost 60. I'm planning to travel.

    Son: _____ alone?

    Dad: No, of course not. I _____ with Mom.

    Son: But she's still _____.

    Dad: She is now. But she's thinking about retiring too. She loves her work, but enough's enough. It's time to have fun.

Technology and the Generation Gap

Before You Read

1. Is it hard for older people to learn about new technology?

2. Do you text a lot?

CD 1, TR 17

A teenager, Marco (M), is visiting his grandmother (G). Read their conversation. Pay special attention to the present continuous tense and the simple present tense.

G: Listen, Marco, I'm **thinking** about getting a new computer. Can you help me pick one out?

M: Sure, Grandma. How about on Saturday?

G: Saturday's good. What's that sound? It **sounds** like rock music **is coming** from your pocket.

M: It's my cell phone. It's my new ring tone. I'm **receiving** a text message now.

G: **Is** it important?

M: It's a message from Dad. See?

G: It **looks** like Greek to me. What **does** it **say**?

M: He's **reminding** me to come home early. He **wants** to give me another driving lesson. I'm **learning** to drive, you know.

G: When I **have** something to say, I **use** the phone. **Don't** you ever **use** your phone anymore?

M: Of course I **do**. But I also **text** at least 20 times a day. It **saves** time. You can text me too, Grandma.

G: OK. It **looks** hard. Teach me.

M: Try it. Grandma, you're **writing** so slowly. And you're **using** whole words. Use abbreviations. And forget about punctuation. You **need** to write fast.

G: You know I'm an English teacher, and I **don't like** to write without punctuation.

M: Everyone **writes** without punctuation.

G: I **don't think** I can do it.

M: But you **send** e-mail.

G: That's different. I **write** slowly and **check** my spelling before I **send**.

M: You're so old-fashioned!

G: No, I'm not. I'm still **learning** new things. I'm **studying** photo editing at the senior center. I'm **making** a digital family album. I **love** it!

M: I'm proud of you, Grandma.

G: Thanks. Life **is** different today. But one thing **is** the same: 16-year-olds **want** to get their driver's license.

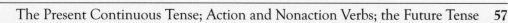

2.4 Contrasting the Simple Present and the Present Continuous

Forms

SIMPLE PRESENT TENSE	PRESENT CONTINUOUS TENSE
Grandma **uses** e-mail.	Marco **is receiving** a message.
She **doesn't use** text messages.	He **isn't receiving** a phone call.
Does she **use** the Internet?	**Is** he **receiving** a message from his friend?
Yes, she **does**.	No, he **isn't**.
When **does** she **use** the Internet?	How **is** he **receiving** a message?
Why **doesn't** she **use** text messages?	Why **isn't** he **receiving** a message from his friend?

Use

EXAMPLES	EXPLANATIONS
a. Most people **have** a computer. a. Young people **like** to send text messages. b. Grandma often **e-mails** her friends. b. Marco sometimes **visits** his grandmother. c. Many people **text** without punctuation. c. People **use** abbreviations in text messages.	Use the **simple present tense** to talk about: a. a general truth b. a habitual activity c. a custom
a. Dad **is reminding** me to put gas in the tank. a. You**'re writing** so slowly. b. Marco **is learning** to drive. b. I**'m making** a family album. c. People **are living** longer these days. c. People **are retiring** earlier these days.	Use the **present continuous tense** for: a. an action that is in progress now b. a longer action that is in progress at this general time c. recent trends in society
Compare: a. My grandparents **live** in a retirement village. b. My sister **is living** in a dorm this semester.	a. *Live* in the simple present shows a person's home. b. *Live* in the present continuous shows a temporary, short-term residence.

Compare:
a. **What does she do (for a living)?**
   She's an English teacher.
b. **What is she doing now?**
   She's talking to her grandson.
	Sentence (a) asks about a job or profession. It uses the simple present tense.
	
	Sentence (b) asks about an activity now. It uses the present continuous tense.

EXERCISE 11 Fill in the blanks with the simple present or the present continuous tense of the verb in parentheses ( ).

1. **A:** What _____are you eating_____? Is it a hamburger?
(example: you/eat)

    B: No, it isn't. It's a veggie burger. I never _____ meat.
(1 eat)

    Where's your lunch?

    A: I don't want to eat lunch. I _____ too much weight.
(2 gain)

    I _____ to lose weight. I _____
(3 try) (4 eat)

    only twice a day—breakfast and dinner.

    B: But you _____ a soda now.
(5 drink)

    A: It's a diet cola.

2. **A:** What _____?
(6 you/do)

    B: I _____ in the answers.
(7 fill)

    A: Why _____ a pen? A pencil is better. What if
(8 you/use)

    you make a mistake?

    B: I never _____ mistakes. My grammar is perfect!
(9 make)

    A: That's not true. We all _____ mistakes. That's
(10 make)

    why we're in this class.

    B: I'm just kidding. Of course I _____ mistakes all
(11 make)

    the time.

3. **A:** What _____ for a living?
(12 your father/do)

    B: He's a commercial artist. He _____ for a big
(13 work)

    company downtown. But this week he's on vacation.

    A: What _____ this week?
(14 he/do)

    B: He _____ golf with his friends.
(15 play)

(continued)

A: Is your mom on vacation too?

B: No. She _____ a vacation every December.
(16 take)

4. **A:** Where _____?
(17 the teacher/go)

B: She _____ to her office.
(18 go)

A: She _____ heavy books. Let's help her.
(19 carry)

B: I'm late for my next class. My math teacher always

_____ on time. He _____ angry
(20 start)   (21 get)

if someone is late.

5. **A:** You _____, Daniel. Wake up.
(22 sleep)

B: I'm so tired. I never _____ enough sleep.
(23 get)

A: How many hours _____ a night?
(24 you/sleep)

B: Only about 4 or 5.

A: That's not enough. You always _____ asleep in class.
(25 fall)

B: I know. But I _____ 18 credit hours this semester.
(26 take)

A: That's too much. I never _____ more than 12.
(27 take)

2.5 Action and Nonaction Verbs

Some verbs are action verbs. These verbs show physical or mental activity (*run*, *play*, *study*, *drive*, *eat*, etc.). Some verbs are nonaction verbs. These verbs describe a state, condition, or feeling, not an action.

EXAMPLES	EXPLANATION
Marco **wants** to get a driver's license. Grandma **loves** her class.	With nonaction verbs, we use the simple present tense, even when we talk about now. We do not usually use a continuous form with these verbs.
Marco is **looking** at his cell phone. He **sees** a message from his father.	*Look* is an action verb. *See* is a nonaction verb.
Grandma **is listening** to her grandson. She **hears** his ring tone.	*Listen* is an action verb. *Hear* is a nonaction verb.
Judy **is meeting** new people. She **knows** a lot of people.	*Meet* is an action verb. *Know* is a nonaction verb.
Grandma **is thinking** about getting a new computer. She **thinks** that using the phone is better than texting.	When you think *about* or *of* something, *think* is an action verb. *Think that* shows an opinion about something. It is a nonaction verb.
Grandma **is having** a good time in her photo class. She**'s having** lunch now. Grandma **has** free time now. She **has** five grandchildren. Marco **has** a cold now.	When *have* means to experience something or to eat or drink something, it is an action verb. When *have* shows possession, relationship, or illness, it is a nonaction verb.
She**'s looking** at her photo album. She**'s smelling** the coffee. I want to learn to text, but it **looks** hard. Your ring tone **sounds** loud.	When the sense-perception verbs describe an action, they are action verbs. When the sense-perception verbs describe a state, they are nonaction verbs.

Nonaction Verbs:

like	remember	see	seem
love	believe	cost	prefer
hate	think (that)	own	know
want	care (about)	have	mean
need	understand	matter	

Sense-Perception Verbs:

smell	taste	feel	look	sound

Fill in the blanks with the simple present or the present continuous tense of the verb in parentheses ( ).

CD 1, TR 18

1. **A:** Grandpa volunteers his time. Twice a week he _____**reads**_____
(example: read)

   for blind people.

   B: My grandmother _____ part-time in a bookstore.
(1 work)

   She _____ books. She usually _____
(2 love)   (3 ride)

   her bike to work. She _____ the exercise.
(4 like)

   A: Where is she now? _____ now?
(5 she/work)

   B: Now she's on vacation. She _____ in Florida.
(6 sail)

2. **A:** Can I borrow your dictionary?

   B: I'm sorry. I _____ it now. Where's your dictionary?
(7 use)

   A: I never _____ it to class. It's too heavy.
(8 bring)

   B: _____ to use my dictionary all the time?
(9 expect)

   You _____ an electronic dictionary. It's very light.
(10 need)

3. **A:** What _____?
(11 the teacher/say)

   She _____ too fast, so I _____ her now.
(12 talk)   (13 not/understand)

   B: I don't know. I _____. I _____
(14 not/listen)   (15 think)

   about my grandparents.

   A: I _____ you are a very good grandson.
(16 think)

   B: Yes. I _____ about visiting them next weekend.
(17 think)

4. **A:** What _____?
(18 you/write)

   B: I _____ a composition about
(19 write)

   my grandparents. I _____ them very much.
(20 love)

A: _____ with you?
(21 they/live)

B: No, they don't. They live in Pakistan. They

_____ us once a year.
(22 visit)

A: _____ them e-mail?
(23 you/ever/send)

B: Sometimes I do. But right now their computer _____.
(24 not/work)

Anyway, they _____ handwritten letters.
(25 prefer)

5. A: Look at that girl. Who is she?

B: She's in my math class. I _____ her pretty well.
(26 know)

A: What _____?
(27 she/wear)

B: She _____ a dress and army boots.
(28 wear)

A: She _____ strange. _____
(29 look)   (30 she/always/wear)

a dress and army boots?

B: No, not always. Sometimes she _____ sandals.
(31 wear)

And sometimes she _____ any shoes at all.
(32 not/wear)

6. A: _____ that guy over there? Who is he?
(33 you/see)

B: That's my English teacher.

A: He _____ jeans and gym shoes. And he
(34 wear)

_____ an earring in his ear.
(35 have)

He _____ like a student.
(36 look)

B: I _____. Everyone _____ he's a student.
(37 know)   (38 think)

But he's a very professional teacher.

A: What level _____?
(39 he/teach)

(continued)

B: He teaches level four. But now he _____ for (40 look)

another job because he _____ a full-time job (41 not/have)

here. He _____ to work full-time. (42 want)

7. A: What _____ this semester? (43 you/study)

B: English, math, and biology.

A: _____ well in all your courses? (44 you/do)

B: I _____ well in English and math. But biology (45 do)

is hard for me. I _____ to drop it. (46 need)

I _____ the teacher very well. (47 not/understand)

He _____ too fast for me. (48 talk)

8. A: What _____ for a living? (49 your mother/do)

B: She's retired now.

A: _____ old? (50 she/be)

B: No, she's only 58.

A: What _____ with her free time? (51 she/do)

B: She does a lot of things. In fact, she _____ any (52 not/have)

free time at all. She _____ two art courses at the (53 take)

art center this semester. Right now she _____ a (54 paint)

beautiful picture of me. She also _____ at a (55 volunteer)

hospital twice a week.

A: That's wonderful. A lot of retired people _____ (56 volunteer)

these days.

EXERCISE 13 This is a phone conversation between two friends, Patty (P) and Linda (L). Fill in the blanks with the missing words. Use the simple present or the present continuous tense.

CD 1, TR 19

P: Hello?

L: Hi, Patty. This is Linda.

P: Hi, Linda. What ___are you doing___ now?
  (example: you/do)

L: Not much. _____ to meet for coffee?
  (1 you/want)

P: I can't. I _____. I _____
  (2 cook)   *(3 have)*
  dinner in the oven now, and I _____ for it to be
  (4 wait)
  finished. What _____?
  (5 you/do)

L: I _____ for a test. But I _____
  (6 study)   *(7 want)*
  to take a break now. Besides, I _____ to talk to
  (8 need)
  someone. I usually _____ to my roommate when
  (9 talk)
  I _____ a problem, but
  (10 have)
  she _____ some friends in New York now.
  (11 visit)

P: We can talk while I _____ dinner.
  (12 prepare)
  It _____ serious.
  (13 sound)

L: My parents _____ to put Grandma in a nursing home.
  (14 plan)

P: But why?

L: My mom _____ she'll receive better care there.
  (15 think)

P: I _____ that's such a good idea. In my family,
  (16 not/think)
  we _____ our parents and grandparents in a nursing
  (17 never/put)
  home. We _____ of them at home.
  (18 always/take care)

L: My mom _____ what else to do. Grandma
  (19 not/know)
  _____ all the time.
  (20 fall)

P: Maybe she _____ a cane or a walker.
  (21 need)

L: Her memory is terrible too. She _____ where she
  (22 never/remember)
  puts things.

P: I _____ my husband coming in the door, and
  (23 hear)
  dinner is almost ready. I'll call you later when we can talk more about it.

L: Thanks for listening. Talk to you later.

The Present Continuous Tense; Action and Nonaction Verbs; the Future Tense **65**

The Graying of America

Before You Read

1. In your native culture, who takes care of people when they get old?

2. Do old people in your native culture get a lot of respect?

CD 1, TR 20

Read the following magazine article. Pay special attention to future tense verbs.

The overall population of the U.S. is growing slowly. In the year 2009, the American population was 303 million. By the middle of this century, it **is going to be** 404 million. Even though this is not a big growth, one group is growing very fast—the elderly (65 years old and over). By 2030, 20 percent of the American population **will be** 65 or over. Today there are three million people 85 or older. In 2050, 28 million **will be** 85 or older.

There are two reasons for this sudden rise in the number of older Americans. First, life expectancy is increasing. In 1900, when the life expectancy was 47, 1 in 25 Americans was elderly. In 2000, with a life expectancy of 79.5 years for women and 74 for men, 1 in 8 was elderly. By 2050, 1 in 5 **will be** elderly.

The second reason for this growth is the aging of the "baby boomers." In the 18 years after World War II, from 1946 to 1964, a large number of babies were born—75 million. The people born during this period, known as the baby boomers, are now middle-aged and **will** soon **be** elderly. The average age of the population is increasing as the baby boomers get older and live longer. The median age of Americans in 1970 was 28; in 2000 it was 35.3. By 2050, it **will be** 41.1.

What does this mean for America? First, there **will be** a labor shortage as the baby boomers retire. There are fewer younger people to take their place at work. For taxpayers, the aging of Americans means that they **are going to pay** more taxes as one-fifth of the population uses one-half of the resources. Also, the country **will see** an increase in the number of nursing homes and the need for people to work in them.

The housing market **will have** to respond to the needs of the baby boomers too. As their children grow up and move out, many baby boomers **will sell** their bigger houses and **move** to smaller ones. Others **will convert** extra bedrooms to offices and home gyms. Also, we **will see** more and more retirement villages for active seniors. Some seniors **will move** from the suburbs to the city. "We live in a suburb of Chicago now," says Paula Hoffman, 52, "because the schools for our teenage children are good. But when they go away to college, we **are going to move** back into the city. There's much more activity for us there."

Susan Brecht, a housing consultant in Philadelphia, Pennsylvania, says, "Baby boomers do not view retirement the way their parents and grandparents did. For starters, they're much more active. My 55 is not my mother's 55," Brecht stated. "I think there is a change in how different generations respond to the aging process. And that's what we're seeing now and **will see** in a dramatic way for the next 10 to 20 years."

It **will be** interesting to see how the baby boomers **are going to continue** to influence the future of America.

2.6 The Future Tense with *Will*

EXAMPLES	EXPLANATION
We **will move** back to the city. You **will see** a big change in the next 10 to 20 years.	We use *will* + the base form for the future tense.
I *will* **always** *help* my parents. My parents *will* **never** *go* to a nursing home.	We can put a frequency word between *will* and the main verb.
I'll be 72 in 2050. **You'll** take care of your elderly parents.	We can contract *will* with the subject pronouns. The contractions are *I'll, you'll, he'll, she'll, it'll, we'll,* and *they'll.*
The population **will not** go down. I **won't** live with my grown children.	To form the negative, put *not* after *will.* The contraction for *will not* is *won't.*

Compare affirmative statements and questions with *will.*

Wh- Word	Will	Subject	Will	Verb (Base Form)	Complement	Short Answer
		She	**will**	live	with her daughter.	
	Will	she		live	with her son?	No, she **won't.**
When	**will**	she		live	with her daughter?	Soon.

(continued)

The Present Continuous Tense; Action and Nonaction Verbs; the Future Tense   **67**

Compare negative statements and questions with *will*.

Wh- Word	Won't	Subject	Won't	Verb (Base Form)	Complement
		They	won't	need	a large house.
Why	won't	they		need	a large house?

EXERCISE 14 Fill in the blanks with an appropriate verb in the future tense. Use *will*. Answers may vary.

EXAMPLE   In the future, people _____will live_____ longer.

1. The population of old people _____.

2. There _____ more older people by 2050.

3. Where _____ you _____

   when you are old?

4. _____ your children _____

   care of you?

5. How old _____ you _____ in 2050?

6. Many baby boomers are middle-aged now. They _____

   soon _____ elderly.

EXERCISE 15 A 30-year-old woman is saying good-bye to her 60-year-old parents. They are leaving on a trip in their recreational vehicle (RV). Fill in the blanks to complete this conversation. Use the future tense with *will*. Answers may vary.

CD 1, TR 21

A: I'm worried about you. You _'ll be_____ gone for a long time.
   (example)

B: Don't worry. We _____ only _____
   (1)   (2)

   gone for the summer months.

A: You _____ alone on the road.
   (3)

B: We _____ on the road all the time.
   (4)

   We _____ at campsites with lots of other
   (5)

   RVs and campers.

A: How _____ your clothes?
   (6)

B: The RV has a washing machine.

A: Where _____ your food?
   (7)

68   Lesson 2

B: We'll buy food at a supermarket on the way and cook it in the RV. The RV has everything—a stove, a microwave, a dishwasher. Sometimes we _____ (8) a fire and cook on the grill. Other times we _____ (9) out in restaurants.

A: Where _____ (10) first?

B: First, we'll go to the Grand Canyon.

A: That's fabulous! _____ (11) me a postcard from there?

B: Of course we _____ (12). And we _____ (13) send you e-mail too.

A: How _____ (14) e-mail?

B: From our computer, of course. We _____ (15) it with us.

A: Where _____ (16) electricity for all these things?

B: At the campsites. There are electrical hookups.

A: You _____ (17) all the comforts of home. Why, then, are you leaving?

B: We can't see the Grand Canyon from our home.

A: _____ (18) pictures?

B: Yes, we'll take lots of pictures. We'll have our digital camera with us. There _____ (19) a lot of beautiful things to take pictures of. We _____ (20) them to you by e-mail.

A: Have a good time. I _____ (21) you.

B: We'll miss you too.

2.7 The Future Tense with *Be Going To*

EXAMPLES	EXPLANATION
People **are going to live** longer. They **are going to need** help from their children. There **are going to be** more elderly people in 50 years.	We use a form of *be* + *going to* + the base form to form the future tense.
I**'m not** going to live with my grown children. He **isn't** going to retire.	To form the negative, put *not* after *am, is,* or *are.*
We're **going to go** on a long trip in the RV. We're **going** on a long trip in the RV.	We often shorten *going to go* to *going.*
We're going to return **in** two months. I'm going to retire **in** ten years.	We use the preposition *in* with the future tense to mean *after.*

Pronunciation Notes:
1. In informal speech, *going to* before another verb often sounds like "gonna." In formal English, we don't write "gonna." Listen to your teacher's pronunciation of *going to* in the following sentences.
   Where's he going to live? (Where's he "gonna" live?)
   He's going to live in a dorm. (He's "gonna" live in a dorm.)
2. Only *going to* before another verb sounds like "gonna." We don't pronounce "gonna" before a noun.
   Where is he going?
   He's going to the bookstore.

Compare affirmative statements and questions with *be going to*.

Wh-Word	Be	Subject	Be	Going to + Verb (Base Form)	Complement	Short Answer
		They	are	**going to sell**	their house.	
	Are	they		**going to sell**	it soon?	Yes, they **are**.
Why	are	they		**going to sell**	it?	Because it**'s** too big.

Compare negative statements and questions with *be going to*.

Wh-Word	Be + n't	Subject	Be + n't	Going to + Verb (Base Form)	Complement
		She	isn't	**going to retire**	from her job.
Why	isn't	she		**going to retire?**	

EXERCISE 16 Fill in the blanks with an appropriate verb in the future tense. Use *be going to*. Answers may vary.

EXAMPLE _____*Are*_____ your children _*going to take care of*_ you?

1. The cost of health care _____.

2. People _____ higher taxes.

3. How old _____ your daughter _____ in 2050?

4. _____ you _____ care of your elderly parents?

5. A lot of people _____ over 100 years old in 2050.

EXERCISE 17 Two co-workers are talking. Fill in the blanks with the future using *be going to*.

🔊

CD 1, TR 22

A: I'm so excited. I _*'m going to retire*_ at the end of this year.
      (example: retire)

B: That's wonderful news. What _____ next?
      (1 you/do)

A: I don't really know yet. I _____ new things.
      (2 explore)

B: For example, what _____?
      (3 you/explore)

A: I think I have a talent for art. I _____ art classes.
      (4 take)

B: _____ part-time?
      (5 you/work)

A: No way! I _____ exactly what I
      (6 do)
      want to do, when I want to do it.

B: Is your husband happy about your retirement?

A: Yes. He _____ too.
      (7 retire)

B: But you're not that old.

A: I'm 58 and he's 56. Our children aren't going to
      need us much anymore.

B: Why _____ you?
      (8 not/need)

A: Our youngest son _____ from college in June. And
      (9 graduate)
      the other two are already on their own. The oldest _____
      (10 get)
      married next year, and the middle one has her own apartment and a job.

B: I _____ you at work.
      (11 miss)

A: I _____ you too. But I _____ the boss
      (12 miss)   (13 not/miss)
      and the long hours.

The Present Continuous Tense; Action and Nonaction Verbs; the Future Tense   **71**

EXERCISE 18 Do you have questions for the teacher about this semester, next semester, or his or her life in general? Write three questions to ask the teacher about the near or distant future.

EXAMPLES   What time are you going to leave today?

When are you going to give us a test?

Are you going to retire soon?

1. _____

2. _____

3. _____

2.8 Choosing *Will* or *Be Going To*

In many cases, you can use either *will* or *be going to*. But in a few cases, one is preferred over the other.

EXAMPLES	EXPLANATION
A: When is Grandpa going to move into the retirement home? B: He**'s going to move** next summer. He needs help. **I'm going to rent** a moving truck and help him.	If the decision or plan was made before this conversation takes place, use *be going to*.
A: What are you going to do when you retire? B: I don't know. **I'll cross** that bridge when I come to it.[8]	Speaker B is thinking about the future at the time of talking. There is no previous plan. If there is no previous plan, use *will*.
Grandma: I don't know how to send a text message. Grandson: No problem. **I'll teach** you. Grandma: I need to buy a cell phone. What should I buy? Grandson: Don't worry. **I'll help** you.	The grandson is making an offer to help at the time of talking. He had no previous plan. If there is an offer to help, use *will*.
Grandma: I'm lonely. Grandson: **I'll visit** you on the weekend. Grandma: You always say that. But you never have time. Grandson: **I'll make time**. I promise.	The grandson is making a promise. If there is a promise, use *will*.

Language Notes:
1. For predictions, facts about the future, or scheduled events, you can use either *will* or *be going to*.
   The movie **will begin** at 8 PM. = The movie **is going to begin** at 8 PM.
   Technology **will improve** in the future. = Technology **is going to improve** in the future.
2. We sometimes use the present continuous tense with a future meaning. We can do this with planned events in the near future. We do this especially with verbs of motion.
   My grandmother **is moving** into a retirement home on Friday.
   I'm helping her move on Friday.

[8]This is an expression that means: I'll worry about it when the time comes, not before.

EXERCISE 19 Choose *be going to* or *will* + the verb to fill in the blanks. In some cases, both are possible.

1. **A:** Where are you going?

   B: I'm going to the park this afternoon. I **'m going to meet** _____
   (example: meet)

   my friend and play tennis with her. I have to return some videos to

   the video store, but I don't have time.

   A: Give them to me. I _____ that way.
   (1 pass)

   I _____ them for you.
   (2 return)

2. **A:** I have to go to the airport. My sister's plane

   _____ at four o'clock this afternoon.
   (3 arrive)

   B: I _____ with you. I _____
   (4 go)   (5 stay)

   in the car while you go into the airport. That way, you

   _____ pay for parking.
   (6 not/have to)

3. **A:** My sister's birthday is next week.

   B: _____ her a birthday present?
   (7 you/give)

   A: Of course I _____.
   (8)

   B: What _____ her?
   (9 you/give)

   A: She loves the theater. I _____ her tickets to a play.
   (10 buy)

   B: How old _____?
   (11 be)

   A: She _____ 21 years old.
   (12 be)

4. **Teacher:** Next week we _____ our midterm test.
   (13 have)

   Student: _____ hard?
   (14 it/be)

   Teacher: Yes, but I _____ you prepare for it.
   (15 help)

(continued)

The Present Continuous Tense; Action and Nonaction Verbs; the Future Tense **73**

5. Wife: I won't have time to pick up the children this afternoon. I have

to work late.

Husband: Don't worry. I _____ them up.
(16 pick)

Wife: I won't have time to cook either.

Husband: Just relax. I _____ dinner tonight.
(17 prepare)

6. Man: I want to marry you.

Woman: But we're only 19. We're too young.

Man: I _____ 20 in April.
(18 be)

Woman: But you don't even have a job.

Man: I _____ a job.
(19 find)

Woman: Let's wait a few years.

Man: I _____ for you forever. I _____ you.
(20 wait)   (21 always/love)

7. A: Do you want to watch the football game with me on Saturday?

B: I can't. My brother _____. I _____ him.
(22 move)   (23 help)

A: Do you need any help?

B: We need boxes. Do you have any?

A: No, but I _____ for boxes. I _____
(24 look)   (25 go)

to the supermarket this afternoon. I _____
(26 get)

boxes there. I _____ them to your house.
(27 bring)

B: Thanks.

8. A: I'm so excited! I _____ a puppy.
(28 get)

B: That's a big responsibility. You're never home. How

_____ care of it?
(29 take)

A: My cousin lives with me now. She doesn't have a job.

She _____ me take care of the dog.
(30 help)

B: What about your landlord? Is it OK with him?

A: I _____ him.
　　　　　 (31 not/tell)

B: You have to tell him. He _____ if you have a
　　　　　　　　　　　　　　　　　　 (32 know)

dog. You _____ take the dog out
　　　　　 (33 have to)

three times a day. And the dog _____.
　　　　　　　　　　　　　　　　　　　　 (34 bark)

2.9 Future Tense + Time/*If* Clause[9]

Some future sentences have two clauses: a main clause and a time or *if* clause.

Time or *If* Clause (Simple Present Tense)	Main Clause (Future Tense)	Explanation
When the children **grow** up,	we **will move** back to the city.	We use the *future* only in the main clause; we use the *simple present tense* in the time/*if* clause.
If I **am** healthy,	I **will continue** to work for the rest of my life.	
Main Clause (Future Tense)	**Time or *If* Clause (Simple Present Tense)**	We can put the time/*if* clause before the main clause. Or we can put the main clause before the time/*if* clause.
He **will move** to a warm climate	as soon as he **retires**.	
My parents **are going to travel**	if they **take** an early retirement.	

Punctuation Note: If the time/*if* clause comes before the main clause, we use a comma to separate the two parts of the sentence. If the main clause comes first, we don't use a comma.

EXERCISE 20 Connect the sentences using the word in parentheses ( ).

EXAMPLE I will retire. I will play golf. (when)

_____When I retire, I will play golf._____ OR _____I will play golf when I retire._____

1. I will retire. I'm not going to live with my children. (when)

_____

2. I will be old. I will take care of myself. (when)

_____

---

[9]A *clause* is a group of words that has a subject and a verb. Some sentences have more than one clause.

(continued)

3. I won't be healthy. I'll live with my children. (if)

_____

4. I won't have money. I will get help from the government. (if)

_____

5. My parents will die. I'll move to another city. (after)

_____

6. I will get a pension. I won't need to depend on my children. (if)

_____

7. I'll retire. I'm going to save my money. (before)

_____

EXERCISE **21** **ABOUT YOU** **Think about a specific time in your future (when you graduate, when you get married, when you have children, when you find a job, when you return to your native country, when you are old, etc.). Write three sentences to tell what will happen at that time. Find a partner who is close to your age. Compare your answers to your partner's answers.**

EXAMPLES When I have children, I won't have as much free time as I do now.

When I have children, I'm going to have a lot more responsibilities.

When I have children, my parents will be very happy.

1. _____

2. _____

3. _____

EXERCISE **22** **A Korean student (K) is talking to an American (A) about getting old. Fill in the blanks with the correct form of the verb to complete this conversation. In many cases, you can use either _be going to_ or _will_.**

CD 1, TR 23

K: How's your grandfather?

A: He's OK. I _'m going to visit_____ him this afternoon.
    (example: visit)

K: How's he doing?

A: He's in great health. Next week he _____
                                            _(1 go)_

    to Hawaii to play golf.

K: How old is he?

A: He _____ 78 next month. Did I tell you?
(2 be)

In June, he _____ married to
(3 get)

a widow he met in the retirement home.

K: That seems so strange to me.

Why _____ that?
(4 he/do)

A: Why not? They like each other, and they want to be together.

K: What _____ when he's no longer
(5 you/do)

able to take care of himself?

A: We never think about it. He's in such great shape that we think

he _____ healthy forever. I think
(6 be)

he _____ us all.
(7 outlive)

K: But he _____ help as he gets older.
(8 probably/need)

A: We _____ that bridge when we come
(9 cross)

to it. Do you have plans for your parents as they get older?

K: They're in their 50s now. But when they _____
(10 be)

older, they _____ with me and my wife.
(11 live)

In our country, it's an honor to take care of our parents.

A: That sounds like a great custom. But I think older people should

be independent. I'm glad that Grandpa doesn't depend on us.

And when I _____ old, I _____
(12 be)   (13 take)

care of myself. I don't want to depend on anyone.

K: You _____ your mind when
(14 change)

you _____ old.
(15 be)

A: Maybe. I have to catch my bus now. Grandpa is waiting for me.

I _____ you later.
(16 see)

K: Wait. I have my car. I _____ you to your
(17 drive)

grandfather's place.

A: Thanks.

EXERCISE **This is a conversation between two co-workers. They are talking about retirement. Fill in the blanks with the correct form and tense of the verb in parentheses ( ).**

A: I hear you're going to retire this year.

B: Yes. Isn't it wonderful? I __'ll be__ 65 in September.
(example: be)

A: What _____ after you _____?
(1 you/do)   (2 retire)

B: I'm trying to sell my house now. When I _____
(3 sell)

it, I _____ to Florida and buy a condo.
(4 move)

A: What _____ in Florida?
(5 you/do)

B: I _____ a sailboat and spend most of my time on the water.
(6 buy)

A: But a sailboat is expensive.

B: When I _____ 65, I _____ to use my
(7 be)   (8 start)

savings. Also, I _____ a lot of money
(9 get)

when I _____ my house.
(10 sell)

What _____ when you _____?
(11 you/do)   (12 retire)

A: I'm only 45 years old. I have another 20 years until I _____.
(13 retire)

B: Now is the time to start thinking about retirement. If you

_____ your money for the next 20 years,
(14 save)

you _____ a comfortable retirement.
(15 have)

But if you _____ about it until the time
(16 not/think)

_____, you _____
(17 come)   (18 not/have)

enough money to live on.

A: I _____ about it when the time _____.
(19 worry)   (20 come)

I'm too young to worry about it now.

B: If you _____ until you _____ 65 to
(21 wait)   (22 be)

think about it, you _____ a poor old man.
(23 be)

On Monday morning when we _____ at work,
(24 be)

I _____ you to a woman who can explain the
(25 introduce)

company's savings plan to you. After you _____
(26 talk)

to her, I'm sure you _____ your mind about
(27 change)

when to worry about retirement.

Summary of Lesson 2

Use of Tense

Simple Present Tense	
General truths, facts	Many people **retire** in their sixties. Retirees **get** Social Security.
Regular activities, habits, customs	Jack **plays** golf twice a week. I **always** visit my grandparents on the weekend.
Place of origin	My grandfather **comes** from Mexico. My grandmother **comes** from Peru.
In a time clause or in an *if* clause of a future statement	When she **retires**, she will enjoy life. If Grandma **needs** help, she will live with her daughter.
With nonaction verbs	I **care** about my grandparents. Your grandfather **needs** help now. My grandfather **prefers** to live alone now.

Present Continuous Tense (with action verbs only)	
Now	We**'re comparing** verb tenses now. I**'m looking** at page 79 now.
A long-term action in progress at this general time	Judy **is earning** money by making dolls. Jack is retired now. He **is starting** a new career.
A trend in society	The population of the U.S. **is getting** older. Americans **are living** longer.
A plan in the near future	She **is retiring** next month. She **is going** on a long trip soon.
A descriptive state	Mary **is standing** over there. She **is wearing** jeans and a T-shirt.

Future Tense

	will	*be going to*
A plan		He **is going to retire** in two years.
A fact	The number of old people **will increase**.	The number of old people is **going to increase**.
A prediction	I think you **will enjoy** retirement.	I think you **are going to enjoy** retirement.
A promise	I **will** take care of you when you're old.	
An offer to help	Grandma, I'**ll carry** your grocery bags for you.	
A scheduled event	Dance instruction **will begin** at 8 PM on Saturday.	Dance instruction **is going to begin** at 8 PM on Saturday.

Editing Advice

1. Always include *be* in a present continuous tense verb.

   is
   She working now.

2. Don't use the present continuous tense with a nonaction verb.

   e
   I ~~am~~ liking your new car.

3. Don't use *be* with another verb for the future.

   I will ~~be~~ go back to my native country in five years.

4. Include *be* in a future sentence that has no other verb.

   be
   He will angry.

   be
   There will a party soon.

5. Don't combine *will* and *be going to*.

   He will ~~going to~~ leave. *OR He's going to leave.*

6. Don't use the future tense after a time word or *if*.

When they ~~will~~ go home, they are going to watch TV.

am
If I ~~will be~~ late, I'll call you.

7. Use a form of *be* with *going to*.

is
He ∧ going to help me.

8. Use the correct word order in questions.

will you
When ~~you will~~ go back to your native country?

isn't she
Why ~~she isn't~~ going to buy a new car?

Editing Quiz

Some of the shaded words and phrases have mistakes. Find the mistakes and correct them. If the shaded words are correct, write *C*.

My grandfather is retired now and he's not happy. He wakes up every day

will I
and says, "What I will do today?" On the other hand, my grandmother
(example)

C
is very busy. My grandparents live in a retirement village and Grandma
(example)

is learning how to draw. She's also take singing lessons, and she
(1)   *(2)*   *(3)*

studying photography. Next month, she going to take a trip to India with
(4)   *(5)*

a group of older people. When Grandma will get back from India,
(6)

she's going to make a photo slideshow of her trip.
(7)

Grandpa doesn't want to travel. He says, "What I'm going to do
(8)

in India?" I'm thinking that Grandpa is needing to find a hobby.
(9)   *(10)*

Grandma always tells him, "You will happy if you find something to
(11)

do." Will I going to have a hard time like Grandpa when I will retire?
(12)   *(13)*

I'll be cross that bridge when I come to it.
(14)   *(15)*

Lesson 2 Test/Review

PART 1 Mary (M) is talking to her friend Sue (S) on the phone. Fill in the blanks with the correct tense and form of the words in parentheses ( ). Use the simple present, present continuous, or future tense. In some cases, more than one answer is possible.

S: Hi, Mary.

M: Hi, Sue. How are you?

S: Fine. What are you doing?

M: I **'m packing** _____ now. We _____
       (example: pack)   *(1 move)*
       next Saturday.

S: Oh, really? Why? You _____ such a lovely
                              (2 have)
       apartment now.

M: Yes, I know we do. But my father _____
                                        (3 come)
       soon, so we _____ a bigger apartment.
                    (4 need)

S: When _____?
             (5 come)

M: He _____ as soon as he _____
           (6 come)   *(7 get)*
       his visa. That'll probably be in about four months.

S: But your present apartment _____ an extra bedroom.
                                   (8 have)

M: Yes. But my husband _____ to have an extra room
                           (9 always/like)
       for an office. He usually _____ a lot of work home.
                                  (10 bring)
       He _____ a place where he can work without noise.
           (11 need)

S: _____ his own apartment after he
       (12 your father/get)
       _____ a job?
       (13 find)

M: He's retired now. He _____ with us.
                            (14 live)
       He _____ to live alone.
           (15 not/like)

S: Do you need help with your packing?

M: No, thank you. Bill and I _____ home this week to
                                 (16 stay)
       finish the packing. And my sister _____ me now too.
                                          (17 help)

S: I _____ over next Saturday to help you move.
         (18 come)

M: We _____ professional movers on
                    (19 use)

Saturday. We don't want to bother our friends.

S: It's no bother. I _____ to help.
                              (20 want)

M: Thanks. There probably _____ a few things you
                                          (21 be)

can help me with on Saturday. I have to go now. I

_____ Bill. He _____ me.
        (22 hear)   (23 call)

He _____ me to help him in the basement.
          (24 want)

I _____ you back later.
          (25 call)

S: You don't have to call me back. I _____ you on
                                                    (26 see)

Saturday. Bye.

PART 2 **Fill in the blanks with the negative form of the underlined verb.**

EXAMPLE   Mary _is_ busy. Sue _____isn't_____ busy.

1. Sue _is talking_ to Mary. She _____ to her husband.

2. Mary _is going to move_ to a bigger apartment. She _____
   to a house.

3. Mary's husband _needs_ an extra room. He _____ a big
   room.

4. Sue _will go_ to Mary's house on Saturday. She _____
   tomorrow.

5. Mary _will move_ the small things. She _____
   the furniture.

6. Her new apartment _has_ an extra room for her father. Her old apartment
   _____ an extra room.

7. Her father _likes_ to live with family. He _____ to live
   alone.

The Present Continuous Tense; Action and Nonaction Verbs; the Future Tense   83

PART 3   Write a *yes/no* question about the words in parentheses ( ).
Then write a short answer based on the conversation in Part 1
on pages 82–83.

EXAMPLE   Mary is busy. (her husband)
<u>Is her husband busy? Yes, he is.</u>

1. Mary's husband is helping her pack. (her sister)

   _____

2. Her husband works in an office. (at home)

   _____

3. Her present apartment has an extra room for an office. (for her father)

   _____

4. Professional movers will move the furniture. (her friends)

   _____

5. Mary is staying home this week. (her husband)

   _____

6. Mary's going to move. (Sue)

   _____

PART 4   Write a *wh-* question about the words in parentheses ( ). An answer
is not necessary.

EXAMPLE   Mary's packing now. (why)

   <u>Why is she packing?</u>

1. They're going to move to a bigger apartment. (why)

   _____

2. Her husband needs an extra room. (why)

   _____

3. She doesn't need her friends to help her move. (why)

   _____

4. Her father is going to come soon. (when)

   _____

5. Bill is calling Mary now. (why)

   _____

6. They'll use professional movers. (when)

Expansion

Classroom Activities

❶ Check (✓) your predictions about the future. Form a small group and discuss your predictions with your group. Give reasons for your beliefs.

a. _____ People are going to have fewer children than they do today.

b. _____ People will live longer.

c. _____ People will have healthier lives.

d. _____ People are going to be happier.

e. _____ People will be lonelier.

f. _____ People will be more educated.

g. _____ Everyone is going to have a computer.

h. _____ There will be a cure for cancer and other serious illnesses.

i. _____ There will be a cure for the common cold.

❷ Check (✓) the activities that you plan to do soon. Form a group of between five and seven students. Ask questions about the items another student checked.

EXAMPLE __✓__ move
When are you going to move?
Why are you moving?
Are your friends going to help you?
Are you going to rent a truck?
Where are you going to move to?

a. _____ send e-mail

b. _____ visit a friend

c. _____ invite guests to my house

d. _____ buy something new

e. _____ take a vacation

f. _____ celebrate a birthday or holiday

g. _____ go to a concert or sporting event

h. _____ transfer to another school

i. _____ move

j. _____ take the citizenship test

k. _____ start a new job

l. _____ have an out-of-town visitor

m. _____ get married

Talk
About It

❶ What is the attitude toward older people in your native country or culture? Do they get a lot of respect?

❷ Is it hard for older people to keep up with all the changes in technology?

❸ How can retired people use their time? Do you know anyone who is retired? How does this person use his/her time?

Write
About It

❶ Write a short composition telling how you think your life will be when you are 10 years older than you are now.

Sample beginning: I'm 25 years old now. When I'm 35 years old, I think I will . . .

❷ Write a short composition describing the life of an old person you know—a family member, a friend, a neighbor, etc.

> ### My Great-Uncle
>
> My great-uncle is 85 years old now and he lives alone, but I think he's going to need help soon. He sometimes falls. Also his memory is not good. My aunt thinks she'll have to put him in a nursing home . . .

 For more practice using grammar in context, please visit our Web site.

Grammar
Habitual Past with *Used To*
The Simple Past Tense

Context
Working Toward Equality

Martin Luther King Jr., 1929–1968

Equal Rights for All

1. In your native country, does the government give equality to everyone?

2. Is there one group of people that has a harder life than other groups? Which group? What kinds of problems do these people have?

CD 1, TR 25

Read the following textbook article. Pay special attention to simple past tense verbs and *used to* + base form.

Rosa Parks

Did You
Know?

Martin Luther King Jr., was interested in the ideas of Mahatma Gandhi of India. He studied and used Gandhi's technique of nonviolent protest.

Today all people in the United States have equal rights under the law. But this **was** not always the case, especially for African-Americans.[1] Even though slavery in the U.S. **ended** in 1865, blacks **continued** to suffer discrimination[2] and segregation,[3] especially in the South. Many hotels, schools, and restaurants **were** for whites only. Many businesses there **used to have** signs in their windows that **said** "Blacks Not Allowed." Black children **used to go** to separate, and often inferior, schools. Many professions **were** for whites only. Even in sports, blacks could not join the major leagues; there **used to be** separate leagues for blacks.

In many places in the South, buses **used to reserve** the front seats for white people. One evening in December of 1955, a 42-year-old woman, Rosa Parks, **got** on a bus in Montgomery, Alabama, to go home from work. She **was** tired when she **sat** down. When some white people **got** on the crowded bus, the bus driver **ordered** Ms. Parks to stand up. Ms. Parks **refused** to leave her seat. The bus driver **called** the police, and they **came** and **arrested** Ms. Parks.

Martin Luther King Jr.,[4] a black minister living in Montgomery, Alabama, **wanted** to put an end to discrimination. When King **heard** about Ms. Parks's arrest, he **told** African-Americans in Montgomery to boycott[5] the bus company. People who **used to** ride the bus to work **decided** to walk instead. As a result of the boycott, the Supreme Court **outlawed**[6] discrimination on public transportation.

---

[1] *African-Americans*, whose ancestors came from Africa as slaves, are sometimes called "blacks." They used to be called "negroes" or "colored."

[2] *Discrimination* means giving some people unfair treatment, especially because of race, age, religion, etc.

[3] *Segregation* means separation of the races.

[4] When a father and son have the same name, the father uses *senior* (Sr.) after his name; the son puts *junior* (Jr.) after his name.

[5] To *boycott* is to refuse to do business with a company.

[6] *To outlaw* means to make an action illegal or against the law.

In 1964, about 100 years after the end of slavery, Congress **passed** a new law that officially **gave** equality to all Americans. This law **made** discrimination in employment and education illegal. King **won** the Nobel Peace Prize[7] for his work in creating a better world.

In 1968, a great tragedy **occurred**. Someone **shot** and **killed** King when he was only 39 years old.

In 1983, Martin Luther King's birthday (January 15) **became** a national holiday.

African-American Firsts

1947 Jackie Robinson was the first African-American to play on a major-league baseball team.

1983 Guion Bluford was the first African-American to go into space.

1989 Oprah Winfrey became the first African-American to own her own television and film production company.

1997 Tiger Woods, whose father is African-American and whose mother is Thai, became both the first African-American and the first Asian-American to win the Masters golf tournament.

2001 Halle Berry became the first African-American woman to win an Oscar for best actress.

2001 General Colin Powell became the first African-American secretary of state.

2005 Condoleezza Rice became the first female African-American secretary of state.

2009 Barack Obama became the first African-American president.

Oprah Winfrey

Colin Powell and Condoleezza Rice

[7]The *Nobel Peace Prize* is one of six prizes given once a year for great work in promoting peace. Other prizes are for literature, science, and economics.

3.1 Habitual Past with *Used To*

EXAMPLES	EXPLANATION
Black children **used to** have separate schools. Many professions **used to** be for white people only. There **used to** be separate baseball teams for black people.	*Used to* + a base form shows a habit or custom over a past period of time. This custom no longer exists.

Language Notes:

1. *Used to* is for past habits or customs. It is not for an action that happened once or a few times.

   Many restaurants **used to** serve white people only. (This happened over a period of time.)

   Rosa Parks **used to** ride the bus to work. (This happened over a period of time.)

   In 1955, Rosa Parks **got** on the bus and **refused** to stand. (This happened one time.)

   The bus driver **called** the police. (This happened one time.)

2. For negatives, omit the *d* in *used to*.

   Some restaurants **didn't use** to serve African-Americans.

EXERCISE 1   **ABOUT YOU** Tell which of the following you used to do when you were a child.

EXAMPLE   cry a lot
I used to cry a lot.

1. enjoy school
2. obey my parents
3. attend religious school
4. play with dolls
5. play soccer
6. fight with other children
7. draw pictures
8. have a pet
9. tell lies
10. read mystery stories
11. live on a farm
12. live with my grandparents
13. watch a lot of TV
14. read comic books

EXERCISE 2   **ABOUT YOU** Name something. Practice *used to*.

EXAMPLE   Name something you used to know when you were in elementary school.

I used to know the names of all the presidents (but I don't know them anymore).

1. Name something you used to do when you were a child.
2. Tell what kind of stories you used to enjoy when you were a child.

3. Name something you used to believe when you were a child.

4. Name something you used to like to eat when you were a child.

5. Tell about some things your parents, grandparents, or teachers used to tell you when you were a child.

6. Tell about some things you used to do when you were younger.

EXERCISE 3 **ABOUT YOU** Write sentences comparing the way you used to live with the way you live now. Share your sentences with a partner or with the entire class.

EXAMPLES I used to live with my whole family. Now I live alone.

I used to work in a restaurant. Now I'm a full-time student.

I didn't use to speak English at all. Now I speak English pretty well.

Ideas for sentences:
school   job   hobbies   apartment/house   family life   friends

1. _____

_____

2. _____

_____

3. _____

_____

EXERCISE 4 A young man is comparing how his life used to be five years ago and how his life is now. Complete his statements. Answers may vary.

EXAMPLE I used to _____ *be lazy* _____. Now I work hard.

1. I used to _____. Now I save my money.
2. I used to _____. Now I'm a serious student.
3. I used to _____. Now I live alone.
4. I used to _____. Now I almost never watch TV.
5. I used to _____. Now I come home after work and study.
6. I used to _____. Now I have short hair.
7. I used to _____. Now I have a car and drive everywhere.
8. I used to _____. Now I'm on a diet and I'm losing weight.

(continued)

Habitual Past with *Used To*; The Simple Past Tense   **91**

9. I used to _____. Now I make my own decisions.

10. I used to _____. Now I use my credit card for most of my purchases.

George Dawson—Life Is So Good

Before You Read

1. Is it necessary to know how to read in order to have a good life?

2. Is it hard for old people to learn new things?

CD 1, TR 26

Read the following magazine article. Pay special attention to the simple past tense.

George Dawson **lived** in three centuries—the end of the nineteenth, all through the twentieth, and the start of the twenty-first. He **was** born in 1898 in Texas, the grandson of slaves. He **was** the oldest of five children. His family **was** very poor, so George **had** to go to work to help his family. He **started** working full-time for his father when he **was** four years old. As a result, he **didn't attend** school. He **worked** at many jobs during his lifetime: he **chopped** wood, **swept** floors, **helped** build the railroad, and **cleaned** houses.

George Dawson (1898–2001)

For most of his adult life, he **ran** farm machinery at a dairy farm.[8]

In his lifetime, great technological changes **occurred:** cars, television, airplanes, spaceships, and computers **came** into being. He **saw** several wars and political changes in the U.S. He **outlived**[9] four wives and two of his seven children.

He **lived** at a time when African-Americans **had** fewer opportunities than they do today. And he **lived** in the South, where there **was** a lot of discrimination against African-Americans; African-Americans **were** segregated from others, and job possibilities **were** limited. By the end of his life, he **saw** others have the opportunities that he **didn't have** when he **was** young. He **witnessed** the success of many African-Americans.

Because he **didn't know** how to read or write, he **signed** his name with an X. Then, when he **was** 98 years old, Dawson **started** attending school. He **went** to adult literacy classes in Dallas County. The teacher **asked** him, "Do you know the alphabet?" He **answered,** "No." Over the next few years,

[8]On a *dairy farm*, cows are used to produce milk and milk products.
[9]*To outlive* means to live longer than others.

his teacher, Carl Henry, **taught** Dawson to read and write. Dawson **said,** "Every morning I get up and I wonder what I might learn that day."

In 1998, an elementary school teacher, Richard Glaubman, **read** an article about Dawson in the newspaper. He **wanted** to meet Dawson. Together Glaubman and Dawson **wrote** a book about Dawson's life, called *Life Is So Good.* In this book, Dawson tells about what makes a person happy. Dawson **had** a close family and never **felt** lonely. He **learned** from his father to see the good things in life. His father **told** him, "We **were** born to die. You **didn't come** here to stay, and life is something to enjoy." He **taught** his children to see the richness in life. Dawson says in the book, "We make our own way. Trouble is out there, but a person can leave it alone and just do the right thing. Then, if trouble still finds you, you've done the best you can. . . . People worry too much. Life is good, just the way it is."

> **Excerpt from Dawson's book:**
> "My first day of school **was** January 4, 1996. I **was** ninety-eight years old and I'm still going. . . . I'm up by five-thirty to make my lunch, pack my books, and go over my schoolwork. Books was[10] something missing from my life for so long. . . . I **learned** to read my ABC's in two days—I **was** in a hurry. . . . Now I am a man that can read."

3.2 Past Tense of *Be*

The past tense of *be* has two forms: *was* and *were*.

EXAMPLES	EXPLANATION

Life **was** hard for George Dawson.
He **was** poor.
His grandparents **were** slaves.
	The past tense of the verb *be* has two forms: *was* and *were*.
	    I, he, she, it ⟶ was
	    we, you, they ⟶ were

There **was** discrimination in the South. There **were** many changes in the twentieth century.	After *there*, use *was* or *were* depending on the noun that follows. Use *was* with a singular noun. Use *were* with a plural noun.
Dawson's life **wasn't** easy. Education and books **weren't** available to Dawson as a child.	To make a negative statement, put *not* after *was* or *were*. The contraction for *was not* is *wasn't.* The contraction for *were not* is *weren't.*
Dawson **was born** in 1898.	Use a form of *be* with *born.*
Dawson **was** married four times. He **was** never bored.	Use *be* with adjectives that end in *-ed: crowded, tired, bored, interested, worried, married, divorced, allowed,* and *permitted.*

[10]These are Dawson's exact words. However, this sentence is not grammatically correct. The correct way is: Books *were* . . . .

(continued)

Compare affirmative statements and questions.

Wh- Word	Was/Were	Subject	Was/Were	Complement	Short Answer
		Dawson	**was**	poor.	
	Was	he		a slave?	No, he **wasn't**.
Where	**was**	he		from?	

Compare negative statements and questions.

Wh- Word	Wasn't/Weren't	Subject	Wasn't/Weren't	Complement
		Dawson	**wasn't**	in school.
Why	**wasn't**	he		in school?
		There	**weren't**	many opportunities.
Why	**weren't**	there		many opportunities?

EXERCISE 5 Fill in the blanks with an appropriate word. Some answers may vary.

EXAMPLE George Dawson ___was___ poor.

1. Dawson was _____ in 1898.

2. At that time, there _____ a lot of discrimination.

3. His parents _____ poor.

4. Life for most African-Americans in the South was _____.

5. Job possibilities for African-Americans _____ limited.

6. When he was _____, he learned how to read.

7. Dawson's father used to tell him, "We _____ born to die."

8. He was poor, but he wasn't _____.

EXERCISE 6 Fill in the blanks with the correct word(s).

EXAMPLE   Martin Luther King Jr. _____was_____ a great American.

1. Martin Luther King Jr. _____ born in Georgia.

2. He (not) _____ born in Alabama.

3. He and his father _____ ministers.

4. There _____ discrimination on public transportation.

5. _____ discrimination in employment? Yes, there _____.

6. Rosa Parks was a citizen of Montgomery, Alabama. _____ an African-American? Yes, she was.

7. She was tired and took a seat on the bus. Why _____ tired?

8. African-Americans weren't allowed to sit down on a crowded bus in Montgomery. Why _____ allowed to sit down?

9. George Dawson wasn't able to write his name. Why _____ able to write his name?

10. George Dawson (not) _____ lonely.

11. How old _____ when he learned to read? He was 98 years old.

12. _____ slavery when Dawson was born? No, there wasn't.

3.3 The Simple Past Tense of Regular Verbs

To form the simple past tense of regular verbs, add -ed to the base form.[11]

EXAMPLES	EXPLANATION
Dawson **signed** his name with an X. Dawson **learned** a lot from his father. African-Americans **suffered** discrimination. Dawson **lived** to be 103 years old.	**Base Form** **Past Form** sign sign**ed** learn learn**ed** suffer suffer**ed** live live**d** If the verb ends in an *e*, add only -*d*. The past forms are the same for all persons.
Dawson **learned** *to read* and *write*. A teacher **wanted** *to meet* Dawson.	The verb after *to* does not use the past form.

[11]For a review of the spelling and pronunciation of the *-ed* past form, see Appendix A.

EXERCISE 7   Fill in the blanks with the past tense of the verb in parentheses ( ).

EXAMPLE   Dawson ___learned___ to read when he was 98.
                     (learn)

1. He _____ for many, many years.
      (live)

2. He _____ his name with an X.
      (sign)

3. He _____ all his wives.
      (outlive)

4. Many changes _____ during his long life.
      (occur)

5. He _____ school when he was 98.
      (attend)

6. His teacher _____, "Do you know the alphabet?"
      (ask)

7. Dawson _____ from his father to enjoy life.
      (learn)

8. Richard Glaubman _____ to meet Dawson.
      (want)

EXERCISE 8   Fill in the blanks with the simple past tense of the verb in parentheses ( ).

EXAMPLE   King ___lived___ in the South.
           (live)

1. Slavery _____ in 1865, but discrimination _____.
      (end)   (continue)

2. King _____ equality for all people.
      (want)

3. King _____ as a minister.
      (work)

4. In many places, the law _____ whites from blacks.
      (separate)

5. Black children _____ separate schools.
      (attend)

6. A bus driver _____ Rosa Parks to stand up, but she _____.
      (order)   (refuse)

7. The bus driver _____ the police.
      (call)

8. The police _____ Ms. Parks.
      (arrest)

9. King _____ a peaceful protest.
      (organize)

10. In 1964, Congress _____ the law.
      (change)

11. In 1968, a great tragedy _____. Someone _____ King.
      (occur)   (kill)

Black students entering
a school in Clinton,
Tennessee, in 1956

3.4 The Simple Past of Irregular Verbs[12]

Many past tense verbs are irregular. They do not have an *-ed* ending.

Verbs With No Change				Final *d* Changes to *t*	
beat	fit	put	spit	bend—bent	send—sent
bet	hit	quit	split	build—built	spend—spent
cost	hurt	set	spread	lend—lent	
cut	let	shut			

Verbs with Vowel Changes

feel—felt	mean—meant[13]	dig—dug	sting—stung
keep—kept	sleep—slept	hang—hung	strike—struck
leave—left	sweep—swept	spin—spun	swing—swung
lose—lost	weep—wept	stick—stuck	win—won
awake—awoke	speak—spoke	begin—began	sing—sang
break—broke	steal—stole	drink—drank	sink—sank
choose—chose	wake—woke	ring—rang	spring—sprang
freeze—froze		shrink—shrank	swim—swam
bring—brought	fight—fought	blow—blew	grow—grew
buy—bought	teach—taught	draw—drew	know—knew
catch—caught	think—thought	fly—flew	throw—threw
arise—arose	rise—rose	bleed—bled	meet—met
drive—drove	shine—shone	feed—fed	read—read[14]
ride—rode	write—wrote	flee—fled	speed—sped
		lead—led	
sell—sold	tell—told	find—found	wind—wound
mistake—mistook	take—took	lay—laid	say—said[15]
shake—shook		pay—paid	
swear—swore	wear—wore	bite—bit	light—lit
tear—tore		hide—hid	slide—slid
become—became	forgive—forgave	fall—fell	run—ran
come—came	give—gave	hold—held	sit—sat
eat—ate	lie—lay		see—saw
forget—forgot	shoot—shot	stand—stood	
get—got		understand—understood	

Miscellaneous Changes

be—was/were	go—went	hear—heard
do—did	have—had	make—made

[12]For an alphabetical list of irregular verbs, see Appendix M.
[13]There is a change in the vowel sound. *Meant* rhymes with *sent*.
[14]The past form of *read* is pronounced like the color *red*.
[15]*Said* rhymes with *bed*.

EXERCISE 9 Fill in the blanks with the past tense of the verb in parentheses ( ).

EXAMPLE Dawson ___had___ a hard life.
(have)

1. He _____ to work for his father when he was four years old.
(begin)

2. He _____ many changes in his lifetime.
(see)

3. He _____ interested in reading when he was 98.
(become)

4. He _____ to the adult literacy program in Dallas County.
(go)

5. His teacher _____ him the alphabet.
(teach)

6. Dawson _____, "I wonder what I might learn today."
(say)

7. Dawson _____ a book.
(write)

EXERCISE 10 Fill in the blanks with the past tense of the verb in parentheses ( ).

EXAMPLE King ___fought___ for the rights of all people.
(fight)

1. King _____ born in 1929.
(be)

2. King _____ a minister.
(become)

3. He _____ married in 1953.
(get)

4. He _____ a job in a church in Montgomery, Alabama.
(find)

5. Rosa Parks was tired and _____ down on the bus.
(sit)

6. Some white people _____ on the bus.
(get)

7. The bus driver _____ Parks to stand up.
(tell)

8. Police _____ and arrested Parks.
(come)

9. King _____ about her arrest.
(hear)

10. In 1963, he _____ a beautiful speech in Washington, D.C.
(give)

11. Many people _____ to see King in Washington in 1963.
(go)

12. King _____ an important prize for his work.
(win)

13. A man _____ King in 1968.
(shoot)

Barack Obama and *Dreams from My Father*

Before
You Read

1. Where were you at the time of the 2008 election of Barack Obama?

2. Are there or were there any unusual leaders in your native country?

CD 1, TR 27

Read the following magazine article. Pay special attention to the negative form of past-tense verbs.

On January 20, 2009, Barack Obama became the first African-American president.

He was born in Hawaii in 1961, the son of a Kenyan father and an American mother. But Barack **didn't know** his father as he was growing up. When he was two years old, his parents separated and his father went back to Africa. Obama saw his father one more time in his life, when his father visited Hawaii. His father died in a car accident in 1982 when Barack was 21 years old. In 1995, he wrote about his life in *Dreams from My Father*. He realized that he **didn't belong** completely to a white world and he **didn't belong** completely to a black world. When he was young, he **didn't have** a clear racial identity.

Barack Obama with his mother

His mother married again, this time to an Indonesian man, and for a while Barack lived with her in Indonesia. But he returned to Hawaii when he was ten to live with his grandparents. His mother returned too, but she **didn't stay** for long. She went back to Indonesia, where she stayed for the rest of her life. For many years he **didn't live** with his mother. She died in 1995.

Barack Obama adored his grandmother but, sadly, she **didn't live** to see him become president. She died one day before the election.

3.5 Negative Statements

Compare affirmative and negative statements with past tense verbs.

EXAMPLES	EXPLANATION
Obama **lived** with his mother's parents. He **didn't live** with his father's parents. Obama **grew** up in Hawaii. He **didn't grow** up in Africa. Obama **knew** his mother. He **didn't know** his father well.	For the negative past tense, we use *didn't* + base form for ALL verbs (except *be*), regular and irregular. **Compare:** lived—didn't live grew—didn't grow knew—didn't know

EXERCISE 11   **Fill in the blanks with the negative form of the underlined word.**

EXAMPLE   Obama <u>spent</u> many years in Hawaii. He _____didn't spend_____ many years in Kenya.

1. Obama <u>wrote</u> about his life. He _____ a novel.

2. He <u>was</u> born in Hawaii. He _____ born in Illinois.

3. He <u>lived</u> in the U.S. He _____ in Kenya.

4. He <u>knew</u> his mother. He _____ his father very well.

5. His mother <u>went</u> to Indonesia. His grandparents _____ to Indonesia.

6. He <u>saw</u> his grandparents a lot. He _____ his father a lot.

7. He <u>grew</u> up with his grandparents. He _____ up with his father.

8. He <u>studied</u> law. He _____ engineering.

9. He <u>became</u> a senator of Illinois. He _____ a senator of Hawaii.

10. His grandmother <u>died</u> before the election. She _____ after the election.

Questions and Answers about Barack Obama

Before You Read

1. What facts do you know about Barack Obama?
2. What facts do you know about the president/prime minister of your native country?

CD 1, TR 28

Read the following questions and answers about Barack Obama. Pay special attention to past tense questions and answers.

> **Q:** **What did Obama do** before he became president?
>
> **A:** He **was** a senator from Illinois.
>
> **Q:** **When did he get** married?
>
> **A:** He **got** married in 1989.
>
> **Q:** **Who did he marry?**
>
> **A:** He **married** Michelle Robinson.
>
> **Q:** **Where did he meet her?**
>
> **A:** He **met** her at a law office.
>
> **Q.** **Did he work** there?
>
> **A:** Yes. They both **worked** there.
>
> **Q:** **Did he ever teach?**
>
> **A:** Yes. He **taught** law at the University of Chicago.
>
> **Q:** **Did he live** in Chicago?
>
> **A:** Yes, he **did**. He also **lived** in Springfield, the capital of Illinois, when he was a senator from Illinois.
>
> **Q:** **Did he win** every election?
>
> **A:** No, he **didn't**. In 2000, he **wanted** to be a U.S. Representative from Illinois, but he **didn't win**.

3.6 Questions with the Simple Past Tense

Compare affirmative statements and questions.

Wh- Word	Did	Subject	Verb	Complement	Short Answer
		Obama	**lived**	with his grandparents.	
	Did	he	**live**	in New York?	No, he didn't.
Where	**did**	he	**live?**		In Hawaii.
		Obama	**went**	to Africa.	
	Did	he	**go**	to Kenya?	Yes, he did.
When	**did**	he	**go**	to Kenya?	In 1988.

Language Note: The base form is used in questions after *did*.

Compare negative statements and questions.

Wh- Word	Didn't	Subject	Didn't	Base Form	Complement
		Obama	**didn't**	**live**	with his father.
Why	**didn't**	Obama		**live**	with his father?
		His father	**didn't**	**stay**	in the U.S.
Why	**didn't**	he		**stay**	in the U.S.?

EXERCISE 12   Read each statement. Write a *yes/no* question with the words in parentheses ( ). Give a short answer.

EXAMPLE   Obama lived in Hawaii. (with his grandparents) (yes)
<u>**Did he live with his grandparents? Yes, he did.**</u>

1. His grandmother died before he became president. (his mother) (yes)

_____

2. His father went to Kenya. (his mother) (no)

_____

3. Michelle Robinson became his wife. (his law partner) (no)

_____

4. He met his wife in a law office. (in Hawaii) (no)

_____

5. He lived in Hawaii. (in Indonesia) (yes)

_____

6. He lost the election for representative of Illinois. (senator of Illinois) (no)

_____

7. He taught at the University of Chicago. (law) (yes)

_____

EXERCISE 13 **Read each statement. Write a _wh-_ question about the words in parentheses ( ). Then answer the question.**

EXAMPLE Obama went to high school. (where) (in Hawaii)

**Where did he go to high school?**

**He went to high school in Hawaii.**

1. His mother met his father. (where) (in college)

_____

_____

2. His mother went to Indonesia. (why) (to be with her husband)

_____

_____

3. Obama returned to Hawaii. (when) (in 1971)

_____

_____

4. He studied law. (where) (at Harvard University)

_____

_____

5. He wrote a book. (what kind of book) (about his life)

_____

_____

6. Obama became president. (when) (in 2009)

_____

_____

7. Obama's grandmother died. (when) (in November 2008)

_____

_____

8. Obama didn't work in Hawaii. (why) (because he lived in Illinois)

_____

_____

EXERCISE 14 A student is interviewing her teacher about Martin Luther King Jr. Fill in the blanks with the correct form of the verb and any other necessary words.

🔊
CD 1, TR 29

S: Do you remember Martin Luther King Jr.?

T: Of course I do. I ____**saw**____ him on TV many times when
(example: see)

I _____ young.
(1 be)

S: _____ him on TV when he was in Washington, D.C.?
(2 see)

T: Yes, I _____. I remember his famous speech in Washington in 1963.
(3)

S: What _____ about?
(4 speak)

T: He _____ about equality for everyone.
(5 speak)

S: _____ to Washington?
(6 a lot of people/go)

T: Oh, yes. 250,000 people _____ to Washington.
(7 go)

S: Do you remember when he died?

T: I was in high school when he _____. The principal
(8 die)

_____ to our class and _____ us the news.
(9 come)   (10 tell)

S: What _____ when you heard the news?
(11 do)

T: At first we _____ it. Then we all started to
(12 not/believe)

_____. We _____ home from
(13 cry)   (14 go)

school and _____ the news on TV.
(15 watch)

S: Where _____ he when he died?
(16 be)

T: He _____ on the balcony of a hotel in Memphis when a man
(17 be)

_____ and _____ him. It was terrible. But we should remember
(18 come)   (19 shoot)

King for his life, not his death. We celebrate Martin Luther King Jr.'s birthday.

S: Really? I _____ that. When is it?
(20 not/know)

T: He _____ born on January 15. The third Monday in January
(21 be)

_____ a national holiday.
(22 become)

S: _____ a holiday right after he died?
(23 this date/become)

T: No. It _____ a holiday in 1983.
(24 become)

S: How do you remember so much about King?

T: I _____ a paper on him when I was in college.
(25 write)

EXERCISE 15 **ABOUT YOU** Check (✓) the things you did this past week. Exchange books with another student. Ask the other student about the items he or she checked.

EXAMPLE ___✓___ I made a long-distance phone call.

A: I made a long-distance phone call.

B: Who(m) did you call?

A: I called my father in Mexico.

B: How long did you talk?

A: We talked for about 15 minutes.

1. ____ I made a long-distance phone call.

2. ____ I shopped for groceries.

3. ____ I met someone new.

4. ____ I got together with a friend.

5. ____ I wrote a letter.

6. ____ I bought some new clothes.

7. ____ I went to the bank.

8. ____ I read something interesting (a book, an article).

9. ____ I went to the post office.

10. ____ I did exercises.

11. ____ I received a letter.

12. ____ I went to an interesting place.

Summary of Lesson 3

1. Simple Past Tense

   Be

   Dawson **was** happy.
   He **wasn't** rich.
   Was he from a large family? Yes, he **was.**
   Where **was** he born?
   Why **wasn't** he in school?

   Regular Verb

   Dawson **lived** for 103 years.
   He **didn't live** during the time of slavery.
   Did he **live** in the North? No, he **didn't.**
   Where **did** he **live?**
   Why **didn't** he **live** in the North?

Irregular Verb

Dawson **felt** happy.

He **didn't feel** lonely.

Did he **feel** good when he learned to read? Yes, he **did.**

How **did** he **feel** about his life?

Why **didn't** he **feel** lonely?

2. Habitual Past with *Used To*

Obama **used to** live in Hawaii.

Black children and white children **used to** go to separate schools. Now schools are for all children.

Editing Advice

1. Use *was/were* with *born.*

   was

   He born in Germany.
   ^

2. Don't use *was/were* with *die.*

   He ~~was~~ died two years ago.

3. Don't use a past form after *to.*

   leave

   I decided to ~~left~~ early.

   I wanted to go home and ~~watched~~ TV.

4. Don't use *was* or *were* to form a simple past tense.

   went

   He ~~was go~~ home yesterday.

5. Use *there* when a new subject is introduced.

   There w

   ~~Was~~ a big earthquake in 1906.

6. Use a form of *be* before an adjective. Remember, some *-ed* words are adjectives.

   were

   They excited about their trip to America.
   ^

7. Don't use *did* with an adjective. Use *was/were.*

   were

   Why ~~did~~ you afraid?

8. Use the correct word order in a question.

didn't you

Why ~~you didn't~~ return?

9. Use *did* + the base form in a question.

did   buy

What kind of car ˰ you ~~bought~~?

10. Use the base form after *didn't*.

He didn't ~~worked~~ work yesterday.

11. Don't forget the *d* in *used to*.

d

She use˰ to live in Miami.

12. Don't add the verb *be* before *used to* for habitual past.

~~I'm~~ used to play soccer in my country.

Editing Quiz

Some of the shaded words and phrases have mistakes. Find the mistakes and correct them. If the shaded words are correct, write C.

come   *C*

A: I didn't ~~came~~ to class last week. I missed two days. What we studied?
        (example)   *(example)*   *(1)*

B: Why you didn't come to class?
        (2)

A: I had to worked overtime, so I tired.
            (3)   *(4)*

B: We had a great lesson. We learn about racial progress in the U.S.
        (5)   *(6)*

We talked about Martin Luther King Jr., George Dawson, and Barack
    (7)

Obama.

A: Who was George Dawson?
        (8)

B: He was an amazing man. He born at the end of the 1800s.
        (9)   *(10)*

He didn't learned to read when he was young. He started to learn
    (11)   *(12)*

when he was 98 years old.

(continued)

---

*Habitual Past with *Used To*; The Simple Past Tense*   **107**

A: Wow! Is he still alive?

B: No, he was died in 2001. And we also learned about Martin Luther
     (13)   (14)

King's life.

A: I use to read about him in my country, India. King was studied
     (15)   (16)

the ideas of our leader, Gandhi. When I was in my country,

I'm used to study a lot of history.
     (17)

B: And was a story about Barack Obama in our book too.
     (18)

A: I know. I read it at home. It made me sad.
            (19)

B: Why did you sad?
       (20)

A: Because his grandmother didn't lived to see him become president.
                              (21)

B: Yeah, that part was sad.

A: Was any homework?
     (22)

B: Yes, there was. We had to wrote a composition about a famous person.
           (23)   (24)

A: Thanks for filling me in.

Lesson 3 Test/Review

PART 1 **Write the past form of the following verbs.**

EXAMPLE   draw ___*drew*___

1. eat _____   8. take _____   15. sit _____

2. put _____   9. bring _____   16. go _____

3. give _____   10. talk _____   17. make _____

4. write _____   11. know _____   18. hear _____

5. send _____   12. find _____   19. feel _____

6. listen _____   13. stand _____   20. fall _____

7. read _____   14. leave _____   21. get _____

PART 2   **Write the negative form of the underlined word.**

EXAMPLE   Rosa Parks <u>lived</u> in Alabama. She _____ *didn't live* _____ in Washington.

1. She <u>was</u> tired when she got out of work. She _____ sick.

2. She <u>went</u> to work by bus. She _____ to work by car.

3. The bus driver <u>told</u> African-Americans to stand. He _____ white Americans to stand.

4. Some African-Americans <u>stood</u> up. Rosa Parks _____ up.

5. The police <u>came</u> to the bus. They _____ to her house.

6. They <u>took</u> her to jail. They _____ her to her house.

7. Many people <u>had</u> the opportunity for education. George Dawson _____ the opportunity for education.

8. George Dawson <u>wrote</u> a book. He _____ it alone.

9. Barack Obama <u>spent</u> a lot of time with his grandparents. He _____ a lot of time with his father.

PART 3   **Write a question beginning with the words given. An answer is not necessary.**

EXAMPLE   Martin Luther King Jr. lived in the South.

Where _____ *did he live?* _____

1. King became a minister.
   Why _____

2. King was born in Georgia.
   When _____

3. Black children went to separate schools.
   Why _____

4. Some restaurants didn't permit black people to eat there.
   Why _____

(continued)

5. King was in jail many times because of his protests.

How many times _____

6. King won the Nobel Peace Prize.

When _____

7. Rosa Parks worked in Montgomery.

Where _____

8. She was tired.

Why _____

9. She went home by bus.

How many times _____

10. She didn't want to obey the law.

Why _____

11. The police took her to jail.

Why _____

12. Dawson learned to read.

When _____

13. Dawson didn't feel lonely.

Why _____

14. Obama didn't know his father very well.

Why _____

15. Obama won the election.

When _____

16. Obama's father wasn't born in the U.S.

Where _____

17. Obama wrote a book.

What _____ about?

PART 4 **Write two sentences with *used to* comparing your life ten years ago with your life today.**

1. _____

2. _____

Expansion

Classroom
Activities

1 **Check (✓) the sentences that are true for you. Find a partner and exchange books. Give each other more information about the things you checked. Ask each other questions about these activities.**

a. ____ I bought a CD in the past week.

b. ____ I worked last Saturday.

c. ____ I rode a bike this past week.

d. ____ I went to a party last weekend.

e. ____ I got a driver's license in the past year.

f. ____ I took a trip in the past year.

g. ____ I got married in the last two years.

h. ____ I found a job this month.

i. ____ I spent more than $50 today.

j. ____ I received some money this week.

k. ____ I ate pizza in the past month.

l. ____ I bought a car in the past year.

m. ____ I came to the U.S. alone.

2 **Who did it?**

Teacher: Pass out an index card to each student.

Students: Write something you did last weekend. It can be something unusual or something ordinary. (Examples: I went fishing. I baked a pie. I did my laundry.)

Teacher: Collect the cards. Pull out one card at a time and read the sentence to the class. The students have to guess who wrote the card.

❸ Who used to do it?

Teacher: Pass out an index card to each student.

Students: Think of some things you used to be, wear, do, etc. when you were younger. Think of things that other students would not guess about you. Write two or three of these things on the card.

Teacher: Collect the cards. Pull out one card at a time and read the sentences to the class. The students have to guess who wrote the card.

EXAMPLES I used to hate studying a foreign language.
I used to have very long hair.
I used to be a terrible student.

❹ Bring in a picture of yourself when you were younger. Describe how you were at that time and compare yourself to how you are now.

EXAMPLE I used to play soccer all day with my friends. Now I don't have time for it.

❺ Fill in the blank. Discuss your answers in a small group or with the entire class.

Before I came to the U.S., I used to believe that _____

_____, but now I know it's not true.

❻ With a partner, write a few questions to ask George Dawson.

EXAMPLES Why didn't you go to school?
What kinds of jobs did you have?
What was the first book you read?

Talk
About It
In a small group or with the entire class, discuss the following:

❶ Changes in daily life: Compare how life used to be when you were younger with how it is now.

❷ Fashion: Talk about different styles or fashions in the past.

EXAMPLE In the 1960s, men used to wear their hair long.

Write

About It   Choose one of the following topics to write a short composition.

❶ Write a paragraph or paragraphs telling about changes in your native country. Compare how life used to be with how it is now.

❷ Write about an ordinary person who did something extraordinary (like George Dawson). It can be someone you read about or someone you know.

❸ Write a paragraph or paragraphs telling about your childhood.

My Childhood

When I was a child, I lived in a big house with my parents, grandparents, sisters, brothers, aunts, and uncles. My parents went to work and my grandparents took care of me. I always had a good time with them. My grandmother used to tell me a lot of stories. My grandfather used to take me fishing…

 For more practice using grammar in context, please visit our Web site.

Grammar
Possessive Forms

Object Pronouns

Reflexive Pronouns

Questions

Context
Weddings

A Traditional American Wedding

Before You Read

1. What kind of clothes do a bride and groom wear in your native culture?

2. At what age do people usually get married in your native culture?

CD 2, TR 01

Read the following magazine article. Pay special attention to object pronouns and possessive forms.

Did You Know?

- Most American weddings (80%) take place in a church or synagogue.
- The average number of guests is 175.
- Hawaii is the favorite honeymoon destination.
- August is the most popular month for weddings.
- Money is the most desired wedding gift.
- About 43 percent of marriages end in separation or divorce within 15 years.

Many young couples consider **their** wedding to be one of the most important days of **their** life. They save for **it** and often spend a year planning for **it**: finding a place, selecting a menu and cake, buying a wedding dress, ordering invitations and sending **them** to friends and relatives, selecting musicians, and much more. The bride chooses **her** maid of honor and bridesmaids, and the groom chooses **his** best man[1] and groomsmen. The bride and groom want to make this day special for themselves and for **their** guests.

When the day arrives, the groom doesn't usually see the bride before the wedding. It is considered bad luck for **him** to see **her** ahead of time. The guests wait with excitement to see **her** too. When the wedding begins, the groom and groomsmen enter first. Then the bridesmaids enter. When the bride finally enters in **her** white dress, everyone turns around to look at **her**. Sometimes guests stand up when the bride enters. Often the **bride's** father or both of **her** parents walk **her** down the aisle to the groom's side.

During the ceremony, the bride and groom take vows.[2] They promise to love and respect each other for the rest of their lives. The groom's best man holds the rings for **them** until they are ready to place **them** on each **other's** fingers. At the end of the ceremony, the groom lifts the **bride's** veil and kisses **her**.

[1]The *best man* is the man who stands beside the groom and helps him.
[2]A *vow* is a promise.

There is a party after the ceremony. People make toasts,[3] eat dinner, and dance. The bride and groom usually dance the first dance alone. Then guests join **them**.

Before the bride and groom leave the party, the bride throws **her** bouquet over **her** head, and the single women try to catch **it**. It is believed that the woman who catches **it** will be the next one to get married.

The newlyweds[4] usually take a trip, called a honeymoon, immediately after the wedding.

4.1 Possessive Forms of Nouns

We use possessive forms to show ownership or relationship.

NOUN	ENDING	EXAMPLES
Singular noun: bride groom	Add apostrophe + **s**.	The **bride's** dress is white. The **groom's** tuxedo is black.
Plural noun ending in **-s**: parents guests	Add apostrophe only.	She got married in her **parents'** house. The **guests'** coats are in the coat room.
Irregular plural noun: men women	Add apostrophe + **s**.	The **men's** suits are black. The **women's** dresses are beautiful.
Names that end in **-s**: Charles	Add apostrophe + **s**.	Do you know **Charles's** wife? **Note:** Sometimes you will see only an apostrophe when a name ends in *s*. Do you know **Charles'** wife?
Inanimate objects: the church the dress	Use "*the _____ of the _____.*" Do not use apostrophe + **s**.	St. Peter's is **the name of the church**. **The front of the dress** has pearls.

[3]A *toast* is a wish for good luck, usually while holding a glass.
[4]For a short time after they are married, the bride and groom are called *newlyweds*.

EXERCISE 1 Fill in the blanks to make the possessive form of the noun.

EXAMPLE   The bride's__ grandfather looks very handsome.

1. The groom ____ mother is very nice.
2. The bride ____ flowers are beautiful.
3. The bridesmaids ____ dresses are blue.
4. They invited many guests to the wedding. They didn't invite the guests ____ children.
5. The women ____ dresses are very elegant.
6. Charles ____ sister is a bridesmaid.
7. The newlyweds ____ picture is in the newspaper.
8. Do you know the children ____ names?

EXERCISE 2 Fill in the blanks with the two nouns in parentheses ( ). Put them in the correct order. Use the possessive form of one of the nouns, except with nonliving things.

EXAMPLES   The _____bride's name_____ is Lisa.
                              (name/the bride)
           The __door of the church__ is open.
                      (door/church)

1. The _____ came to the wedding from London.
       (bride/grandmother)

2. The _____ has a red carpet.
       (church/floor)

3. The _____ are very beautiful.
       (windows/church)

4. The _____ is crying.
       (bride/mother)

5. The _____ is Saint Paul's.
       (church/name)

6. The _____ are black.
       (men/tuxedos)

7. The _____ is white.
       (limousine/color)

8. The _____ are pretty.
       (dresses/girls)

9. Who chose the _____?
                    (flowers/color)

10. Some people get married in their _____.
                                      (house/parents)

4.2 Possessive Adjectives

Possessive adjectives show ownership or relationship.

EXAMPLES	EXPLANATION
My brother is getting married. Your gift is wonderful. The groom chooses his best man. The bride chooses her bridesmaids. The restaurant has its own reception hall. Our cousins came from out of town. The wedding is the most important day of their lives.	<table><tr><td>Subject Pronouns</td><td>Possessive Adjectives</td></tr><tr><td>I</td><td>my</td></tr><tr><td>you</td><td>your</td></tr><tr><td>he</td><td>his</td></tr><tr><td>she</td><td>her</td></tr><tr><td>it</td><td>its</td></tr><tr><td>we</td><td>our</td></tr><tr><td>they</td><td>their</td></tr></table>

My sister loves her husband.
 	
My uncle lives with his daughter.
	Be careful not to confuse *his* and *her*.
	  Wrong: My sister loves *his* husband.
	  Wrong: My uncle lives with *her* daughter.

The **bride's mother's** dress is blue.	We can use two possessive nouns together.
My brother's wife did not attend the wedding.	We can use a possessive adjective (*my*) before a possessive noun (*brother's*).

EXERCISE 3 Fill in the blanks with a possessive adjective.

EXAMPLE   I love _____my_____ parents.

1. I have one sister. _____ sister got married five years ago.

2. She loves _____ husband very much.

3. He's an accountant. He has _____ own business.

4. They have one child. _____ son's name is Jason.

5. They bought a house last year. _____ house isn't far from my house.

6. My sister and I visit _____ parents once a month. They live two hours away from us.

7. My sister said, "My car isn't working this week. Let's visit them in _____ car."

EXERCISE 4 Fill in the blanks with a possessive adjective.

CD 2, TR 02

A: What are you going to wear to ___your___ sister's
(example)
wedding?

B: I'm going to wear _____ new blue dress.
(1)

A: Did your sister buy a new dress for her wedding?

B: No. She's going to borrow _____ best friend's dress.
(2)

A: Will the wedding be at your home?

B: Oh, no. We live in an apartment. _____ apartment
(3)
is too small. We're going to invite more than 200 guests. The wedding
is going to be at a church. Afterwards, we're going to have a dinner in a
restaurant. The restaurant has _____ own
(4)
reception hall.

A: Are the newlyweds going on a honeymoon after the wedding?

B: Yes. They have friends who have a cottage. They're going to stay at
_____ friends' cottage in the country for a week.
(5)

A: Is the groom's mother a nice woman?

B: I don't know _____ mother. I'll meet her at the
(6)
wedding for the first time.

4.3 Possessive Pronouns

We can use possessive pronouns (*mine, yours, his, hers, ours, theirs*) to show ownership or relationship.

POSSESSIVE ADJECTIVE	POSSESSIVE PRONOUN	EXPLANATION
Her dress is white. **Their wedding** was big. We had **our wedding** in a church.	**Mine** is blue. **Ours** was small. They had **theirs** in a garden.	When we omit the noun, we use a possessive pronoun. *mine* = my dress *ours* = our wedding *theirs* = their wedding
The groom's parents look happy.	**The bride's** do too.	After the possessive form of a noun, we can omit the noun. *The bride's* = the bride's parents

Compare the three forms below.

SUBJECT PRONOUN	POSSESSIVE ADJECTIVE	POSSESSIVE PRONOUN
I	my	mine
you	your	yours
he	his	his
she	her	hers
it	its	—
we	our	ours
they	their	theirs

EXERCISE **5** **Fill in the blanks with an appropriate possessive adjective or pronoun.**

CD 2, TR 03

A: I heard your brother got married last month. How was the wedding? Was it anything like your wedding? I remember ___**yours**___ *(example)* very well.

B: My brother's wedding was very different from _____. His was a very formal wedding *(1)* in a church last month. _____ was very *(2)* informal, in a garden.

A: I enjoyed your wedding. I prefer informal weddings. At most weddings, I have to get dressed up in a suit and tie. At _____, I wore *(3)* comfortable clothes.

B: _____ brother and _____ bride had a very different *(4)* *(5)* honeymoon too. Our honeymoon was a two-day trip. _____ was a *(6)* two-week stay in a luxury hotel in Hawaii. Their honeymoon was expensive. _____ was very economical. We drove to Chicago and *(7)* stayed in a motel there.

A: I remember your wife made her own dress. You saved a lot of money.

B: My sister-in-law, Gina, spent a lot of money on _____ dress. *(8)* _____ cost over $1,000. My wife's was only about $100. *(9)*

(continued)

A: The cost of a wedding isn't the most important thing. The most important thing is the happiness that follows. My uncle's wedding cost over $30,000. _____ was the most beautiful
(10)
wedding you can imagine. But his marriage lasted only eight months.

EXERCISE 6 Fill in the blanks with *I, I'm, me, my,* or *mine.*

1. _____ a student.
2. _____ live in an apartment near school.
3. _____ apartment is on the first floor.
4. _____ parents often visit _____.
5. They don't have a computer. They use _____.

EXERCISE 7 Fill in the blanks with *we, we're, us, our,* or *ours.*

1. _____ classroom is large.
2. _____ study English here.
3. _____ foreign students.
4. The teacher helps _____ learn English.
5. The teacher brings her book, and we bring _____.

EXERCISE 8 Fill in the blanks with *you, you're, your,* or *yours.* Pretend you are talking directly to the teacher.

1. _____ the teacher.
2. _____ come from the U.S.
3. My first language is Polish. _____ is English.
4. _____ pronunciation is very good.
5. We see _____ every day.

EXERCISE 9 Fill in the blanks with *he, he's, his,* or *him.*

1. I have a brother. _____ name is Paul.
2. _____ married.
3. _____ has four children.
4. My apartment is small. _____ is big.
5. I see _____ on the weekends.

EXERCISE 10 Fill in the blanks with *she, she's, her,* or *hers.*

1. I have a sister. _____ name is Marilyn.
2. I visit _____ twice a week.
3. _____ lives in a suburb.
4. _____ a teacher. _____ husband is a doctor.
5. My children go to private school. _____ go to public school.

EXERCISE 11 Fill in the blanks with *it, it's,* or *its.*

1. The school has a big library. _____ comfortable and clean.
2. _____ has many books and magazines.
3. _____ hours are from 8 a.m. to 8 p.m.
4. I use _____ every day.
5. _____ on the first floor.

EXERCISE 12 Fill in the blanks with *they, they're, them, their,* or *theirs.*

1. My parents rent _____ apartment.
2. My apartment is small, but _____ is big.
3. _____ very old now.
4. _____ live in a suburb.
5. I visit _____ on the weekends.

4.4 Questions with *Whose*

Whose + a noun asks a question about ownership.

WHOSE + NOUN	AUXILIARY VERB	SUBJECT	VERB	ANSWER
Whose dress	did	the bride	borrow?	She borrowed her sister's dress.
Whose flowers	are	those?		They're the bride's flowers.
Whose last name	will	the bride	use?	She'll use her husband's last name.

EXERCISE 13   Write a question with *whose*. The answer is given.

EXAMPLE   <u>Whose flowers are these?</u>

They're the bride's flowers.

1. _____

That's my father's car.

2. _____

Those are the newlyweds' gifts.

3. _____

She's wearing her sister's necklace.

4. _____

I'm wearing my friend's suit.

5. _____

I follow my parents' advice.

6. _____

The bride borrowed her sister's dress.

4.5 Object Pronouns

We can use an object pronoun (*me, you, him, her, it, us,* or *them*) after the verb.

OBJECT NOUN	OBJECT PRONOUN	EXPLANATION
Daniel loves **Sofia**. Sofia loves **Daniel**. You met **my parents**.	He loves **her** very much. She loves **him** very much. You met **them** last night.	We can use an object pronoun to substitute for an object noun.
Do you know **the guests**? The bride and groom sent **invitations**.	Yes, we know **them**. They sent **them** last month.	We use *them* for plural people and things.
I see **the bride**. The bride is with **her father**.	Everyone is looking *at* **her**. She will dance *with* **him**.	An object pronoun can follow a preposition (*at, with, of, about, to, from, in,* etc.).

Compare subject and object pronouns.

SUBJECT	OBJECT	EXAMPLES		
		Subject	**Verb**	**Object**
I	me	You	love	me.
you	you	I	love	you.
he	him	She	loves	him.
she	her	He	loves	her.
it	it	We	love	it.
we	us	They	love	us.
they	them	We	love	them.

EXERCISE 14 Fill in the blanks with an object pronoun in place of the underlined words.

EXAMPLE The groom doesn't walk down the aisle with <u>the bride</u>. Her father walks with _____**her**_____.

1. <u>The bride</u> doesn't enter with <u>the groom</u>. He waits for _____, and she goes to _____.

2. The groom takes <u>the ring</u>. He puts _____ on the bride's hand.

3. <u>The bride</u> wears <u>a veil</u>. The groom lifts _____ to kiss _____.

4. The bride doesn't throw <u>the bouquet</u> to all the women. She throws _____ to the single women only.

5. People make toasts to <u>the bride and groom</u>. They wish _____ health and happiness.

6. <u>The groom</u> promises to love the bride, and the bride promises to love _____.

EXERCISE 15 Fill in the blanks with the correct subject pronoun, object pronoun, or possessive adjective.

CD 2, TR 04

A: How was your cousin Lisa's wedding last Saturday?

B: _____**It**_____ was great.
    (example)

A: How many guests were there?

B: Maybe about 200. I couldn't count _____.
                             (1)

A: Wow! That's a lot. It sounds like an expensive wedding. How did they pay for _____?
                                     (2)

(continued)

B: Lisa and Ron worked when _____ graduated from college
(3)

and saved money for _____ wedding. _____
(4)   (5)

parents helped _____ a little, but they couldn't depend on
(6)

_____ too much. _____ parents aren't wealthy.
(7)   (8)

A: Did Lisa wear a traditional white dress?

B: Yes. In fact, _____ wore _____ mother's
(9)   (10)

wedding dress. She looked beautiful in _____.
(11)

A: Where did _____ go on their honeymoon?
(12)

B: They went to Hawaii. I was surprised—they sent _____
(13)

a postcard. They had a great time.

A: I hope _____ will be happy. The wedding and honeymoon
(14)

are important, but the marriage that follows is what really counts.

B: I agree with _____. But I'm sure they'll be happy.
(15)

She loves _____ and _____
(16)   (17)

loves _____ very much.
(18)

A: Did you take pictures?

B: Yes. Do you want to see _____? I took _____
(19)   (20)

with my new digital camera.

A: I don't have time now. Can you show _____ the pictures
(21)

tomorrow?

B: I'll e-mail _____ to _____ later this evening.
(22)   (23)

New Wedding Trends

1. American wedding customs are changing. Are wedding customs changing in your native culture?

2. In your native culture, what kind of vows do the bride and groom make to each other?

CD 2, TR 05

Read the following Web article. Pay special attention to direct and indirect objects after verbs.

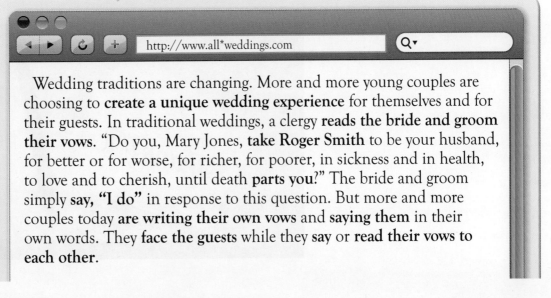

http://www.all*weddings.com

Wedding traditions are changing. More and more young couples are choosing to **create a unique wedding experience** for themselves and for their guests. In traditional weddings, a clergy **reads the bride and groom their vows.** "Do you, Mary Jones, **take Roger Smith** to be your husband, for better or for worse, for richer, for poorer, in sickness and in health, to love and to cherish, until death **parts you?**" The bride and groom simply **say, "I do"** in response to this question. But more and more couples today **are writing their own vows** and **saying them** in their own words. They **face the guests** while they **say** or **read their vows to each other.**

(continued)

Churches and synagogues are still the most popular places for a wedding. But some couples are choosing to **have a destination wedding.** They get married on the beach, on a mountain top, or other unusual place. These weddings **have fewer guests** because of the expense of traveling. Often the bride and groom **pay for the hotel rooms** of their guests. They **tell their guests the date** at least three to four months in advance. Often they **send them "save-the-date" cards** so that their guests can **make plans** to **attend the wedding.**

Another new trend in weddings is to **create a wedding** based on the couple's ethnic background. For example, in an African-American wedding, some couples want to **show respect to their ancestors**[5] by jumping over a broom, a tradition coming from the time of slavery. The jumping of the broom **symbolizes a new beginning** by sweeping away the old and welcoming the new. Some African-Americans **use colorful clothing** inspired by African costumes, rather than a white dress for the bride and a suit or tuxedo for the groom.

One thing stays the same. The newlyweds **send the guests thank-you cards** by mail to **thank them** for attending the wedding and for the gifts they gave.

[5]*Ancestors* are your grandparents, great-grandparents, great-great-grandparents, etc.

4.6 Direct and Indirect Objects

Some verbs are followed by both a direct and an indirect object. The order of the objects sometimes depends on the verb.[6] It sometimes depends on pronoun use.

EXAMPLES	EXPLANATION
Pattern A: | Subj.	Verb	Indirect Obj.	Direct Obj. | |---|---|---|---| | We | gave | the couple | a wedding gift. | | They | sent | us | a thank-you card. | | She | read | the groom | her vows. | | They | showed | me | their pictures. |	With the following verbs, we follow Pattern A or Pattern B. bring read show give sell tell offer send write pay (e-)mail
Pattern B: | Subj.	Verb	Direct Obj.	*To* Indirect Obj. | |---|---|---|---| | We | gave | a wedding gift | to the couple. | | She | read | her vows | to the groom. |	In Pattern A, we put the indirect object before the direct object. In Pattern B, we put the direct object first and then use *to* + the indirect object.
Ed gave Ann a ring. He gave **it** to Ann on her birthday. Do you have the pictures? Can you show **them** to me?	When the direct object is a pronoun, we follow Pattern B.
	Direct Obj.	*To* **Indirect Obj.** Please explain wedding customs to me. Please describe the wedding to us.	With the following verbs, we follow Pattern B: direct object *to* indirect object. announce mention say describe prove suggest explain report

---

EXERCISE 16 Fill in the blanks with the words in parentheses ( ). Put them in the correct order. Add *to* if necessary. In some cases, more than one answer is possible.

🔊 CD 2, TR 06

A: How was your cousin's wedding? Can you describe ___**it to me**___?
(example: it/me)

B: It was beautiful. The bride read _____,
(1 a lovely poem/the groom)
and then the groom read _____ too.
(2 a poem/her)

A: Did they get married in a church?

B: No. They got married in a beautiful garden. Why didn't you go? I thought they sent _____?
(3 an invitation/you)

[6]For a more detailed list of verbs and the order of direct and indirect objects, see Appendix I.   *(continued)*

A: They did. But I couldn't go. I wrote _____ and

(4 a letter/them)

I explained _____. I had to take an important

(5 them/my problem)

exam for college that day. But I sent _____.

(6 a lovely present/them)

B: I'm sure they'll appreciate it. It's too bad you couldn't go.

A: I'm sure I mentioned _____ a few weeks ago.

(7 you/it)

B: You probably did, but I forgot.

A: Do you have pictures from the wedding?

B: I took a lot of pictures. I'll e-mail _____ tonight.

(8 you/them)

A: Thanks.

4.7 *Say* and *Tell*

Say and *tell* have the same meaning, but we use them differently.

EXAMPLES	EXPLANATION
Compare: a. She **said** her name. b. She **told** me her name. c. She **said** her name to me. d. They **told** the musicians to start the music.	a. We *say* something. b. We *tell* someone something. c. We *say* something to someone. d. We *tell* someone to do something.
The bride and groom **say** "I do." They **say** "thank you" to the guests.	*Say* is followed by a direct object.
They **told** the guests the wedding date. **Tell** me the bride's name.	*Tell* is followed by an indirect object and a direct object.
Tell the truth, do you love me?	We can use *tell the truth* or *tell a lie* without an indirect object.

EXERCISE 17 Fill in the blanks with the correct form of *say* or *tell*.

EXAMPLES The bride ___said___, "I love you."

They ___told___ me the date of the wedding.

1. You _____ me the groom's name, but I forgot it.

2. Can you _____ me where the wedding is?

3. _____ the truth, do you like the bride's dress?

4. The bride hates to _____ good-bye to her family.

5. During the ceremony, the bride and groom _____, "I do."

6. We _____ the band to play romantic music.

7. My neighbor wants to come to the wedding. I wasn't planning on inviting her, but I can't _____ no.

8. We _____ our daughter to economize on her wedding, but she _____ she wanted a fancy wedding.

Economizing on a Wedding

Before You Read

1. Does a wedding have to be expensive?

2. How can people economize on their weddings?

CD 2, TR 07

Read the following magazine article. Pay special attention to the reflexive pronouns.

The average cost of a wedding in the U.S. today is $28,800. In days past, the bride's parents usually paid for the wedding. But as today's brides and grooms are older when they get married, they often pay for things **themselves**. There are many couples who put **themselves** in debt[7] to create a dream wedding.

Some recently married people give advice on how to economize on a wedding and still have a lovely, memorable event. Here are their tips:

- "I always pictured **myself** in a beautiful white dress. But when I went shopping and saw that most dresses are at least $1,000, I decided to look for a secondhand dress. I found something for $200, and it was lovely. When my sister got married, she made her dress **herself** and spent only $100 on fabric and lace. It isn't necessary to spend so much money on a dress. A bride is always beautiful."

- "We were going to use a professional printer for the invitations, but we decided to make the invitations **ourselves**. We designed them on the computer and added ribbons. The guests told us that they were beautiful and original."

Did You Know?

The average age of marriage is 27 for men and 25 for women.

[7]When you are *in debt*, you owe money and have to pay it back.

(continued)

- "I always wanted live music at my wedding. But when I saw the cost of musicians, I was shocked. My cousin plays piano well, so I asked her to play the piano for the wedding. And we used a DJ[8] for the dancing afterwards. We had to remind **ourselves** that the music wasn't the focus for the day—our marriage was."
- "Most couples want to get married in the summer. Ask **yourself** how important a summer wedding really is. You can cut costs by having a wedding at a less popular time. For example, a wedding in January is cheaper than a wedding in August."

According to some couples, it is not good to economize on some things:

- "Don't try to save money by sending invitations or thank-you cards through e-mail. Guests are offended. You should use postal mail."
- "We asked a friend to take pictures at our wedding but were very disappointed with the results. Our advice: Hire a professional photographer. You want to look at **yourselves** and guests for years to come."

The best way to economize is to cut the guest list and invite only your closest relatives and friends.

Although most young couples want a perfect wedding, the most important thing is to have a good marriage.

4.8 Reflexive Pronouns

We use reflexive pronouns for the object when the subject and object are the same. Compare:

> **The groom loves her. (object pronoun)**
> **The bride loves herself. (reflexive pronoun)**

EXAMPLES	EXPLANATION
a. I pictured **myself** in a beautiful white dress. (D.O.) b. We tell **ourselves** that money makes us happy, but it's not true. (I.O.) c. They like to look at **themselves** in their wedding photos. (O.P.)	A reflexive pronoun can be a. a direct object (D.O.) b. an indirect object (I.O.) c. the object of a preposition (O.P.)
She made the dress **all by herself**. The bride and groom made the invitations **by themselves**.	We often use a reflexive pronoun to mean alone, without help. We often add *all by* or *by* before the reflexive pronoun.
We enjoyed **ourselves** at the wedding. Help **yourself** to more cake. Make **yourself** at home.	We use reflexive pronouns in a few idiomatic expressions.

[8]A *DJ* is a disk jockey, a person who plays recorded music.

EXERCISE **Frank and Sylvia are like many American couples. They have problems balancing their relationship, children, careers, families, and other responsibilities. Read each one's story and fill in the blanks with a reflexive pronoun.**

CD 2, TR 08

Sylvia's Story:

Now that I'm married, I don't have time for ___**myself**___ anymore.

(*example*)

We used to spend time with each other. Now that we have kids, we never

have time for _____. We both work, but Frank doesn't

(1)

help me with housework or with the kids. I have to do everything all by

_____. My husband thinks only of _____. When he wants

(2)   (3)

something, like a new digital camera or new software, he buys it.

He never buys me flowers or presents anymore. I tell _____ that

(4)

he still loves me, but sometimes I'm not so sure. Sometimes I think the

problem is his fault, but sometimes I blame _____.

(5)

Frank's Story:

Sylvia never has time for me anymore. We used to do things together.

Now I have to do everything by _____. If I want to go to a movie,

(6)

she says that she's too busy or too tired or that the kids are sick. I rarely go

to the movies, and if I do, I go by _____. It seems like all I do is

(7)

work and pay bills. Other married people seem to enjoy _____ more

(8)

than we do. She says she wants me to help her with the housework, but she

(continued)

really prefers to do everything _____ because she doesn't like
(9)

the way I do things. She wants us to see a marriage counselor, but I don't

like to tell other people about my problems. I like to solve my problems

_____.
(10)

What do you think Frank and Sylvia should do?

EXERCISE **19** **ABOUT YOU** Write two sentences telling about things you like to do by yourself. Write two sentences telling about things you don't like to do by yourself.

EXAMPLES   I like to shop by myself. I prefer to visit art museums by myself.

I don't like to eat by myself. I don't like to go for a walk by myself.

_____

_____

_____

_____

EXERCISE **20** **Fill in the blanks with the correct pronoun or possessive form.**

Frank and Sylvia used to do a lot of things together. ___**They**___ went
(example)

to movies, went out to restaurants, and took vacations together. But now

_____ are always too busy for each other. _____ have two
(1)   (2)

children and spend most of _____ time taking care of _____.
(3)   (4)

Frank and Sylvia bought a house recently and spend _____ free
(5)

time taking care of _____. It's an old house and needs a lot of work.
(6)

When Frank and Sylvia have problems, _____ try to solve
(7)

_____ by _____. But sometimes Sylvia goes to _____
(8)   (9)   (10)

mother for advice. Frank never goes to _____ mother. He doesn't
(11)

want to bother _____ with _____ problems. Frank often
(12)   (13)

complains that Sylvia cares more about the kids and the house than

about _____.
(14)

Sylvia wants to go to a marriage counselor, but Frank doesn't want to

go with _____. He always says to Sylvia, "We don't need a marriage
(15)

134   Lesson 4

counselor. We can solve _____ problems by _____. You just
              (16)   (17)

need to pay more attention to _____. If you want to see a counselor,
                              (18)

you can go by _____. I'm not going." Sylvia feels very frustrated. She
              (19)

thinks that the marriage isn't going to get better by _____.
                                                      (20)

Questions and Answers about an American Wedding

Before
You Read

1. Do you have any questions about American weddings?

2. How is a traditional American wedding different from a wedding in your native culture?

CD 2, TR 09

Read the following questions and answers about American weddings. Pay special attention to questions.

Q: Who pays for the wedding?

A: In the past, the bride's parents paid for most of the wedding. Today only about 20 percent of weddings are the responsibility of the bride's parents. As men and women are getting married after starting careers and earning money, more and more weddings are becoming the responsibility of the bride and groom.

Q: What is a shower?

A: A shower is a party for the bride (and sometimes the groom) before the wedding. The purpose of the party is to give the couple gifts that will help them start their new home. Typical gifts are towels, cookware, linens,[9] and small kitchen and household appliances.

Q: Who hosts the shower?

A: Usually the maid of honor hosts the shower. She invites friends and relatives of the bride and groom.

Q: When do they have the shower?

A: Usually the shower is two to six weeks before the wedding.

[9]*Linens are sheets, pillowcases, and tablecloths.*

(*continued*)

Q: How long does it take to plan a wedding?

A: Most couples plan their wedding for seven to twelve months.

Q: When do the couples send invitations?

A: They usually send the invitations about eight weeks before the wedding.

Q: When guests come in from out of town, **who pays for their hotel and transportation?**

A: The out-of-town guests pay for their own hotel. However, the groom pays for the hotel for his groomsmen and the bride pays for her bridesmaids. The guests usually pay for their own transportation.

Q: **Whom does the groom choose as his best man?**

A: Often the groom chooses his brother or best friend. However, he chooses the man he feels closest to. The groom chooses other close friends or male relatives as the groomsmen.

Q: **When do the bride and groom open their gifts?**

A: They open their gifts at home, not at the wedding.

Q: **How do the guests know what the bride and groom want as gifts?**

A: The bride and groom usually register for gifts at stores. They list the gift items they want and need for their new home, such as dishes, cookware, small appliances, and towels. When the guests go to buy a gift, they check the registry in the store. Of course, money is always a popular gift.

Q: **How do I know how much money to give?**

A: Most guests spend about $100 on a gift. People who are closer to the bride or groom often spend more. Casual friends usually spend less.

4.9 Questions about the Subject or Complement

Questions about the complement include *do, does,* or *did*. Questions about the subject do not include *do, does,* or *did*.

EXAMPLES	EXPLANATION
Who wears a white dress? The bride **does.** **Who paid** for the wedding? The parents **did.** **Whose ring has** a diamond? The bride's ring **does.**	We usually answer a subject question with a subject and an auxiliary verb.
What happened after the wedding? The bride and groom **went** on a honeymoon.	*What happened* is a subject question. We usually answer with a different verb.
a. Who **has** the prettiest dress? b. Which woman **has** the prettiest dress? c. Which women **have** the prettiest dresses? d. How many people **want** to dance? e. What **happens** at the reception?	For the simple present tense: a. Use the *-s* form after *who*. b. Use the *-s* form after *which* + singular noun. c. Use the base form after *which* + plural noun. d. Use the base form after *how many* + plural noun. e. Use the *-s* form after *what*.

Compare these statements and related questions.

Wh- Word	Do/Does/Did	Subject	Verb	Complement
What	did	The groom the bride	paid for pay for?	the rings.
		Someone Who	paid for paid for	the wedding. the wedding?
Whom	does	The groom he	chooses choose?	a best man.
		The bride Who	chooses chooses	her dress. the rings?
Why	do	Out-of-town guests they Who	stay stay stays	at a hotel. at a hotel? at a hotel?
Whose dress	did	The bride she	borrowed borrow?	a dress.
		Someone's dress Whose dress	looks looks	beautiful. beautiful?
		Something What	happened happened	next. next?

Language Note: In a question about the object, *whom* is very formal. Informally, many Americans say *who*.

Formal: *Whom* did your brother marry?
Informal: *Who* did your brother marry?

EXERCISE **21** **Read each statement. Then write a question about the words in parentheses ( ). No answer is necessary.**

EXAMPLE   Someone takes the bride to the groom. (who)
<u>**Who takes the bride to the groom?**</u>

1. Someone holds the rings. (who)

_____

2. Someone's car has a "just married" sign. (whose car)

_____

3. Two people say, "I do." (how many people/"congratulations")

_____

4. One woman wore a black dress. (which woman)

_____

5. The bride pays for her white dress. (who/the bridesmaids' dresses)

_____

EXERCISE 22 **ABOUT YOU** Use the simple present tense of the verb in parentheses ( ) to ask a question about this class. Any student may volunteer an answer.

EXAMPLES Who (ride) a bike to school?

A: Who rides a bike to school?

B: I do.

How many students (have) the textbook?

A: How many students have the textbook?

B: We all do.

1. Who (explain) the grammar?

2. How many students (speak) Spanish?

3. What usually (happen) after class?

4. Who (need) help with this lesson?

5. Which students (walk) to school?

6. Who (have) a digital camera?

7. Who (live) alone?

8. Whose last name (have) over ten letters?

EXERCISE 23 **ABOUT YOU** Use the simple past tense of the verb in parentheses ( ) to ask a question. Any student may volunteer an answer.

EXAMPLE Who (buy) a used textbook?

A: Who bought a used textbook?

B: I did.

1. Who (move) last year?

2. Who (understand) the explanation?

3. Whose family (take) a trip recently?

4. Who (bring) a dictionary to class today?

5. Who (pass) the last test?

6. Which students (come) late today?

7. Which student (arrive) first today?

8. How many students (do) today's homework?

9. How many students (study) English in elementary school?

10. How many students (bring) a cell phone to class?

EXERCISE 24 Read each statement. Then write a question about the words in parentheses ( ). Some of the questions are about the subject. Some are not. No answer is necessary.

EXAMPLES The bride wears a white dress. (what/the groom)
What does the groom wear?

The bride enters last. (who/first)
Who enters first?

1. The bride throws the bouquet. (when)

   _____

2. Some women try to catch the bouquet. (which women)

   _____

3. The groom puts the ring on the bride's finger. (on which hand) OR (which hand . . . on)

   _____

4. The band plays music. (what kind of music)

   _____

5. Someone dances with the bride. (who)

   _____

6. Guests give presents. (what kind of presents)

   _____

7. Some people cry at the wedding. (who)

   _____

8. There's a dinner after the ceremony. (what/happen/after the dinner)

   _____

EXERCISE 25 In the conversation below, two women are talking about their families. Fill in the blanks to complete the questions. Some of the questions are about the subject. Some are about the object. In some cases, more than one answer is possible.

CD 2, TR 10

A: How do you have time to work, go to school, and take care of a family?

B: I don't have to do everything myself.

A: Who ___ **helps you** ___?
   (example)

B: My husband helps me.

A: I usually cook in my house. Who _____?
   (1)

B: Sometimes my husband cooks; sometimes I cook. We take turns.

(continued)

A: I usually clean. Who _____?
(2)

B: I usually clean the house.

A: How many _____?
(3)

B: I have five children.

A: How many _____?
(4)

B: Three children go to school. The younger ones stay home.

A: Do you send them to public school or private school?

B: One of my sons goes to private school.

A: Which _____?
(5)

B: The oldest does. He's in high school now.

A: It's hard to take care of so many children. How do you find the time to go to class?

B: As I said, my husband helps me a lot. And sometimes I use a babysitter.

A: I'm looking for a sitter. Who(m) _____?
(6)

B: I recommend our neighbor, Susan. She's 16 years old, and she's very good with our children.

A: Maybe she's too busy to help me. How many families

_____?
(7)

B: I think she works for only one other family. I'll give you her phone number. If she's not busy, maybe she can work for you too.

A: Thanks. I could use some help.

EXERCISE **26** **Fill in the blanks with *who, whom, who's,* or *whose.***

1. _____ did you invite to the wedding?

   I invited all my friends and relatives.

2. _____ took pictures?

   My brother did. He borrowed a camera because his is broken.

3. _____ camera did he borrow?

   He borrowed my aunt's camera. She has a fantastic camera.

4. _____ your aunt?

   She's that woman over there.

Summary of Lesson 4

1. Pronouns and Possessive Forms

SUBJECT PRONOUN	OBJECT PRONOUN	POSSESSIVE ADJECTIVE	POSSESSIVE PRONOUN	REFLEXIVE PRONOUN
I	me	my	mine	myself
you	you	your	yours	yourself
he	him	his	his	himself
she	her	her	hers	herself
it	it	its	—	itself
we	us	our	ours	ourselves
you	you	your	yours	yourselves
they	them	their	theirs	themselves
who	whom	whose	whose	—

EXAMPLES

They came from Canada.
I invited **them**.
Their wedding was outdoors.
My wedding was small. **Theirs** was big.
They paid for the wedding **themselves**.

Who came from Canada?
Who(m) did you invite?
Whose wedding was outdoors?
Someone's wedding was big.
  Whose was big?

2. Possessive Form of Nouns

Singular Nouns
  the **bride's** dress
  my **father's** house
  the **child's** toy
  the **man's** hat
  Charles's wife

Plural Nouns
  the **bridesmaids'** dresses
  my **parents'** house
  the **children's** toys
  the **men's** hats

3. *Say* and *Tell*

  He **said** his name.
  He **told** me his name.

He **said** good-bye to his friends.
He **told** them to write often.

4. Questions about the Subject

Simple Present:
  Who has the rings?
  How many bridesmaids have a pink dress?
  Which bridesmaid has a red dress?
  Which bridesmaids have pink flowers?
  What happens after the wedding?

Simple Past:
  Who kissed the bride?
  Which man kissed the bride?
  What happened next?
  How many people came to the wedding?
  Whose mother cried?

Editing Advice

1. Don't confuse *you're* (you are) and *your* (possessive form).

   You're
   ~~Your~~ late.

   Your
   ~~You're~~ class started ten minutes ago.

2. Don't confuse *he's* (he is) and *his* (possessive form).

   He's
   ~~His~~ married.

   His
   ~~He's~~ wife is a friend of mine.

3. Don't confuse *it's* (it is) and *its* (possessive form).

   It's
   This college is big. ~~Its~~ a state university.

   Its
   ~~It's~~ library has many books.

4. Don't confuse *his* (masculine possessor) and *her* (feminine possessor).

   her
   My sister loves ~~his~~ son.

   his
   My brother loves ~~her~~ daughter.

5. Don't confuse *my* and *mine*.

   my
   I don't have ~~mine~~ book today.

   mine
   You can borrow ~~my~~.

6. Don't confuse *they're* and *their*.

   Their
   ~~They're~~ last name is Williams.

   They're
   ~~Their~~ from California.

7. Use the correct pronoun (subject or object).

   her
   I have a daughter. I love ~~she~~ very much.

8. For a compound subject, use "another person and I." Don't use *me* in the subject position.

   I
   My father and ~~me~~ like to go fishing.
   My father and I
   ~~Me and my father~~ like to go fishing.

9. For a compound object, use "another person and me." Don't use *I* in the object position.

   me
   My parents gave my brother and ~~I~~ a present.

10. Don't use an apostrophe to make a plural form.

    guests
    They invited many ~~guest's~~ to the wedding.

11. Don't use an auxiliary verb in a question about the subject.

    s
    Who ~~does~~ speak Spanish?

12. Don't separate *whose* from the noun.

    Whose is this book?

13. Don't confuse *whose* and *who's*.

    Whose
    ~~Who's~~ coat is that?

14. Use the correct word order for possession.

    My wife's mother
    ~~Mother my wife~~ helps us a lot.

15. Put the apostrophe after the *s* of a plural noun that ends in *s*.

    parents'
    My ~~parent's~~ house is small.

16. The *s* in a possessive pronoun is not for a plural.

    Theirs parents live in Canada.

17. Don't use a form of *be* with *what happened*.

    What ~~was~~ happened to your new car?

18. Use the correct word order with direct and indirect objects.

    the grammar to me
    She explained ~~me the grammar.~~
    it to him
    I gave ~~him it.~~

Editing Quiz

Some of the shaded words and phrases have mistakes. Find the mistakes and correct them. If the shaded words are correct, write C.

A: I heard you got married recently. Tell me about ~~you're~~ *your* wedding. Did you have a lot of guests? *(example)* C *(example)*

B: It was a small wedding. Sara's (1) parents wanted a big wedding, and hers (2) parents offered to pay for it (3). But we wanted to be responsible and pay for it ourself (4). We explained them the situation (5), and they agreed. So we just had our (6) immediate families: parents, grandparents, sisters, brothers, aunts, and uncles. But grandfather Sara (7) didn't come.

A: Why not? What was happened (8) to he (9)?

B: Nothing. His (10) grandfather lives in Mexico. His (11) very old and couldn't travel. But her (12) grandmother came and stayed at Sara's aunt's house (13).

A: Your (14) grandparents are old too, aren't they? Did they come?

B: Yes, they did. Mine (15) live nearby. And their (16) in great health.

A: That's good. So you (17) didn't spend a lot of money on your wedding?

B: No. No big ceremony, no big party. Just a small dinner at Sara's parent's (18) house. Aunts of Sara (19) made a beautiful dinner. We even saved money on the wedding dress because Sarah borrowed a dress.

A: Who's (20) dress did she borrow?

B: She wore her (21) mothers (22) wedding dress. And I didn't rent a tuxedo. I wore my (23) new blue suit. You know the tradition: "Something old, something new, something borrowed, something blue." My suit is new and blue. Sara's (24) dress is old and borrowed.

A: Did you hire a photographer?

B: No. We (25) saved money there too. Mine (26) uncle is a photographer. He (27) took all the picture's (28) and gave us them (29) on disk. We printed they (30) and made an album.

A: Did you go on a honeymoon?

B: We saved money there too. Sara's uncle has a vacation home in Miami.

Me and Sara stayed there for a week. (His uncle wasn't there at the
(31)   (32)

time.)

A: Its hot in Miami at this time of the year.
(33)

B: Yes, it is. But there was a swimming pool. We used it every day.
(34)

A: What are you going to do with all the money you saved?

B: We have to pay our college loans. We also want to buy a house and car,

so we're saving for its.
(35)   (36)

A: You're a wise man! When Lisa and I get married after we graduate, I'd
(37)   (38)

like to do the same thing. But I think Lisa won't agree.

B: Who know? Maybe she'll like the idea.
(39)

Lesson 4 Test/Review

PART 1 **Choose the correct word to complete each sentence.**

EXAMPLE Do you like __c__ neighbors?

  a. you   **b.** you're   **c.** your   **d.** yours

1. Where do your parents live? _____ live in Colombia.

  a. My   **b.** Mine   **c.** Mine's   **d.** Mines

2. _____ coat is that?

  a. Whose   **b.** Who's   **c.** Who   **d.** Whom

3. _____ went to Hawaii for our honeymoon.

  a. My wife and I   **c.** Me and my wife

  b. I and my wife   **d.** My wife and me

4. My sister's daughter is 18. _____ son is 16.

  a. His   **b.** Her   **c.** Hers   **d.** Her's

5. What's _____?

  a. the name your son   **c.** the name your son's

  b. your son's name   **d.** your the son's name

6. Look at those dogs. Do you see _____?

  a. they   **b.** its   **c.** them   **d.** it's

7. We have your phone number. Do you have _____?

  a. us   **b.** our   **c.** ours   **d.** our's

8. What is _____?

  a. that building name   **c.** the name that building

  b. the name of that building   **d.** the name's that building

9. Someone left a sweater. _____?

  a. Whose is this sweater?   **c.** Whose sweater is this?

  b. Who's is this sweater?   **d.** Who's sweater is this?

10. _____ the correct answer?

  a. Who's knows   **b.** Whom knows   **c.** Who does know   **d.** Who knows

11. They have my address, but I don't have _____.

  a. their   **b.** them   **c.** they're   **d.** theirs

12. We did it by ____.

    a. self   **b.** oneself   **c.** ourself   **d.** ourselves

13. They can help ____.

    a. theirself   **b.** theirselves   **c.** themself   **d.** themselves

14. I know ____ very well.

    a. myself   **b.** mineself   **c.** meself   **d.** self

15. My teacher speaks Spanish. My ____ teacher doesn't.

    a. husbands   **b.** husbands'   **c.** husband's   **d.** the husband's

PART 2   **Fill in the blanks with *said* or *told*.**

1. She _____, "Excuse me."

2. She _____ them to study.

3. She _____ him the truth.

4. She _____ "hello" to her neighbor.

5. She _____ them the answers.

6. She _____ us about her trip.

7. She _____ the answer out loud.

8. She _____ "good-bye."

PART 3   **Complete the question. Some of these questions ask about the subject. Some do not. The answer is underlined.**

EXAMPLES   What _*does the bride wear?*_____

The bride wears <u>a white dress and a veil</u>.

Who _*usually cries at the wedding?*_____

<u>The bride's mother</u> usually cries at the wedding.

  1. When _____

     She throws the bouquet <u>at the end of the wedding party</u>.

  2. Which women _____

     <u>The single women</u> try to catch the bouquet.

  3. On which hand _____

     The groom puts the ring <u>on the bride's left hand</u>.

  4. Whom _____

     The groom kisses <u>the bride</u>.

(continued)

5. Whose _____

The bride's ring has a diamond.

6. Whose _____

The bride uses her husband's last name.

7. Who _____

A professional photographer took pictures at my wedding.

8. Whose _____

I borrowed my sister's dress.

9. Whose _____, yours or your sisters?

My sister's wedding was bigger.

10. How many people _____

Over 250 people came to the wedding.

11. Who _____

The bride and groom cut the cake.

PART 4 **Fill in the blanks with a reflexive pronoun.**

EXAMPLE   She likes to talk about __herself__ .

1. I made the cake all by _____.

2. The bride made her dress _____.

3. They prepared _____ financially before getting married.

4. We helped _____ to another piece of cake.

5. The groom bought _____ a new pair of shoes.

6. All of you should help _____ to more cake and coffee.

7. Did you go to the wedding by _____ or did your wife go with you?

Expansion

Classroom Activities

❶ Form a small group. The group should have people from different cultures and countries, if possible. Talk about weddings and marriages in your native cultures and countries.

a. Who chooses a husband for a woman?

b. Who pays for the wedding?

c. What happens at the wedding?

d. What happens after the wedding?

e. Do the guests bring gifts to the wedding? What kind of gifts do they give? Where do the bride and groom open the gifts?

f. How many people attend a wedding?

g. Where do people get married?

h. Do people dance at a wedding?

i. Who takes pictures?

j. What color dress does the bride wear?

k. At what age do people usually get married?

❷ In a small group, interview one person who is married. Ask this person questions about his or her wedding.

EXAMPLES   Where did you get married?
How many people did you invite?
How many people came?
Where did you go on your honeymoon?

❸ According to an American tradition, the bride should wear:

Something old,
Something new,
Something borrowed,
Something blue.

Do you have any traditions regarding weddings in your native culture?

❹ Do you have a video of a wedding in your family? If so, can you bring it to class and tell the class about it? The teacher may have a video of an American wedding to show the class.

5 Write some advice for newlyweds in each of the following categories. Discuss your sentences in a small group.

home
children
housework
careers
family obligations

problem solving
mother-in-law
money
time together/time apart

Talk

About It

1 What kind of problems do most married people have today? Do you think American married couples have the same problems as couples in other countries?

2 Do you think married couples can solve their problems by themselves? At what point should they go to a marriage counselor?

3 Do you think married people should spend most of their time together, or should they spend some time by themselves?

4 Do you think young people are realistic about marriage? How can they prepare themselves for the reality of marriage?

Write

About It

1 Write about the different ways in which a person can economize on a wedding.

2 Write about a typical wedding in your native culture, or describe your own wedding or the wedding of a family member or friend.

Weddings in China

In my country, China, weddings are different from weddings in the U.S. On the day of the wedding, the groom goes to the bride's house with his groomsmen. At the bride's house, the bride's friends play a "door game." They block the door until the men offer red packets of money . . .

For more practice using grammar in context, please visit our Web site.

Grammar

Singular and Plural

Count and Noncount Nouns

There + Be

Quantity Words

Context

Thanksgiving, Pilgrims, and Native Americans

A Typical Thanksgiving

1. When you celebrate a holiday, what kind of food do you prepare?

2. Do you think a holiday meal is a healthy meal?

CD 2, TR 11

Read the following Web article. Pay special attention to singular and plural nouns.

> http://www.all*about*holidays.com

Thanksgiving is a very special American **holiday**. We celebrate it on the fourth Thursday of November. **People** get together with **family** and **friends**. **Airports** are especially crowded as people travel to be with their **families** on this **day**. In fact, there are more **travelers** on the Sunday after Thanksgiving than any other day in the **year**.

On Thanksgiving, people eat a very big **meal**. While waiting for the **guests** to arrive, the host family usually puts out **snacks**, such as **potato chips** and **nuts**. The main **part** of the meal is **turkey**. Most people stuff the turkey with a **mixture** of **bread**, **onions**, **celery**, **nuts**, and **spices**. Some people add **fruit**, such as **apples** or **apricots**, to the **stuffing**. Other **parts** of the meal include **sweet potatoes**, **mashed potatoes**, **gravy**,[1] **corn**

Thanksgiving Day Parade

---

[1]*Gravy* is a sauce made from meat drippings, flour, water, and sometimes bacon fat.

bread, and **cranberry sauce**. Then there is **dessert**. **Pumpkin pie** with whipped **cream** is a favorite dessert. The typical Thanksgiving meal contains more than 3,000 **calories** and is 45 percent **fat**. Many people talk about going on **a diet** the day after Thanksgiving.

In addition to eating a big meal, many people relax and watch TV. It is a typical **tradition** to watch professional football on Thanksgiving Day. The **men** are especially interested in football. Many **cities** also have a **parade** on Thanksgiving morning. New York City has a very big parade. **Millions** of people go to see the parade.

5.1 Noun Plurals

We use the plural to talk about more than one. Regular noun plurals add -s or -es.

REGULAR NOUN PLURALS				
Word Ending	**Example Noun**	**Plural Addition**	**Plural Form**	**Pronunciation**
Vowel	bee banana	+ s	bees bananas	/z/
ch, sh, x, s	church dish box class	+ es	churches dishes boxes classes	/əz/
Voiceless consonants	cat month	+ s	cats months	/s/
Voiced consonants	card pin	+ s	cards pins	/z/
Vowel + y	boy day	+ s	boys days	/z/
Consonant + y	lady story	y͟ + ies	ladies stories	/z/
Vowel + o	video radio	+ s	videos radios	/z/
Consonant + o	potato hero	+ es	potatoes heroes	/z/
Exceptions: photos, pianos, solos, altos, sopranos, autos, tuxedos, and avocados				
f or *fe*	leaf knife	f͟ + ves	leaves knives	/z/
Exceptions: beliefs, chiefs, roofs, cliffs, chefs, and sheriffs				

IRREGULAR NOUN PLURALS

Singular	Plural	Examples	Explanation
man woman tooth foot goose	men women teeth feet geese	The **women** cooked the dinner. The **men** washed the dishes.	Vowel change
sheep fish deer	sheep fish deer	There are two **fish** in the bowl.	No change
child mouse person	children mice people	The **children** set the table. We invited a lot of **people** to dinner.	Different word form

Language Note: The plural of *person* can also be *persons*, but *people* is more common.

EXERCISE 1 Write the plural form of each noun. Pronounce each plural form.

EXAMPLE hour ___hours___

1. holiday _____
2. turkey _____
3. cranberry _____
4. potato _____
5. child _____
6. family _____
7. spice _____
8. nut _____
9. guest _____
10. man _____
11. woman _____
12. snack _____

13. apple _____
14. peach _____
15. tomato _____
16. pie _____
17. knife _____
18. deer _____
19. watch _____
20. tax _____
21. month _____
22. goose _____
23. dish _____
24. path _____

EXERCISE **2**   **Fill in the blanks with the plural form of the words in parentheses ( ).**

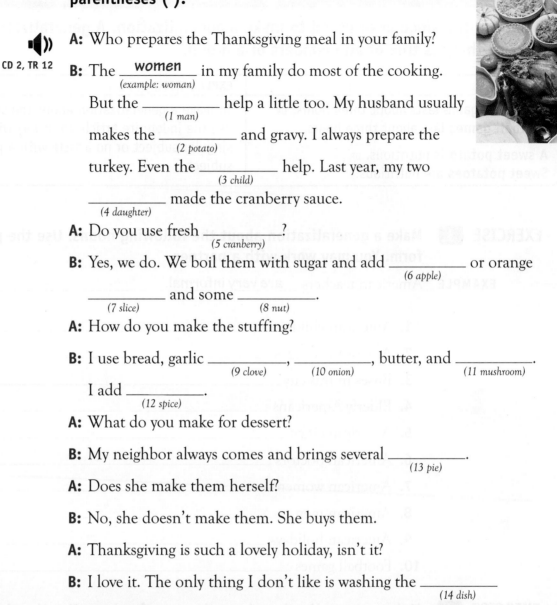

CD 2, TR 12

A: Who prepares the Thanksgiving meal in your family?

B: The _____women_____ in my family do most of the cooking.
           (example: woman)

But the _____ help a little too. My husband usually
      (1 man)

makes the _____ and gravy. I always prepare the
      (2 potato)

turkey. Even the _____ help. Last year, my two
        (3 child)

_____ made the cranberry sauce.
(4 daughter)

A: Do you use fresh _____?
      (5 cranberry)

B: Yes, we do. We boil them with sugar and add _____ or orange
                        (6 apple)

_____ and some _____.
(7 slice)   *(8 nut)*

A: How do you make the stuffing?

B: I use bread, garlic _____, _____, butter, and _____.
                 (9 clove)   *(10 onion)*   *(11 mushroom)*

I add _____.
  (12 spice)

A: What do you make for dessert?

B: My neighbor always comes and brings several _____.
                                        (13 pie)

A: Does she make them herself?

B: No, she doesn't make them. She buys them.

A: Thanksgiving is such a lovely holiday, isn't it?

B: I love it. The only thing I don't like is washing the _____
                                                (14 dish)

afterwards.

A: Why don't the _____ wash the _____?
             (15 man)   *(16 dish)*

B: They're too busy watching the football game. They always say that they'll

wash them later, but the _____ are in a hurry to clean up. So we
                        (17 woman)

do it ourselves.

5.2 Using the Singular and Plural for Generalizations

We can use the singular or plural to make a generalization. A generalization says something is true of all members of a group.

EXAMPLES	EXPLANATION
A football game lasts about three hours. OR **Football games** last about three hours. **A sweet potato** is nutritious. OR **Sweet potatoes** are nutritious.	To make a generalization about the subject, use the indefinite article (*a* or *an*) with a singular subject or no article with a plural subject.

EXERCISE 3 Make a generalization about the following nouns. Use the plural form. You may work with a partner.

EXAMPLE American teachers ___are very informal.___

1. American children _____
2. American colleges _____
3. Buses in this city _____
4. Elderly Americans _____
5. American cities _____
6. American doctors _____
7. American women _____
8. American men _____
9. American holidays _____
10. Football games _____

EXERCISE 4 Make a generalization about these professions. Use the singular form. You may work with a partner.

EXAMPLE A taxi driver ___has a dangerous job.___

1. A teacher _____
2. A doctor _____
3. A nurse _____
4. A garbage collector _____
5. A lawyer _____
6. A musician _____
7. A librarian _____

8. A movie star _____

9. An accountant _____

10. A newspaper reporter _____

5.3 Special Cases of Singular and Plural

EXAMPLES	EXPLANATION
a. The U.S. has more than 300 **million** people.	a. Exact numbers use the singular form.
b. **Millions** of people go shopping the day after Thanksgiving.	b. Inexact numbers use the plural form.
c. My grandfather is in his **seventies**. He was born in the **1940s**.	c. An approximate age or year uses the plural form.
One of my **neighbors** brought a pie to Thanksgiving dinner. One of the **men** helped with the dishes.	We use the plural form in the following expressions: *one of* (*the, my, his, her,* etc.).
Every **guest** brought something. We washed all the **dishes**.	We use a singular noun after *every*. We use a plural noun after *all*.
After dinner, the girl put on her **pajamas** and went to bed. We're wearing our best **clothes** today.	Some words have no singular form: *pajamas, clothes, pants, slacks, (eye)glasses, scissors.*
Let's watch the **news**. It's on after dinner. Let's not discuss **politics** during dinner. It's not a good subject.	Even though *news* and *politics* end in *-s*, they are singular.

Language Note: Do not make adjectives plural.
He made three ***wonderful*** pies.

EXERCISE **5** Find the mistakes with the underlined words and correct them. Not every sentence has a mistake. If the sentence is correct, write C.

EXAMPLES Five ~~man~~ watched the football game.
　　　　　　　　　　 men

Ten <u>guests</u> came to dinner. *C*

1. The <u>childrens</u> helped serve the dinner.

2. One of her <u>daughter</u> came from New York on Thanksgiving.

3. Ten <u>millions</u> people passed through the airports that day.

(continued)

4. <u>Millions</u> of people travel for Thanksgiving.

5. After the news <u>is</u> over, we can watch the football game.

6. His pants <u>is</u> new.

7. Five <u>women</u> prepared the dinner.

8. Every <u>guests</u> stayed to watch the game.

9. Thanksgiving is one of my favorite <u>holiday</u>.

10. <u>Hundreds</u> of people saw the parade.

11. My grandmother came for Thanksgiving. She's in her <u>eighties</u>.

12. Politics <u>is</u> not a good subject to discuss at the dinner table.

13. The boy should go to bed. His pajamas <u>are</u> on the bed.

14. Do you like <u>sweets</u> potatoes?

The Origin of Thanksgiving

Before You Read

1. What do you know about the origin of American Thanksgiving?

2. Do you have a day of thanks in your native culture?

CD 2, TR 13

Read the following textbook article. Pay special attention to count and noncount nouns.

On Thanksgiving, **Americans** come together to give thanks for all the good **things** in their **lives**. Thanksgiving officially began in 1863, when President Lincoln declared that Americans would have a **day** of thanks. What is the **origin** of this great day?

In 1620, a **group** of 120 **men, women,** and **children** left England for America on a **ship** called the Mayflower. They came to America in search of religious **freedom**. They started their new **life** in a deserted[2] Indian **village** in what is now the **state** of Massachusetts. But **half** of the **Pilgrims** did not

[2]*Deserted* means empty of people.

survive their first cold, hard **winter**. In the **spring**, two American **Indians**[3] found the **people** from England in very bad **condition**. They didn't have enough **food**, and they were in bad **health**. Squanto, an English-speaking American Indian, stayed with them for several **months** and taught them how to survive in this new **land**. He brought them deer **meat** and animal **skins**; he showed them how to grow **corn** and other **vegetables**; he showed them how to use **plants** as **medicine**; he explained how to use **fish** for **fertilizer**[4]—he taught them many **skills** for **survival** in their new land.

By the time their second **fall** arrived, the Pilgrims had enough food to get through their second winter. They were in better **health**. They decided to have a Thanksgiving **feast**[5] to celebrate their good **fortune**.

They invited Squanto and neighboring Indian **families** of the Wampanoag **tribe** to come to their **dinner**. The Pilgrims were surprised when 90 Indians showed up. The Pilgrims did not have enough food for so many people. Fortunately, the Indian **chief** sent some of his people to bring food to the **celebration**. They brought five **deer, fish, beans, squash, corn bread, berries**, and many wild **turkeys**. The feast lasted for three **days**. There was a short **time** of **peace** and **friendship** between the Indians and the Pilgrims.

Now on Thanksgiving, we eat some of the traditional **foods** from this **period** in American **history**.

5.4 Count and Noncount Nouns

EXAMPLES	EXPLANATION
Use one **potato** in the recipe. Use three **potatoes** in the soup.	A count noun is something we can count. It has a singular and plural form.
Corn is native to America. The Indians used a lot of **corn**.	A noncount noun is something we don't count. It has no plural form.
We used **rice** in the recipe. We use **beans** in the soup.	*Count* and *noncount* are grammatical terms, but they are not always logical. *Rice* and *beans* are both very small, but *rice* is a noncount noun and *bean* is a count noun.

[3]The native people of America are called *American Indians, Indians,* or *Native Americans.*
[4]We put *fertilizer* in the earth to help plants grow.
[5]A *feast* is a large dinner.

(continued)

There are several types of noncount nouns.

Group A: Nouns that have no distinct, separate parts. We look at the whole.			
milk	juice	bread	electricity
oil	yogurt	meat	lightning
water	pork	butter	thunder
coffee	poultry	paper	cholesterol
tea	soup	air	blood

Group B: Nouns that have parts that are too small or insignificant to count.		
rice	hair	sand
sugar	popcorn	corn
salt	snow	grass

Group C: Nouns that are classes or categories of things. The members of the category are not the same.

money or cash (nickels, dimes, dollars)   mail (letters, packages, postcards, flyers)
furniture (chairs, tables, beds)   homework (compositions, exercises, readings)
clothing (sweaters, pants, dresses)   jewelry (necklaces, bracelets, rings)

Group D: Nouns that are abstractions.					
love	happiness	nutrition	patience	work	nature
truth	education	intelligence	poverty	health	help
beauty	advice	unemployment	music	fun	energy
luck/fortune	knowledge	pollution	art	information	friendship

Group E: Subjects of study.		
history	grammar	biology
chemistry	geometry	math (mathematics*)

*Note: Even though *mathematics* ends with *s*, it is not plural.

EXERCISE 6 Fill in the blanks with a noncount noun from the box below.

advice	snow	freedom✓	friendship
health	work	corn	

EXAMPLE The Pilgrims wanted to find __freedom__ in America.

1. They had poor _____ during their first winter in America.

2. The Indians gave the Pilgrims a lot of _____ about how to grow food.

3. Squanto taught them to plant _____.

4. The first winter was hard. It was cold and there was a lot of _____.

5. Learning American agriculture was hard _____ for the Pilgrims.

6. In the beginning, there was _____ between the Pilgrims and the Indians.

5.5 Nouns That Can Be Both Count or Noncount

Some nouns can be noncount or count, depending on their meaning or use.

NONCOUNT	COUNT
a. I like to spend **time** with my family on the holidays. b. My neighbors invited me to their dinner many **times**. a. Indians had **experience** with American winters. b. The first winter for the Pilgrims was **a** bad **experience**.	The noncount nouns in (a) and the count nouns in (b) have different meanings. In many languages, a completely different word is used.
a. **Life** in America was difficult. b. The Pilgrims had difficult **lives**. a. The Pilgrims had a lot of **trouble** their first winter. b. Do you tell your **troubles** to your friends? a. The men are watching the football game. They're making a lot of **noise**. b. There are some loud **noises** coming from the next room.	Sentences (a) show abstractions. They are noncount nouns. Sentences (b) show specific examples of these nouns. They are count nouns.
a. We put some **fruit** in the cranberry sauce. b. Oranges and lemons are citrus **fruits**. a. We prepare a lot of **food** for Thanksgiving. b. Cranberries and sweet potatoes are typical **foods** for Thanksgiving.	Sentences (a) refer to the nouns in general. They are noncount nouns. Sentences (b) refer to categories of the noun. They are count nouns.
a. We ate some **pie** for dessert. b. My friend brought three **pies** to the Thanksgiving dinner. a. We eat **turkey** on Thanksgiving. b. The Indians brought many **turkeys** to the feast.	Sentences (a) refer to a part of the whole. They are noncount nouns. Sentences (b) refer to the whole. They are count nouns. In the case of animals, the count noun usually refers to the animal rather than the food.

EXERCISE 7 Decide if the noun in parentheses ( ) is count or noncount. If it is a count noun, change it to the plural form. If it is a noncount noun, do not use the plural form.

EXAMPLE   The __Pilgrims__ wanted __freedom__.
(Pilgrim)   (freedom)

1. American Indians have a lot of respect for _____.
(nature)

   They love _____, _____, and _____.
(tree)   (bird)   (fish)

2. Thanksgiving is a celebration of _____ and _____.
(peace)   (friendship)

(continued)

3. On Thanksgiving, Americans eat a lot of _____ and
(food)

sometimes gain weight.

4. Americans sometimes eat _____ for dessert.
(pie)

5. Squanto gave the Pilgrims a lot of _____ about planting
(advice)

_____ and other _____. He had a lot of _____ about
(corn)   (vegetable)   (knowledge)

the land.

6. The Pilgrims didn't have any _____ with American agriculture.
(experience)

7. On the first Thanksgiving, Indians brought _____,
(meat)

_____, _____, and _____.
(bean)   (bread)   (berry)

8. The Pilgrims celebrated because they had a lot of good _____.
(fortune)

9. American Indians use _____ for _____.
(plant)   (medicine)

10. My friends went to the Southwest last summer. They

bought American Indian _____, such as _____
(jewelry)   (ring)

and _____.
(necklace)

11. Do you have a lot of _____ about American _____?
(information)   (holiday)

Recipe for Turkey Stuffing

Before You Read

1. Do you like to cook?

2. What is a favorite recipe of yours?

CD 2, TR 14

Read the following recipe from a magazine. Pay special attention to quantities.

Turkey Stuffing[6]

¼ cup of butter or olive oil
2 cloves of garlic, minced[7]
1 cup of sliced mushrooms
1 onion, chopped
3 stalks of celery, chopped
¼ cup bacon pieces
4 cups of dry bread, cut into cubes
¼ teaspoon of salt
¼ teaspoon of pepper
¼ teaspoon of dry oregano
2 teaspoons of dry parsley
1 cup of hot chicken broth

Brown garlic[8] in butter (or olive oil). Add mushrooms and sauté[9]. Add the rest of the vegetables and cook until they begin to soften. Stir bacon pieces into mixture, then lower heat to medium and add bread cubes and seasonings.

Continue cooking for approximately 5 more minutes, stirring continuously.

Add hot chicken broth and mix well. Cover and cook over low heat for at least 30 minutes, stirring frequently.

Use as turkey stuffing and bake with turkey or place in a covered casserole dish and bake for 30 minutes in a 350–375 degree oven.

[6]Stuffing is often cooked inside the turkey.
[7]*Minced* means cut into very small pieces.
[8]Recipes often leave out articles. For example, this recipe says "brown garlic" instead of "brown the garlic."
[9]To *sauté* means to fry quickly.

5.6 Quantities with Count and Noncount Nouns

We can put a number before a count noun. We cannot put a number before a noncount noun. We use a unit of measure, which we can count—for example, two *cloves* of garlic.

BY CONTAINER	BY PORTION	BY MEASUREMENT[10]	BY SHAPE OR WHOLE PIECE	OTHER
a bottle of water	a slice (piece) of bread	an ounce of sugar	a loaf of bread	a piece of mail
a carton of milk	a piece of meat	a quart of oil	an ear of corn	a piece of furniture
a jar of pickles	a piece of cake	a pound of meat	a piece of fruit	a piece of advice
a bag of flour	a strip of bacon	a gallon of milk	a head of lettuce	a piece of information
a can of soda (pop)	a piece (sheet) of paper	a pint of cream	a candy bar	a work of art
a cup of coffee	a slice of pizza		a tube of toothpaste	a homework assignment
a glass of water	a scoop of ice cream		a bar of soap	
a bowl of soup			a clove of garlic	
			a stalk of celery	

EXERCISE 8   **Fill in the blanks with a specific quantity or unit of measure. Answers may vary.**

EXAMPLE   I drink three _____*glasses of*_____ water a day.

1. I drink a _____ orange juice in the morning.

2. I'm going to buy two _____ meat to make dinner for the family.

3. _____ milk is heavy to carry.

4. She drinks two _____ coffee every morning.

5. Buy _____ bread for dinner.

6. He eats _____ fruit a day.

7. Some people carry _____ water with them.

8. I ate two _____ cake.

9. Let me give you _____ advice before you apply to colleges.

10. How many _____ gas did you buy at the gas station?

11. How many _____ garlic are you going to use in the recipe?

12. The recipe calls for ¼ _____ butter or oil.

13. The recipe calls for ¼ _____ pepper.

[10] For a list of conversions from the American system of measurement to the metric system, see Appendix D.

Taking the Land from the Native Americans

CD 2, TR 15

Before You Read

1. Who were the original inhabitants of your native country?

2. Are there any ethnic minorities in your native country? Do they have the respect of the majority population?

American Indian Reservations in the U.S.

Read the following textbook article. Pay special attention to *there* + a form of *be*.

> **Did You Know?**
>
> Many place names in the U.S. are American Indian names. Chicago, for example, comes from an Indian word meaning "smelly onion."

Before the arrival of Europeans, **there were** between 10 and 16 million Native Americans in America. Today **there are** fewer than 2 million. What happened to these natives of America?

The friendship between the Indians and Europeans did not last for long. As more English people came to America, they did not need the help of the Indians, as the first group of Pilgrims did. The white people started to take the land away from the Indians. As Indians fought to keep their land, many of them were killed. Also, **there were** many deaths from diseases that Europeans brought to America. In 1830, President Andrew Jackson took the Indians' lands and sent them to live on reservations. Indian children had to learn English. Often they were punished for speaking their own language. As a result, **there are** very few Indians today who speak the language of their ancestors.

Today **there are** about 500 tribes in the U.S., each with its own traditions. **There are** about 300 reservations, but less than half of American Indians live on this land. **There is** a lot of unemployment and poverty on many reservations. As a result, many Indians move to big cities to find work. Many return to their reservations only for special celebrations such as powwows, when Indians wear their traditional clothing and dance to traditional music.

It is becoming harder and harder for Indians to keep their traditions and languages alive.

5.7 *There* + a Form of *Be*

We use *there* + a form of *be* to introduce a subject, either count or noncount, into the conversation. After the noun, we often give a time or place.

There	Be	A/An/One	Singular Subject	Complement
There	is	a	reservation	in Wyoming.
There	is	an	onion	in the recipe.
There	will be	a	football game	on TV tonight.
There	was	one	guest	for dinner.

There	Be	(Quantity Word)	Noncount Subject	Complement
There	is	a lot of	unemployment	on some reservations.
There	is	some	garlic	in the recipe for stuffing.
There	was		peace	between the Indians and the Pilgrims.

There	Be	(Quantity Word)	Plural Subject	Complement
There	are	500	Indian tribes	in the U.S.
There	were	many	deaths	from diseases after the Europeans arrived.
There	are	a lot of	calories	in a typical Thanksgiving meal.
There	are		reservations	in California.

Negative Forms

There	Be + Not + A/An	Singular Subject	Complement
There	wasn't a	problem	between the Pilgrims and Indians in 1620.

There	Be + No	Singular Subject	Complement
There	was no	problem	between the Pilgrims and Indians in 1620.

There	Be + Not + (Any)	Noncount Subject	Complement
There	isn't any	milk	in the recipe.

There	Be + No	Noncount Subject	Complement
There	is no	milk	in the recipe.

There	Be + Not + (Any)	Plural Subject	Complement
There	aren't any	reservations	in Illinois.

There	Be + No	Plural Subject	Complement
There	are no	reservations	in Illinois.

5.8 Using *There*

EXAMPLES	EXPLANATION
There's a reservation in Wyoming. **There are** reservations in California and Utah.	The contraction for *there is = there's*. We don't write a contraction for *there are*.
There is one onion and three celery stalks in the recipe. **There are** three celery stalks and one onion in the recipe. **There is** dessert and coffee after the dinner.	If two nouns follow *there*, use a singular verb (*is*) if the first noun is singular. Use a plural verb (*are*) if the first noun is plural.
Informal: There's a lot of reservations in California. **Formal: There are** a lot of reservations in California.	In conversation, you will sometimes hear *there's* with plural nouns.
There are over 500 tribes in the U.S. **They** each have their own traditions. There's a Navajo reservation in Arizona. **It's** very big. There's a Navajo woman in my chemistry class. **She** comes from Arizona.	After we introduce a noun with *there*, we can continue to speak of this noun with a pronoun (*they, it, she*, etc.).
Is there unemployment on some reservations? Yes, there is. **Are there** any reservations in California? Yes, there are. How many Navajo Indians **are there** in Arizona?	Observe the word order in questions with *there*.
Wrong: There's the Grand Canyon in Arizona. *Right:* The Grand Canyon is in Arizona.	Don't use *there* to introduce a specific or unique noun.

EXERCISE **9** **Fill in the blanks with the correct form and tense of _be_.**

EXAMPLE There ____are____ a lot of Indians in Oklahoma.

1. There _____ a lot of reservations in California.

2. There _____ more American Indians 200 years ago than there _____ today.

3. In the beginning, there _____ peace between the Indians and the Pilgrims.

4. Later, there _____ wars between the Indians and the Europeans who took their land.

5. _____ _____ enough food to eat at the first Thanksgiving? Yes, there was.

6. How many people _____ _____ at the first Thanksgiving celebration?

7. Next week there _____ _____ a test on noncount nouns.

8. How many questions _____ _____ _____ on the test?

EXERCISE **10** **Fill in the blanks with a time or place.**

EXAMPLE There was a war __in my country from 1972 to 1975._____

1. There will be a test _____

2. There's a lot of snow _____

3. There's a lot of rain _____

4. There are a lot of people _____

5. There are a lot of reservations _____

6. There was a presidential election _____

7. There are a lot of different languages _____

8. There aren't many students _____

9. There are a lot of books _____

10. There was a war _____

Navajo Code Talkers

Before You Read

1. Are some languages more complicated than others?

2. Why is a code important during wartime?

CD 2, TR 16

Read the following textbook article. Pay special attention to quantity words.

American Indian languages are very complicated. There are **many** different languages and each one has **several** dialects. **Some** languages, like Navajo, have **no** alphabet or symbols.

Philip Johnston was not an Indian but he grew up on the Navajo reservation and learned **a lot of** their language. Later, when Johnston served in World War I, he understood the importance of developing a code that the enemy could not understand. In World War II, the U.S. was at war with Japan. The Japanese were very skillful at breaking codes. In 1942, Johnston met with an American military general and explained his idea of using the Navajo language in code to send messages. Indians living on Navajo land in the southwest U.S. could speak and understand the language. **Very few** non-Navajos could speak or understand it.

The general agreed to try this idea. The U.S. Marines recruited **200** native speakers of Navajo to create a code based on their language. There were **many** military words that did not exist in the Navajo language, so the Navajo recruits had to develop words for these things. For example, the commanding general was a "war chief"; a battleship was a "whale"; a submarine was an "iron fish."

In the first **two** days of code talking, more than **800** messages were sent without **any** errors.

During and after the war, the Navajo code talkers got **little** recognition for their great help in World War II. It wasn't until 1992 that the U.S. government honored the Navajo code talkers for their help in winning major battles of the war.

5.9 Quantity Expressions—An Overview

We can use quantity expressions to talk about the quantity of count and noncount nouns.

EXAMPLES

There are about **two million** American Indians today.
There were about **200** code talkers during World War II.
Very few non-Navajos could speak the Navajo language.
Navajo code talkers got **little** recognition for their work.
The Navajo language has **no** alphabet.
The Navajo language has **several** dialects.
The Pilgrims had **very little** food during the first winter.
The American Indians had **a lot of** knowledge about the land.
The Pilgrims didn't have **much** knowledge about the land.
Many Indians died from disease after the Europeans came.
Some Indians today live on reservations.

EXERCISE 11 Fill in the blanks to complete these statements. Answers may vary.

EXAMPLE There are 500 _____ **tribes** _____ of American Indians in the United States.

1. Two hundred native speakers of _____ served as code talkers.

2. There is no word for "_____" in Navajo.

3. The Navajo language has no _____.

4. Before the arrival of people from Europe, there were at least _____ American Indians.

5. After the first cold winter in America, the Pilgrims didn't have much _____.

6. Many Pilgrims _____ during the first winter.

7. Some _____ helped the Pilgrims.

8. The Indians taught them many _____ to help them survive.

9. The second year in America was much better. They had a lot of _____.

10. As more Europeans came to America, many _____ lost their land.

11. Many Indians can't find work on their reservations. There is a lot of _____ on a reservation.

Native American at a Powwow

5.10 Some, Any, A, No

	EXAMPLES	EXPLANATION
Affirmative	There is **a** big reservation in the Southwest. There is **an** onion in the recipe.	Use *a* or *an* with singular count nouns.
Affirmative	I used **some** raisins in the recipe. I used **some** bread in the recipe.	Use *some* with both plural count nouns and noncount nouns.
Negative	I didn't eat **any** potatoes. I didn't eat **any** gravy.	Use *any* for negatives with both plural count nouns and noncount nouns.
Question	Did the code talkers make **any** mistakes? Did the enemy get **any** information?	Use *any* for questions with both plural count nouns and noncount nouns.
No **vs.** *any*	There isn't **any** sugar in the stuffing. There is **no** sugar in the stuffing. There aren't **any** potatoes in the soup. There are **no** potatoes in the soup.	Use *any* after a negative verb. Use *no* after an affirmative verb. *Wrong:* There *aren't no* potatoes in the soup.

Language Notes:

1. Don't use the indefinite article after *no*.
   Wrong: I have no *an* answer to your question.
   Right: I have no answer to your question.

2. You will sometimes see *any* with a singular count noun.
   Which pen should I use for the test? You can use *any* pen.

   Any, in this case, means whichever you want. It doesn't matter which pen.

EXERCISE 12 **Look at the recipe on page 163. Use *there + be* + the words given to tell about this recipe. If you use *no*, delete the article.**

EXAMPLES salt
There's some salt in the recipe.

a sweet potato
There are no sweet potatoes in the recipe.

1. an onion
2. pepper
3. oil
4. raisins
5. mushrooms
6. nuts
7. carrots
8. milk

EXERCISE **13** **Fill in the blanks with *some*, *any*, *a*, *an*, or *no*.**

EXAMPLE **A:** I put ___some___ salt on the potatoes.

B: Did you put ___any___ pepper on the potatoes?

1. A: Do you know _____ American Indians?

B: No, I don't know _____ American Indians.

2. A: Can you name _____ American Indian tribes?

B: Yes, I can name _____ tribes.

A: I can't name _____.

3. A: Does the Navajo language have _____ alphabet?

B: No. It has _____ alphabet.

4. A: I'll make _____ pie.

B: Can you cook the turkey too?

A: Sorry, I can't. I have _____ experience cooking a turkey.

5. A: I need _____ onion.

B: Do you need _____ carrots?

A: Yes, I need _____ carrots too.

6. A: Do you need _____ butter for your recipe?

B: No. I don't need _____ butter. I'm going to use oil.

7. A: Sugar is not good for you, so there's _____ sugar in this recipe.

B: Is there any honey?

A: No. There isn't _____ honey either.

B: Are there _____ raisins?

A: There are _____ raisins either.

5.11 A Lot Of, Much, Many

	EXAMPLES	EXPLANATION
Affirmative	**A lot of** American Indians served in the military. It takes **a lot of** time to develop a code.	Use *a lot of* with count and noncount nouns.
Affirmative	On Thanksgiving, we give thanks for the **many** good things in our lives. We eat **a lot of** food on Thanksgiving.	Use *many* with count nouns. Use *a lot of* with noncount nouns in affirmative statements. *Much* is rare in affirmative statements.
Negative	Today the Indians don't have **much** land. The Pilgrims didn't have **many** skills.	Use *much* with noncount nouns. Use *many* with count nouns.
Negative	Today the Indians don't have **a lot of** land. The Pilgrims didn't have **a lot of** skills.	Use *a lot of* with both count and noncount nouns.
Question	Did you eat **much** turkey? Did you eat **many** cookies?	Use *much* with noncount nouns. Use *many* with count nouns.
Question	Did you eat **a lot of** turkey? Did you eat **a lot of** cookies?	Use *a lot of* with both count and noncount nouns.
Question	**How much** experience did the code talkers have? **How many** code talkers were in the military?	Use *how much* with noncount nouns. Use *how many* with count nouns.

Language Note:
When the noun is omitted (in the following sentence, **water**), use *a lot*, not *a lot of*.
I usually drink **a lot of** water, but I didn't drink **a lot** today.

EXERCISE 14 Fill in the blanks with *much*, *many*, or *a lot (of)*. Avoid *much* in affirmative statements. In some cases, more than one answer is possible.

CD 2, TR 17

A: Did you prepare ___a lot of___ food for Thanksgiving?
(example)

B: No, I didn't prepare _____.
(1)

A: You didn't? Why not?

B: This year I didn't invite _____ people. I just
(2)
invited my immediate family.

A: How _____ people are there in your immediate family?
(3)

B: Just seven. I bought a twelve-pound turkey. It was more than enough.

(continued)

A: I don't know how to prepare a turkey. Is it _____ work
(4)

to prepare a turkey?

B: Not really. But you have to cook it for _____ hours.
(5)

A: Did you make _____ other dishes, like sweet potatoes
(6)

and cranberry sauce?

B: No. Each person in my family made something. That way I didn't

have _____ work. But we had _____ work cleaning
(7)   (8)

up. There were _____ dirty dishes. I hate washing dishes
(9)

after a big dinner, so I'm planning to buy a dishwasher soon.

A: Does a dishwasher cost _____ money?
(10)

B: Yes, but I'd like to have one for that one day a year.

A: Maybe you should just use paper plates.

B: I know _____ people do that, but I want my dinner to look
(11)

elegant. For me, paper plates are for picnics.

5.12 *A Lot Of* vs. *Too Much/Too Many*

EXAMPLES	EXPLANATION
a. **A lot of** Navajo Indians live in the Southwest. b. My friend left the reservation because there was **too much** unemployment and she couldn't find a job. a. **A lot of** people came to dinner. We all had a great time. b. **Too many** people came to dinner. There wasn't enough food for everyone.	Sentences (a) show a large quantity. No problem is presented. *A lot of* has a neutral tone. Sentences (b) show an excessive quantity. A problem is presented or implied. A sentence with *too much/too many* can have a complaining tone.
I feel sick. I ate **too much**.	We can put *too much* at the end of a verb phrase.

Language Note: Sometimes you can use *a lot of* in place of *too much/too many*.
   Too many people came to dinner. There wasn't enough food for everyone.
   A lot of people came to dinner. There wasn't enough food for everyone.

EXERCISE **15** **Fill in the blanks with *a lot of*, *too much*, or *too many*. In some cases, more than one answer is possible.**

EXAMPLE I love garlic. This recipe calls for ___a lot of___ garlic, so it's going to be delicious.

1. I can't eat this soup. It has _____ salt.

2. A Thanksgiving dinner has about 3,000 calories. Most people eat _____ and don't feel so good afterwards.

3. You put _____ pepper in the potatoes, and they taste terrible.

4. She's going to bake a cherry pie. She needs _____ cherries.

5. I think I ate _____ pieces of pumpkin pie. Now I feel sick.

6. Before the Europeans arrived, there were _____ Indians in America.

7. There are _____ American Indian languages.

8. The Navajo code talkers gave _____ help during World War II.

9. The code talkers sent _____ messages successfully.

EXERCISE **16** **Use *a lot of*, *too much*, or *too many* to fill in the blanks in the story below. In some cases, more than one answer is possible.**

CD 2, TR 18

My name is Coleen Finn. I'm a Ho-chunk Indian. My tribal land is in Wisconsin. But I live in Chicago because there is __too much__ unemployment *(example)* on my tribal land, and I can't find a good job there. There are _____ *(1)* opportunities in Chicago, and I found a job as a secretary in the English Department at Truman College. I like my job very much. I have _____ responsibilities and I love the challenge. *(2)*

I like Chicago, but I miss my land, where I still have _____ relatives *(3)* and friends. I often go back to visit them whenever I get tired of life in Chicago. My friends and I have _____ fun together, talking, *(4)* cooking our native food, walking in nature, and attending Indian ceremonies, such as powwows. I need to get away from Chicago once in a while to feel closer to nature. Even though there are _____ nice *(5)* things about Chicago, there are _____ cars and trucks in the big city *(6)* and there is _____ pollution. A weekend with my tribe gives me *(7)* time to relax and smell fresh air.

EXERCISE 17 **ABOUT YOU** Fill in the blanks after *too* with *much* or *many*. Then complete the statement.

EXAMPLE   If I drink too ___much___ coffee, ___I won't be able to sleep tonight.___

1. If I try to memorize too _____ words, _____
   _____

2. If I make too _____ mistakes on my homework, _____
   _____

3. If I spend too _____ money on clothes, _____
   _____

4. If I spend too _____ time with my friends, _____
   _____

5.13 A Few, Several, A Little

	EXAMPLES	EXPLANATION
Count	The Navajo language has **several** dialects. She speaks **a few** languages. Put **a few** teaspoons of salt in the potato recipe.	Use *a few* or *several* with count nouns or with quantities that describe noncount nouns (*teaspoon, cup, bowl, piece,* etc.).
Noncount	He put **a little** salt in the potatoes. Please add **a little** milk to the coffee.	Use *a little* with noncount nouns.

EXERCISE 18 Fill in the blanks with *a few*, *several*, or *a little*. In some cases, more than one answer is possible.

EXAMPLE   We have ___a little___ information about American Indians.

1. _____ Indians came to help the Pilgrims.
2. They taught the Pilgrims _____ skills for planting.
3. The article gave us _____ information about the code talkers.
4. _____ Navajo Indians developed a code.
5. It took _____ time to develop the code.
6. The Navajos had to create _____ new words.
7. There were _____ Japanese experts at code breaking.

5.14 *A Few* vs. *Few*; *A Little* vs. *Little*

A few and *a little* have a neutral tone. *Few* and *little* (without *a*) have a negative emphasis.

EXAMPLES	EXPLANATION
a. **A few** Indians helped the Pilgrims. b. **Few** non-Navajos could speak the Navajo language. c. **Very few** young American Indians speak the language of their ancestors.	In example (a), *a few* means some or enough. *A few* has a neutral tone. In examples (b) and (c), *few* and *very few* mean not enough; almost none. We often use *very* before *few*.
a. There's **a little** food in the refrigerator. Let's make a sandwich. b. The Navajo code talkers got **little** recognition for their help in World War II. c. The Pilgrims had **very little** food the first winter.	In example (a), *a little* means some or enough. *A little* has a neutral tone. In examples (b) and (c), *little* and *very little* mean not enough; almost none. We often use *very* before *little*.

Language Note: Whether something is enough or not enough does not depend on the quantity. It depends on the perspective of the person. Is the glass half empty or half full?
☺ One person may say the glass is half full. He sees something positive about the quantity of water in the glass: The glass has *a little* water.
☹ Another person may say the glass is half empty. He sees something negative about the quantity of water in the glass: The glass has (*very*) *little* water.

EXERCISE 19 Fill in the blanks with *a little, very little, a few,* or *very few*.

EXAMPLE 1. **A:** We read about American Indians in this lesson. Did you know that

Eskimos are Native Americans too?

B: Really? I know __very little__ about Eskimos.
(example)
In fact, I know almost nothing.

A: They live in Alaska, Canada, and Greenland.

They make their houses out of ice.

B: What do they eat? _____ plants grow
(1)

in the cold regions.

A: They use a lot of sea animals for food. They

eat whale, seal, and fish.

B: I like to eat _____ fish, but I can't imagine eating it all the
(2)

time. And I really can't imagine eating whale and seal. How do you

know so much about Eskimos?

(continued)

A: I saw the movie *Eskimo*. I learned _____ about Eskimos from
the movie. And I read _____ books. Do you want to borrow
my books?

B: Uh, no thanks.

2. **A:** Let's prepare the Thanksgiving dinner together. I always like to get
_____ help for the Thanksgiving holiday.

B: I don't think I'm going to be much help. You know I have
_____ experience in the kitchen.

A: Don't worry. You can be my assistant.

B: OK. What can I do?

A: I need to put _____ oil on the turkey.

B: There's _____ oil in the house. I don't think it's going to be
enough.

A: Don't worry. I have another bottle. Can you get _____ things
out of the cabinet for me?

B: Sure.

A: Get the spices. We're going to put _____ spices on the turkey.

B: What else do you need?

A: I need _____ string to tie the legs. Then the turkey will be
ready to go into the oven.

B: Is there anything else I can do?

A: Yes. I need you to go to the store and get _____ things for me.
Here's a list.

B: Shopping! That's something I can do well.

A: Why is it that _____ men cook the turkey? In fact, I almost
never see a man prepare the Thanksgiving dinner. It seems like it's
always a woman's job.

3. **A:** Do you speak another language?

B: I speak _____ Spanish. I also studied Latin in high school.

A: Who speaks Latin?

B: No one does anymore. It's dead as a spoken language. That's why
_____ high schools offer Latin classes.
(15)

A: Is it like the Navajo language?

B: No. The Navajo language is not a dead language. However, today
_____ people speak it anymore. Most American Indians speak
(16)
English.

EXERCISE 20 **ABOUT YOU** Ask a question with *"Are there . . . ?"* and the words given about another student's hometown. The other student will answer with an expression of quantity. Practice count nouns.

EXAMPLE   museums

A: Are there any museums in your hometown?

B: Yes. There are a lot of (a few, three) museums in my hometown.

OR

No. There aren't any museums in my hometown.

1. department stores   6. open markets
2. fast-food restaurants   7. hospitals
3. homeless people   8. universities
4. skyscrapers   9. American businesses
5. supermarkets   10. bridges

EXERCISE 21 **ABOUT YOU** Ask a question with *"Is there . . . ?"* and the words given about another student's native country or hometown. The other student will answer with an expression of quantity. Practice noncount nouns.

EXAMPLE   petroleum/in your native country

A: Is there much petroleum in your native country?

B: Yes. There's lot of petroleum in my native country.

OR

No. There isn't much petroleum in my native country.

In Your Native Country   **In Your Hometown**

1. petroleum   5. traffic
2. industry   6. rain
3. agriculture   7. pollution
4. tourism   8. noise

EXERCISE 22 **ABOUT YOU** Ask a student a question with "*Do you have . . . ?*" and the words given. The other student will answer. Practice both count and noncount nouns.

EXAMPLES American friends

A: Do you have any American friends?
B: Yes. I have many (OR a lot of) American friends.
   OR
   No. I don't have many American friends.

free time

A: Do you have a lot of free time?
B: Yes. I have some free time.
   OR
   No. I have very little free time.

1. problems in the U.S.

2. friends

3. relatives in New York

4. time to relax

5. brothers and sisters (siblings)

6. experience with small children

7. questions about American customs

8. trouble with English pronunciation

9. information about points of interest in this city

10. knowledge about computer programming

EXERCISE 23 **ABOUT YOU** Cross out the phrase that doesn't fit and fill in the blanks with an expression of quantity to make a true statement about another country you know about. Discuss your answers.

EXAMPLE ~~There's~~/There isn't ___much___ unemployment in ___Korea___.

1. There's/There isn't _____ opportunity to make money in _____.

2. There are/There aren't _____ divorced people in _____.

3. There are/There aren't _____ foreigners in _____.

4. There's/There isn't _____ freedom in _____.

5. There are/There aren't _____ American cars in _____.

6. There are/There aren't _____ political problems in _____.

7. There is/There isn't _____ unemployment in _____.

8. There is/There isn't _____ crime in _____.

Summary of Lesson 5

1. Study the words that are used before count and noncount nouns.

SINGULAR COUNT	PLURAL COUNT	NONCOUNT
a tomato	some tomatoes	some coffee
no tomato	no tomatoes	no coffee
	any tomatoes *(with questions and negatives)*	any coffee
	a lot of tomatoes	a lot of coffee
	many tomatoes	much coffee *(with questions and negatives)*
	a few tomatoes	a little coffee
	several tomatoes	
	How many tomatoes?	How much coffee?

2. Sentences with *there*

Count
> **There's** an onion in the recipe.
> **There are** two carrots in the recipe.

Noncount
> **There's** some oil in the recipe.
> How much salt **is there** in the recipe?

3. *Too Much/Too Many/A Lot Of*
- *A lot of* + count or noncount noun (no problem is presented)
  I cooked **a lot of** potatoes for Thanksgiving dinner.
  I put **a lot of** butter on the potatoes.
- *Too much* + noncount noun (a problem is presented)
  She doesn't qualify for financial aid because her parents make **too much** money.
- *Too many* + count noun (a problem is presented)
  There are **too many** students in the class. The teacher doesn't have time to help everyone.

Editing Advice

1. Some plural forms are irregular and don't take -s.

   She has two childrens.

2. Use a singular noun and verb after *every*.

   Every ~~children~~ need^s love.

3. Use the plural form of the noun after *one of*.

   One of my sister^s is a lawyer.

4. Don't use *a* or *an* before a plural noun.

   She bought ~~a~~ *(some)* new socks.

5. Don't put *a* or *an* before a noncount noun.

   I want to give you ~~an~~ *some* OR *a piece of* advice.

6. A noncount noun is always singular.

   I have ~~many~~ *a lot of* homeworks to do.

   She bought three *pieces of* furnitures.

7. Use *there is* or *there are* to introduce a noun.

   ~~Are~~ *There are* a lot of people in China.

8. Be careful with *there* and *they're*. They sound the same.

   ~~They're~~ *There* are many problems in the world.

9. Don't use a specific noun after *there is/there are*.

   ~~There's~~ *T*he Golden Gate bridge *is* in San Francisco.

10. Include *of* with a unit of measure.

    He bought three tubes *of* toothpaste.

11. Omit *of* after *a lot* when the noun is omitted.

    I have a lot of time, but my brother doesn't have a lot ~~of~~.

12. Use a *little/a few* to mean *some*. Use *little/few* to mean *not enough*.

(very)

He can't help you because he has a little time.

13. Don't use *too much* or *too many* if the quantity doesn't present a problem.

a lot of

He's a lucky man. He has ~~too many~~ friends.

14. Don't confuse *too* and *too much/many*.

The potatoes are too ~~much~~ salty. I can't eat them.

15. Don't use a double negative.

any

He doesn't have ~~no~~ money. OR *He has no money.*

Editing Quiz

Some of the shaded words and phrases have mistakes. Find the mistakes and correct them. If the shaded words are correct, write C.

I love American Thanksgiving. Every years, the whole family comes to our

C

(example)

house for this holiday and a few other holidays. But Thanksgiving is my

(example)

favorite. There are a lot of childrens in my family and they love to see each

(1)   (2)

other on Thanksgiving. They don't have many time to see each other the

(3)

rest of the year because of school. It's so joyful to have too many children

(4)

in the house few times a year. There's a lot of noise in the house when

(5)   (6)   (7)

they're here, but we don't mind.

(8)

We all bring some foods. One of my sister always makes a pumpkin pie.

(9)   (10)   (11)

Her husband always makes a cookies in the shape of turkeys. My other

(12)

sister makes cranberry sauce. She uses a lot of sugars and sometimes it's

(13)

too much sweet, but I never say anything. My brother doesn't like to cook,

(14)

so he brings a lot fresh fruit. My cousin brings about 10 big bottles soda.

(15)   (16)

I prepare the sweet potatoes. My mother always makes the turkey. It takes

(17)

much time to cook a big turkey.

(18)

(continued)

Singular and Plural; Count and Noncount Nouns; There + Be; Quantity Words **183**

We have a lot to prepare before Thanksgiving. My mother has very little
(19)   (20)
time the week before because of her job. But I have a lot of because I don't
(21)
have no homeworks that week. So I clean the house. My father likes to
(22)   (23)
help but he has very few experience in the kitchen, so my mother asks him
(24)
to do the shopping. He doesn't have much experience shopping either, so
(25)
she always gives him an advice about shopping with a list. But he always
(26)
forgets to take the list and buys too much. Last year he bought a 50-pound
(27)
bag of rice that we still haven't finished!

It's always fun to spend Thanksgiving with too many people that we love.
(28)
But there's one thing I don't like: they're are always a lot of dishes to wash
(29)   (30)   (31)
afterwards.

Lesson 5 Test/Review

PART **1** **Fill in the blanks with the singular or plural form of the word in parentheses ( ).**

EXAMPLE   The Pilgrims didn't have a lot of ___experience___ with American land.
(experience)

1. The Indians had many _____ with white _____ over
(war)   (person)

their land.

2. Some _____ have a big problem with _____ and _____.
(reservation)   (unemployment)   (poverty)

There aren't enough _____ for everyone.
(job)

3. My father gave me a lot of _____. He told me that there are
(advice)

more _____ in big _____ than on reservations.
(job)   (city)

4. We like to visit the art museum. We like to see the _____ and
(sculpture)

_____ by famous _____. We like all kinds of _____.
(painting)   (artist)   (art)

5. My brother likes all kinds of _____. He has a large collection
(music)

of _____.
(CD)

PART **2** **Fill in the blanks with an appropriate measurement of quantity. In some cases, several answers are possible.**

EXAMPLE   I bought a ___loaf___ of bread.

1. I drank a _____ of tea.
2. She drank a _____ of milk.
3. I usually put a _____ of sugar in my coffee.
4. There's a _____ of milk in the refrigerator.
5. I'm going to buy a _____ of furniture for my living room.
6. The teacher gave a long homework _____.
7. My father gave me an important _____ of advice.
8. I drank three _____ of water today.
9. I need a _____ of paper to write my composition.
10. We need to buy a _____ of soap.

PART **3** **Read this composition by an American Indian. Circle the correct words to complete the composition.**

My name is Joseph Falling Snow.

I'm (an, *a*, any) Native American from
   (example)
a Sioux[11] reservation in South Dakota.

I don't live in South Dakota anymore

because I couldn't find (a, any, no) job.
                          (1)
There's (a little, a few, very little, very few)
                          (2)
work on my reservation. There's

(much, a lot of, many) poverty. My uncle
   (3)
gave me (a, an, some, any) good advice.
         (4)

He told me to go to Minneapolis to find (a, an, some) job. Minneapolis is a
                                              (5)
big city, so there are (much, many, any) job opportunities there. It was easy
                          (6)
for me to find a job as a carpenter. I had (no, not, any) trouble finding a job
                                              (7)
because I have (a lot of, many, much) experience.
                  (8)

[11]Sioux is pronounced /su/.

(continued)

My native language is Lakota, but I know (*any*, *a few*, *very few*) words in
my language. Most of the people on my reservation speak English.

(*A few*, *Any*, *A little*) older people still speak Lakota, but the language is
dying out as the older people die.

(*A few*, *A little*, *Few*, *Little*) times a year, I go back to the reservation for
a powwow. We wear our native costumes and dance our native dances. It
gets very crowded at these times because (*much*, *any*, *a lot of*) people from
our reservation and nearby reservations attend this celebration. We have
(*much*, *many*, *a lot of*) fun.

Expansion

Classroom

Activities

**❶ Work with a partner. Imagine that you have to spend a few weeks
alone on a deserted island. You can take 15 things with you. What will
you need to survive? Give reasons for each item.**

EXAMPLE I'll take a lot of water because I can't drink ocean water. It has salt in it.

❷ Game: Where am I?

**Teacher: Write these words on separate index cards: *at the airport,
downtown, at the library, at a supermarket, at a department store,
on the highway, at the zoo, at church, at the beach, at home, on an
elevator, on a bus, on an airplane, at the post office,* and *in the school
cafeteria.***

**Students: One student picks an index card with a place name and says,
"Where am I?" Other students have to guess where he/she is by asking
questions.**

EXAMPLES Are you indoors or outdoors?
Are there a lot of cars in this place?
Is it noisy in this place?
Are there a lot of people in this place?

**❸ Find a partner. Talk about the food you eat on a holiday or special
day. Describe the ingredients of this food.**

Read the following quotes and discuss what they mean to you.

❶ "Once I was in a big city and I saw a very large house. They told me it was a bank and that the white men place their money there to be taken care of, and that by and by they got it back with interest. We are Indians and we have no such bank. When we have plenty of money or blankets, we give them away to other chiefs and people, and by and by they return them with interest, and our hearts feel good. Our way of giving is our bank."

—Chief Maquinna, Nootka tribe

❷ "Treat the Earth well. It was not given to you by your parents; it was loaned to you by your children." (*Kenyan proverb*)

❸ "Today is a time of celebrating for you—a time of looking back to the first days of white people in America. But it is not a time of celebrating for me. It is with a heavy heart that I look back upon what happened to my people. When the Pilgrims arrived, we, the Wampanoags, welcomed them with open arms, little knowing that it was the beginning of the end. . . . Let us always remember, the Indian is and was just as human as the white people."

From a speech by a Wampanoag Indian given on Thanksgiving in 1970 in Massachusetts, at the 350th anniversary of the Pilgrims' arrival in America.

Write

About It ❶ Write about an ethnic minority in your native country or another country you know about. Where and how do these people live? Use expressions of quantity.

❷ Write a paragraph telling about the advantages or disadvantages of living in a city. You may write about pollution, job opportunities, weather, traffic, transportation, and crime. Use expressions of quantity.

3 Write about a holiday in your country. How do you celebrate it?

The New Year Celebration in Vietnam

In my country, Vietnam, we celebrate the New Year (*Tet*) in a very special way. It's the most important day of the year. We follow the lunar calendar and New Year comes at the end of January or the beginning of February. It's not like the American New Year at all. We spend a lot of time preparing for this day…

 For more practice using grammar in context, please visit our Web site.

Grammar
Adjectives

Noun Modifiers

Adverbs

Too/Enough/Very/A Lot Of

Context
Health

Obesity: A National Problem

1. Do you ever eat at fast-food restaurants?

2. What kind of food commercials do you see on TV?

CD 2, TR 19

Read the following Web article. Pay special attention to adjectives and noun modifiers.

http://www.website*reading.com

Everyone knows that it's **important** to eat well and get **enough** exercise. We see **beautiful, thin fashion** models and want to look like them. We see commercials for **exercise** machines on TV showing **fit, thin, smiling** people exercising. **Health** clubs are full of people trying to get in shape. Sales of **diet** colas and low-calorie and low-carbohydrate foods indicate that Americans want to be **thin**. However, two-thirds of **American** adults are **overweight**, and one in six American children is overweight. This is a **large** increase from 30 years ago, when 50 percent of adults and only about 5 percent of children were overweight.

Approximately half of Americans are **concerned** about their weight. They spend billions of dollars on **weight-loss** products and health clubs. But weight is also becoming a **national** problem as health costs go up in response to diseases related to obesity: **heart** disease, **high blood** pressure, diabetes, arthritis, and stroke.

What is the reason for this **growing** problem? First, **today's** lifestyle does not include enough **physical** activity. When the U.S. was an **agricultural** society, farmers ate a **big, heavy** meal, but they burned off the calories by doing **hard physical** labor. **Modern** technology has removed physical activity from our **daily** lives. Seventy-five percent of all trips are less than a mile from home, but Americans drive. Only 15 percent of schoolchildren walk to school even though most of them live within one mile of school. And the **average** American child spends approximately 24 hours a week watching TV. In most physical **education** classes, kids are **active** for just three minutes.

Did You **Know?**

In 1969, approximately half of all schoolchildren walked or bicycled to or from school, and 87% of those living within 1 mile of school walked or bicycled.

Quote
from public
health expert,
Dr. David Katz:
"Today's kids may be
the first generation
in history whose life
expectancy is . . .
less than that of
their parents."

Another reason for the **weight** problem is the American diet. The average child sees more than 10,000 **food** commercials a year. Most of these are for high-calorie foods, such as **sweetened** cereals, **sugary** soft drinks, **salty** chips, and other **snack** foods. We call these **unhealthy** foods "**junk**" food. Children and adults often prefer junk food.

Adults have **busy** lives and depend on **fast** food. The supermarkets are **filled** with **cheap, tasty** food that is **easy** to prepare and **high** in calories.

Obesity is quickly becoming the number one cause of **preventable** death.

What's Your Body Mass Index?

Body Mass Index (BMI) helps to measure if a person is overweight or not.

$$\frac{\text{weight in pounds}}{(\text{height in inches})^2} \times 703$$

Example:

$$\frac{160 \text{ lbs.}}{(69 \text{ in.})^2} \times 703 = 23.6 \text{ BMI}$$

BMI	Status
Below 18.5	Underweight
18.5–24.9	Normal
25.0–29.9	Overweight
30.0–39.9	Obese
40 and above	Extremely obese

6.1 Adjectives

An adjective describes a noun.

EXAMPLES	EXPLANATION
We ate a **big** meal. People need **physical** activity.	An adjective can come before a noun.
a. Farmers ate a **big**, **heavy** meal. a. We see **beautiful**, **thin** models. b. People used to do **hard physical** labor. b. The **average American** child watches a lot of TV.	Two adjectives can come before a noun. In examples (a), we put a comma between the two adjectives because we can reverse the order of the adjectives without changing the meaning. In examples (b), we don't use a comma because we can't reverse the order of the adjectives.
Fast food is **cheap**. Chips are **salty**. Burgers taste **delicious**. You look **healthy**.	An adjective can come after *be, seem,* and the sense-perception verbs: *look, sound, smell, taste,* or *feel.*
It is **important** to eat well. It is **easy** to gain weight if you eat junk food.	An adjective can come after impersonal expressions beginning with *it + be.*
Are you **concerned** about your weight? I'm **tired** after work. Supermarkets are **filled** with easy-to-prepare foods.	Some -*ed* words are adjectives: *tired, worried, located, crowded, married, divorced, excited, disappointed, finished, frightened, filled,* and *concerned.*
We read an **interesting** article about weight. Obesity is a **growing** problem in the U.S. **Working** parents often don't have time to prepare a good meal for their children.	Some -*ing* words are adjectives: *interesting, growing, exciting, boring,* and *working.*
She is a **thin** model. We often see **thin** models on TV.	Do not make adjectives plural.
Fast food is **very** fattening. I'm **so** tired. Some Americans are **quite** fat. People used to do **extremely** hard physical labor.	*Very, so, quite,* and *extremely* can come before adjectives.
I was **kind of** tired after work, so I just watched TV. We had a **real** delicious meal. I had a **pretty** hard day.	Conversational words that come before adjectives are: *pretty, sort of, kind of,* and *real.*
Do you want a big pizza or a small **one**? Do you prefer the purple grapes or the green **ones**?	After an adjective, we can substitute a singular noun with *one* and a plural noun with *ones.*

EXERCISE 1 Fill in the blanks with an appropriate word. Answers may vary.

EXAMPLE Burgers and fries are ___high___ in calories.

1. Fries are cooked in oil. They are very _____.

2. I ate a terrible meal and I got _____.

3. Do you want a large coffee or a small _____?

4. She's very _____ about her children's health because they prefer candy to fruit.

5. I didn't sleep at all last night. I'm very _____ today.

6. Have a piece of fresh apple pie. I just had a piece. It _____ good.

7. Potato chips are very _____.

8. Ice cream is _____ in calories.

9. Most Americans have _____ lives and don't make the time to eat well.

10. Obesity in the U.S. is a _____ problem. It is a much bigger problem today than it was 30 years ago.

EXERCISE 2 Circle the correct words in italics to complete this conversation.

CD 2, TR 20

A husband (H) and wife (W) are discussing weight.

H: We're gaining weight. We used to be (**thin** / *thins*), but when we got
(*example*)
(*marry* / *married*), we started to gain weight.
(1)

W: Let's go jogging after work. There's
a (*beautiful park* / *park beautiful*)
(2)
where we can go. It's (*locate* / *located*) just a
(3)
few blocks away from our apartment.

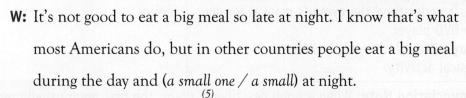

H: But after work I'm always too (*tire* / *tired*).
(4)
I just want to eat dinner and watch TV.

W: It's not good to eat a big meal so late at night. I know that's what
most Americans do, but in other countries people eat a big meal
during the day and (*a small one* / *a small*) at night.
(5)

H: What difference does it make?

(continued)

W: If we eat a big meal in the middle of the day, we have the rest of the day to burn off the calories.

H: I'm sure that's (*an idea very good / a very good idea*) but I don't have
(6)
time to eat a big meal in the middle of the day. My lunch break is
(*kind / kind of*) short.
(7)

W: We should cook more at home. We're always eating out in
(*expensive / expensives*) restaurants that have (*fatty / fattied*) foods.
(8)   (9)

H: Maybe doctors will find a pill that will make us thin with no effort.

W: You know what they say, "No pain, no gain." It takes a lot of effort to lose weight.

6.2 Noun Modifiers

EXAMPLES	EXPLANATION
Do you have an **exercise machine**? A **farm worker** gets a lot of exercise. Some people eat at **fast-food restaurants**. I joined a **health club**. **Fashion models** are very thin.	A noun can modify (describe) another noun. The second noun is more general than the first. An *exercise machine* is a machine. A *leg exercise* is an exercise.
I bought new **running** shoes. Do you ever use the **swimming** pool?	Sometimes a gerund describes a noun. It shows the purpose of the noun.
My **five-year-old** son prefers candy to fruit. **Potato** chips have a lot of grease.	The first noun is always singular. A five-**year**-old son is a son who is five **years** old. **Potato** chips are chips made from **potatoes**.
Very few **schoolchildren** walk to school. I can't read the ingredients without my **eyeglasses**.	Sometimes we write the two nouns as one word. The noun modifier and the noun become a compound word.
Do you have your **driver's** license? I can't understand the **owner's** manual for my new DVD player. **Today's** lifestyle doesn't include much physical activity.	Sometimes a possessive noun describes a noun.

Pronunciation Note: When a noun describes a noun, the first noun usually receives the greater emphasis in speaking.
I wear my **running** shoes when I go to the **health** club and use the **exercise** machines.

EXERCISE 3   Find the noun modifiers in the reading on pages 190–191. Underline them.

EXERCISE 4   A mother (M) and son (S) are shopping at a big supermarket. Fill in the blanks by putting the nouns in parentheses ( ) in the correct order. Remember to use the singular form for the first noun.

CD 2, TR 21

S: What are we going to buy today? Just a few things?

M: No. We need a lot. Let's take a _____shopping cart_____.
   (example: cart/shopping)

S: Can I sit in the _____?
   (1 child/seat)

M: You're much too big. You're a six-

   _____ boy.
   (2 years/old)

S: Mom, buy me that cereal. It looks good.

   I saw it on a _____.
   (3 commercial/TV)

M: Let's read the ingredients on the _____ first. I want to

   see the _____ before we buy it. Let me put on my
   (5 content/sugar)

   _____. Oh, dear. This cereal has 20 grams of sugar.
   (6 glasses/eyes)

S: But I like sugar, Mom.

M: You know it causes _____. Remember what the
   (7 teeth/decay)

   dentist told you?

S: But I brush my teeth once a day.

M: I want you to use your _____ after every meal, not
   (8 teeth/brush)

   just once a day.

S: Mom, can we buy those _____?
   (9 chips/potatoes)

M: They have too much fat.

S: How about some soda?

M: You should drink more juice. How about some _____?
   (10 juice/oranges)

S: I don't like juice.

M: It seems you don't like anything that's good for you. Maybe we

   should shop at the _____ store next time.
   (11 food/health)

S: Oh, Mom, you're no fun.

M: Let's get in the _____ and pay now.
   (12 line/check-out)

Adjectives; Noun Modifiers; Adverbs; *Too/Enough/Very/A Lot Of*   **195**

Obesity: The Solution

Before You Read

1. Where and when do you eat your big meal of the day?

2. When you see commercials for food on TV, do you want to buy that food?

CD 2, TR 22

Read the following Web article. Pay special attention to adverbs.

http://website*reading.com

Millions of Americans are overweight. Health experts agree that the problem comes from a combination of things: the kind of food we eat, our lifestyle, and even technology. Experts have the following recommendations for living a healthier lifestyle:

1. Get active. Ride a bike or walk places instead of driving. Cars and other machines **greatly** reduce the need for physical activity. These machines help us move from place to place **easily** and **quickly** and work **efficiently**, but we don't use much physical energy.

2. Eat a **well**-balanced meal consisting of protein, grains, vegetables, and fruit. Unfortunately, many people often eat alone and **quickly**. Some even just eat snacks all day. Nutritionists recommend that families eat together like they used to. As they eat their big meal together **slowly**, they can discuss the events of their day and enjoy each other's company.

3. Take the soft drink and snack machines out of the schools and educate children **early** about nutrition and exercise. The typical teenager gets about 10 to 15 percent of his or her calories from soft drinks, which have no nutrition at all. Replace the food in the machines with water, juice, and healthy snacks such as raisins.

4. Be careful of the food messages you hear from advertisers that say, "Eat this. Buy that." Technology allows advertisers to send us messages **constantly** through commercials. Many of these foods are high in fat and calories. Choose natural foods, such as fruits and nuts, instead of manufactured foods.

In addition to what individuals can do, communities need to build their housing more **carefully**. In many communities in the U.S., it is hard to walk from place to place **easily** because there are no sidewalks. If we want people to get exercise in their communities, they need sidewalks and bike paths with stores and activities within walking distance.

Can you think of any other ways to solve the problem of obesity?

6.3 Adverbs of Manner

An adverb of manner tells _how_ or _in what way_ a person does something.

EXAMPLES	EXPLANATION
Subject **Verb Phrase** **Adverb** He does his job **efficiently.** They ate lunch **quickly.** We walk together **slowly.**	We form most adverbs of manner by putting -_ly_[1] at the end of an adjective. An adverb usually follows the verb phrase.
Cars **greatly** reduce the need for physical activity. We **constantly** see ads on TV for food.	The -_ly_ adverb of manner can come before the verb. This position is more formal.
Do you eat **well**?	The adverb for _good_ is _well_.
You should eat a **well**-balanced meal. We live in a **carefully** planned community.	An adverb can come before an adjective.
ADJ: He is a **hard** worker. ADV: He works **hard.** ADJ: He wants a **fast** meal. ADV: Don't eat so **fast.** ADJ: He has an **early** class. ADV: We need to educate our children **early.** ADJ: I have a **late** class. ADV: I get home **late.**	Some adjectives and adverbs have the same form: _hard, fast, early,_ and _late._
She worked **hard** to prepare a good meal, but her son **hardly** ate anything.	_Hard_ and _hardly_ are both adverbs, but they have completely different meanings. _She worked_ **hard** means she put a lot of effort into the work. _Hard_ comes after the verb phrase. _He_ **hardly** _ate anything_ means he ate almost nothing. _Hardly_ comes before the verb.
He came home **late** and missed dinner. **Lately,** he doesn't have time to eat a good meal.	_Late_ and _lately_ are both adverbs, but they have completely different meanings. _Late_ means not on time. It comes after the verb phrase. _Lately_ means recently. It comes at the beginning or end of the sentence.
Compare: She is a **friendly** person. She behaves **in a friendly manner.** He is a **lively** person. He dances **in a lively way.**	Some adjectives end in -_ly_: _lovely, lonely, early, friendly, lively, ugly._ They have no adverb form. We use an adverbial phrase (_in a ___-ly way_) to describe the action.
He loses weight **very** _easily._ She cooks **extremely** _well._ He eats **so** _fast._ She exercises **real** _hard._ You eat **quite** _slowly._	_Very, extremely, so, real,_ and _quite_ can come before an adverb.

[1]For the spelling of _-ly_ adverbs, see Appendix C.

EXERCISE 5   **Fill in the blanks with an adverb from the box below (or choose your own adverb). Several answers may be possible.**

cheaply	differently	constantly	poorly
briskly ✓	regularly	quickly	well

EXAMPLE   If you walk __briskly__ every day, you can lose weight.

1. TV gives us messages _____, telling us to buy more junk food.
2. Do you eat _____ or slowly?
3. You should exercise _____ if you want to lose weight.
4. If you eat _____, you will not be healthy and strong.
5. If you eat _____, you will have no need to snack between meals.
6. In a fast-food restaurant, a family can eat _____. In another kind of restaurant, they have to spend a lot of money.
7. Some immigrants eat _____ when they come to the U.S. because they can't find food from their native countries.

EXERCISE 6   **ABOUT YOU**   **Write the adverb form of the word in parentheses ( ). Then check (✓) the activities that you do in this way. Make statements telling how you do these activities.**

EXAMPLES   ✓ shop __carefully__
                 (careful)

I shop carefully. I always try to buy healthy food for my family.

       ____ dance __well__
                (good)

I don't dance well. I never learned how.

1. ____ answer every question _____
                               (honest)
2. ____ walk _____
            (fast)
3. ____ cook _____
             (good)
4. ____ talk _____
           (constant)
5. ____ work _____
            (hard)
6. ____ study _____
            (hard)
7. ____ speak Spanish _____
                   (fluent)
8. ____ type _____
           (fast)
9. ____ exercise _____
               (regular)
10. ____ choose my food _____
                   (careful)

6.4 Adjective vs. Adverb

An adjective describes a noun. An adverb describes a verb (phrase).

EXAMPLES	EXPLANATION
Jim is **serious** about good health. He takes his doctor's advice **seriously**.	*Serious* is an adjective. It describes Jim. *Seriously* is an adverb. It tells how he takes his doctor's advice.
a. Your composition looks **good**. b. The teacher is looking at it **carefully**. a. The soup tastes **delicious**. b. I tasted the soup **slowly** because it was hot.	a. Use an adjective, not an adverb, after the following verbs if you are describing the subject: *smell, sound, taste, look, seem, appear,* and *feel*. b. Use an adverb if you are telling *how* the action (the verb phrase) is done.
a. The children got **hungry**. b. They ate lunch **hungrily**.	Use an adjective, not an adverb, in expressions with *get: get hungry, get tired, get sick, get rich,* etc. a. *Hungry* describes the children. b. *Hungrily* describes how they ate lunch.
Her health is **absolutely** perfect. The refrigerator is **completely** empty. You should eat a **well**-balanced diet.	An adverb can come before an adjective in phrases such as these: completely right extremely important pleasantly surprised well-known perfectly clear absolutely wrong
He's sick. He doesn't feel **well** today.	For health, use *well*. In conversational English, people often use *good* for health. He's sick. He doesn't feel **good** today.
Compare: **As usual**, she cooked dinner. Her husband **usually** cooks on Saturday.	Use the adjective, not the adverb, in the expression *as usual*.

EXERCISE 7 Fill in the blanks with the correct form of the adjective or adverb in parentheses ( ).

Last week I was invited to a "potluck" dinner at my math teacher's house. This is my first month in the U.S., so I didn't know what "potluck" was. A ____good____ friend of mine told me that this is a dinner where
(example: good)
each person brings some food. I wanted to make a _____ impression,
(1 good)
so I prepared my _____ dish from Mexico. I worked _____ hard
(2 favorite)   (3 extreme)
to make it look and taste _____.
(4 good)

Most of the people at the dinner looked at my dish _____.
(5 strange)
They didn't know what it was. They thought _____ that
(6 foolish)
Mexicans just eat tacos. They tasted my food _____, thinking
(7 careful)
that Mexicans make everything very hot and spicy. But I didn't. I know
that some people don't like _____ food, so I put the hot sauce
(8 spicy)
on the side.

A student from India brought Indian food. I was _____ to
(9 surprised)
find out how spicy Indian food is. The taste was very _____ to
(10 strange)
me, but I ate it anyway.

The party was great. I went home very _____. I had to get
(11 late)
up _____ the next morning, so I _____ slept at all that night.
(12 early)   (13 hard)

Adjectives; Noun Modifiers; Adverbs; *Too/Enough/Very/A Lot Of* **201**

Sleep

Before You Read

1. How many hours do you sleep a night?

2. How many hours would you like to sleep a night?

CD 2, TR 23

Read the following magazine article. Pay special attention to phrases with *too, enough, a lot of*, and *very*.

Did You Know?

Albert Einstein said he needed 10 hours of sleep a night to function well.

Most people need eight hours of sleep but don't get enough. Most Americans get less than seven hours a night. Only 30 percent get **enough sleep**. When people aren't rested **enough**, there are bad results. For example, if people drive when they're **too tired**, they can cause serious accidents on the road. According to the National Transportation Administration, sleepy drivers cause 100,000 accidents each year. There are many work-related accidents too. But that's not all. If you stay awake **too long**, your mind and nervous system begin to malfunction.[2] In the long term, if you don't get **enough sleep**, you will have less resistance to infection and disease.

Are we **too busy** to get **enough sleep**? Not always. Besides job and family responsibilities, Americans have **a lot of other things** that keep them out of bed. Twenty-four-hour-a-day Internet and TV keep us awake. Supermarkets, shopping malls, and laundromats are open late.

A lot of Americans, approximately 75 percent, report having trouble sleeping a few nights per week. Maybe they have **too much stress** in their lives or don't have good sleep habits. Sleep experts have some recommendations:

- Don't nap during the day.
- Don't get **too stimulated** before going to bed. Avoid activities such as watching TV or eating before bed.
- Go to bed at the same time every night.
- Avoid caffeine after lunchtime. If you drink **too much coffee** during the day, don't expect to get a good night's sleep.
- Exercise. Physical activity is **very good** for sleep. But if you exercise **too late** in the day, it will interfere with your sleep.

A good night's sleep is **very important**, so turn off the TV, shut down the computer, and sleep well.

[2]*To malfunction* means to function, or work, poorly.

6.5 Too and Enough

Too indicates a problem. The problem is stated or implied. Enough means sufficient.

EXAMPLES	EXPLANATION
adjective I'm **too** *tired* to drive. **adverb** She drove **too** *fast* and got a ticket.	Put *too* **before** adjectives and adverbs.
noncount **noun** a. Children eat **too much** *food* that is high in calories. **count** **noun** b. You spend **too many** *hours* watching TV.	a. Use *too much* before a noncount noun. b. Use *too many* before a count noun.
He doesn't sleep well because he worries **too much**.	*Too much* can come at the end of the verb phrase.
adjective Five hours of sleep is not *good* **enough**. **adverb** I walked *quickly* **enough** to raise my heart rate.	Put *enough* **after** adjectives and adverbs.
noun Some children don't get **enough** *exercise*. **noun** I don't have **enough** *time* to exercise.	Put *enough* **before** nouns.

Language Notes:
1. An infinitive phrase can follow a phrase with *too* and *enough*.
   He's **too young** *to understand* that candy isn't good for you.
   I don't have **enough money** *to join* a health club.
2. *Too good to be true* shows a surprised or doubtful reaction.
   I just won a million dollars. It's **too good to be true**.

EXERCISE **8** **Fill in the blanks to complete these statements. Answers may vary.**

EXAMPLES   Are Americans too _____busy_____ to get a good night's sleep?

Some people don't get enough ___exercise___, so they're overweight.

1. It's hard to sleep if you exercise too _____ in the evening.

2. If you're too _____ when you drive, you can fall asleep at the wheel.

(*continued*)

3. Some people spend too much _____ on the Internet. They should shut down the computer and go to bed.

4. If you drink too much _____, it can affect your sleep.

5. People drive everywhere. They don't _____ enough.

6. When children eat too _____, they get fat.

7. Children shouldn't drink so much soda, because it contains too many _____.

8. Most Americans don't get enough _____.

9. Many people say, "I don't have enough _____ to do all the things I need to do."

10. It's never too _____ to change your bad habits.

11. His clothes don't fit him anymore because he got too _____.

EXERCISE **9** **ABOUT YOU** **Complete each statement with an infinitive.**

EXAMPLES   I'm too young *to retire.*

I'm not strong enough *to move a piano.*

1. I'm not too old _____

2. I'm too young _____

3. I don't have enough money _____

4. I don't have enough time _____

5. I don't speak English well enough _____

EXERCISE **10** **A person is complaining about the school cafeteria. Fill in the blanks with *too, too much,* or *too many*.**

EXAMPLE   It's __*too*__ noisy, so I can't talk with my friends.

1. They serve _____ junk food there.

2. The fries have _____ grease.

3. The hamburgers have _____ calories.

4. The food is _____ expensive.

5. The tables are _____ dirty.

6. There are _____ people there, and sometimes there's no place to sit.

6.6 *Too* and *Very* and *A Lot Of*

EXAMPLES	EXPLANATION
a. I'm **too** tired to drive. Would you drive for a while? b. I was **very** tired, but I stayed up late and studied for my test. a. The speed limit on the highway is 55, and you're driving 40. You're driving **too** slowly. b. The speed limit on this road is 15 miles per hour. You need to drive **very** slowly. a. My brother is 14 years old. He's **too** old to get into the movie theater at half price. b. My grandmother is 85. She's **very** old, but she's in great health.	Don't confuse *very* and *too*. *Too* always indicates a problem in a specific situation. The problem can be stated or implied. *Very* is a neutral word. In examples (a), *too* shows a problem in a specific situation. In examples (b), *very* does not show any problem.
a. You put **too much** salt in the soup, and I can't eat it. b. She puts **a lot of** sugar in her coffee. She likes it that way. a. I ate **too many** cookies, and now I feel sick. b. She baked **a lot of** cookies for the party. Everyone enjoyed them.	Don't confuse *a lot of* and *too much/too many*. a. *Too* always indicates a problem in a specific situation. b. *A lot of* is a neutral expression.

EXERCISE 11 Fill in the blanks with *too*, *too much*, *too many*, *a lot of*, or *very*.

CD 2, TR 24

A: Your dinner was ____very____ delicious tonight.

(example)

B: I'm _____ glad you liked it.

(1)

A: Everything was great. But the soup had _____ salt.

(2)

B: Oh. I thought you liked everything.

A: I did. Other than the salt, it was good.

And I especially liked the potatoes.

B: I'm glad.

A: But you put a little _____ butter in the

(3)

potatoes. They were _____ greasy.

(4)

B: Oh.

A: But don't worry. I ate them anyway.

(continued)

B: I'm afraid the steak was burned. I left it in the oven _____ long.
(5)

A: Well, no one's perfect. I ate it anyway.

B: What about the cake I made? Did you like that?

A: Yes. It was _____ good. The only problem was it was
(6)

_____ small. I was hoping to have another piece, but
(7)

there was nothing left.

B: I thought you wanted to lose weight. You always say you're

_____ fat and need to go on a diet.
(8)

A: Fat? I'm not fat.

B: But you can't wear your old pants anymore.

A: I'm not _____ fat. My clothes are
(9)

_____ small. When I washed them, the water I used
(10)

was _____ hot and they shrank.
(11)

B: They didn't shrink. You gained weight. You consume _____
(12)

calories.

Summary of Lesson 6

1. Adjectives and Adverbs

ADJECTIVES	ADVERBS
We had a **quick** lunch.	We ate **quickly**.
We had a **late** dinner.	We ate **late**.
She is a **good** cook.	She cooks **well**.
She looks **serious**.	She is looking at the label **seriously**.
As usual, he drank a cup of coffee.	He **usually** drinks coffee in the morning.

2. Adjective Modifiers and Noun Modifiers

ADJECTIVE MODIFIER	NOUN MODIFIER
a **new** machine	an **exercise** machine
old shoes	**running** shoes
a **short** vacation	a **two-week** vacation
a **valid** license	a **driver's** license

3. *Very/Too/Enough/Too Much/Too Many*

He's **very** healthy.
He's **too** young to retire.
I'm relaxed **enough** to drive.
I had **enough** sleep last night.
She doesn't eat ice cream because it has **too much** fat.
She doesn't eat ice cream because it has **too many** calories.
He loves coffee, but when he drinks **too much**, he can't sleep.

Editing Advice

1. Adjectives are always singular.

I had two importants meetings last week.

2. Certain adjectives end with *-ed*.

              ed
He's interest in history.
           ^

3. Put an adjective before the noun.

      very intelligent girl
She is a ~~girl very intelligent~~.

4. Use *one(s)* after an adjective to take the place of a noun.

                              one
He has an old dictionary. She has a new.
                                ^

5. Put a specific noun before a general noun.

              phone call
She made a ~~call phone~~.

6. A noun modifier is always singular.

She took a three-weeks vacation.

7. An adverb describes a verb. An adjective describes a noun.

                             ly
The teacher speaks English fluent.
                             ^

The teacher looks serious~~ly~~.

8. Don't put the *-ly* adverb between the verb and the object.

He opened carefully the envelope.

---

9. Adverbs of manner that don't end in -ly follow the verb phrase.

He ~~late~~ came home.

10. *Too* indicates a problem. If there is no problem, use *very*.

very
Your father is ~~too~~ intelligent.

11. *Too much* and *too many* are followed by a noun. *Too* is followed by an adjective or adverb.

She's too ~~much~~ old to take care of herself.

12. Put *enough* after the adjective.

old enough
He's ~~enough old~~ to get married.

13. Don't confuse *hard* and *hardly*.

I'm tired. I worked hard~~ly~~ all day.

14. Don't use *too much* /*too many* when there is no problem.

a lot of
I love juice. Every day I drink ~~too much~~ juice.

Editing Quiz

Some of the shaded words and phrases have mistakes. Find the mistakes and correct them. If the shaded words are correct, write C.

C   *well*
I exercise regularly and I eat very good most of the time. Luckily, I'm too
     (example)   *(example)*   *(1)*

healthy. I try to eat too many fresh fruits and vegetables every day. I also
           (2)   *(3)*

eat a lot of whole grains. I rarely eat red meat. I eat fish or chicken. But I
       (4)   *(5)*

rarely eat chicken fried because it's too much greasy. Most mornings I
       (6)   *(7)*

have a glass of juice orange and cereal. For lunch, I have a small meal,
         (8)   *(9)*

usually a tuna sandwich. For dinner, I like to eat a nice meal slowly. Most
      (10)   *(11)*

of the time, I cook dinner. But on Fridays I have a three-hours biology
                      (12)

course and I late get home and I'm too much tire to cook. Then I'm not
      (13)   *(14)*   *(15)*

so carefully about what I eat. My roommate offers me his food, but he eats
  (16)

very poorly. He often eats hamburgers and greasy fries from a fast-food
       (17)   (18)
place, or he brings home a sausage pizza. He eats quickly his food. And he
                          (19)   (20)
drinks a lot of sweets colas. He thinks it's enough good, but I don't agree.
                (21)   (22)
When I eat with him, I'm not carefully about what I eat and then I don't
                            (23)
feel well the next day. I think it's important to have a diet very healthy.
     (24)   (25)
I'm going to try hardly to have a better meal on Friday nights.
                 (26)

Lesson 6 Test/Review

PART 1   **Fill in the blanks by putting the words in the correct order and making any other necessary changes.**

EXAMPLE   He ran a _____ten-mile race_____.
                        (race/ten miles)

1. His _____ are getting old.
        (shoes/running)

2. He _____.
      (fast/ran)

3. He didn't run _____ to win the race.
                  (enough/fast)

4. He was _____ when he finished the race.
           (completely/tired)

5. He _____.
      (late/arrived home)

6. He was _____ to eat dinner.
           (too/tired)

7. He took a _____.
              (nap/two hours)

PART 2   **Fill in the blanks with the correct form, adjective or adverb, of the word in parentheses ( ).**

EXAMPLES   She has _____clear_____ pronunciation.
                        (clear)

She pronounces very _____clearly_____.
                        (clear)

1. You need to find time to eat _____. Don't eat food that
                                 (good)

   is _____ for you.
      (bad)

2. Don't drive _____. It's important to arrive _____.
                (fast)   (safe)

                                                          (continued)

Adjectives; Noun Modifiers; Adverbs; *Too/Enough/Very/A Lot Of*   **209**

3. I can't understand you. Could you speak more _____, please?

(slow)

4. Some people learn languages _____.

(easy)

5. Some people think that math is _____, but it's _____

(hard) (easy)

for me.

6. As _____, we will have a test at the end of the lesson.

(usual)

7. She spoke _____, and I couldn't hear her _____.

(soft) (good)

8. I need to learn English _____.

(quick)

9. Do you exercise _____, or are you _____?

(regular) (lazy)

10. You seem _____ today.

(tired)

11. I'm very _____.

(busy)

12. She works very _____, but she's _____ with her job.

(hard) (happy)

13. She is a _____ woman. She's very _____.

(lovely) (friendly)

14. John sounds _____, but he's not angry. He just

(angry)

talks _____.

(loud)

15. You speak English _____ well. You have _____

(extreme) (perfect)

pronunciation. Everything you say is _____ _____.

(absolute) (clear)

Expansion

Classroom Activities

1 Make a list of things that you ate when you were younger that you don't eat now. Make a list of things that you eat now that you didn't eat when you were younger. Form a small group and compare your lists.

Things I ate before that I don't eat now:	Things I eat now that I didn't eat before:

2 Make a list of your lifestyle changes in the past few years. Find a partner. Compare your list with your partner's list. Which of these activities affect your health?

	Things I do (or don't do) now:	Things I did (or didn't do) before:
EXAMPLES	*I watch TV more often.* *I shop once a week.*	*I hardly ever watched TV before.* *I shopped almost every day* *when I lived in my country.*

3 Bad habits: Make a list of bad habits that you or someone in your family has.

EXAMPLES   I don't get enough exercise.
My daughter talks on the phone too much.

4 Take something from your purse, pocket, or bag, but don't show it to anyone. Describe it. Another student will try to guess what it is.

5 In some schools, students evaluate teachers. Work with a partner and write an evaluation form for teachers at this school or for another profession you are familiar with.

		Strongly Agree	Agree	Disagree	Strongly Disagree
EXAMPLES	1. Begins class promptly. 2. Treats students with respect. 3. Explains assignments clearly.				

Talk

About It

❶ In a small group or with the entire class, discuss what kind of food you usually eat. Do you think people eat healthy food in your native culture?

❷ Americans often say, "You are what you eat." What do you think this means?

❸ Do you get enough sleep? How much is enough for you? Do you remember your dreams?

Write

About It

❶ Write a short composition comparing food in your native culture to food in the U.S.

❷ Describe your eating habits.

> ### My Eating Habits
>
> In the U.S., I don't eat as well as I ate back home.
>
> In the morning, I just grab a quick cup of coffee and
>
> a piece of toast. For lunch, I usually eat fast food.
>
> Sometimes I even eat while I'm driving. . .

 For more practice using grammar in context, please visit our Web site.

Grammar
Time Words and Time Clauses

The Past Continuous Tense[1]

Context
Immigrants and Refugees

[1]The *past continuous tense* is also called the *past progressive tense*.

Ellis Island

Before You Read

1. Who was the first member of your family to come to the U.S.?

2. Was the process of entering the U.S. difficult for your family? How was it difficult?

CD 2, TR 25

Read the following textbook article. Pay special attention to time words.

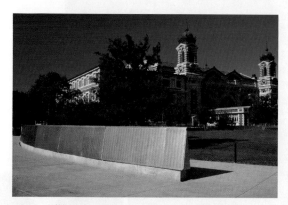

Ellis Island today with Wall of Honor

Did You Know?

Between 1820 and 1966, the largest number of immigrants in the U.S. came from Germany. The largest number of immigrants today come from Mexico, India, the Philippines, and China.

For many years, Ellis Island, an island in New York Harbor, was the main door through which millions of immigrants entered the United States. **From** the time it opened **in** 1892 **until** the time it closed **in** 1924, the U.S. Bureau of Immigration used Ellis Island to receive and process new arrivals. **During** this time, 12 million foreigners passed through this door with the hope of becoming Americans. They came from Italy, Poland, Russia, Germany, China, and many other countries. Sometimes more than 10,000 people passed through the registry room in one 24-hour period. New arrivals often waited **for** many hours **while** inspectors checked to see if they met legal and medical standards. Most did not speak English, and they were tired, hungry, and confused. Two percent (250,000 people) did not meet the requirements to enter the U.S. and had to return to their countries.

After Congress passed an immigration law that limited the number and nationality of new immigrants, immigration slowed down and Ellis Island was closed as an immigration processing center. It remained abandoned **until** 1965, **when** President Lyndon Johnson decided to restore it as a monument. Restoration of Ellis Island was finished **by** 1990. Now visitors to this monument can see the building as it looked **from** 1918 to 1920. In addition, they can see the Wall of Honor with the names of many of those who passed through on their way to becoming American citizens.

7.1 When, Until, While

EXAMPLES	EXPLANATION
When immigration slowed down, Ellis Island was closed.	*When* means *at that time* or *starting at that time.*
When it reopened, visitors could see the history of immigration.	
Ellis Island was closed **until** 1990.	*Until* means *before that time.*
Immigrants could not enter the U.S. **until** they passed an inspection.	
While they waited, they were often tired, confused, and hungry.	*While* means *during that time.*
New arrivals waited **while** inspectors checked their documents.	We can sometimes use *when* in place of *while*:
While they were crossing the ocean, they thought about their uncertain future.	**When** they were crossing the ocean, they thought about their uncertain future.

EXERCISE **1** Fill in the blanks with *when, while,* or *until*. In some cases, more than one answer is possible.

EXAMPLE My grandfather came to the U.S. ____when____ he was 25 years old.

1. _____ he lived in Poland, he had a hard life.

2. _____ he left Poland, he didn't speak English at all.

3. _____ he was at Ellis Island, he had to wait for hours. He was
   nervous _____ he waited.

4. He was nervous _____ he got permission to enter the country.
   Then he felt more relaxed.

5. _____ he passed the inspection, he entered the country.

6. In Poland, he didn't study English. He didn't speak a word of English
   _____ he started to work in the U.S. Then he learned a little.

7. _____ he worked, he saved money to bring his wife and children
   to America.

8. My grandmother couldn't come to the U.S. _____ my grandfather
   had enough money to send for her and their children.

9. My grandfather lived in the U.S. _____ he died in 1968.

EXERCISE 2 **ABOUT YOU** Add a main clause to complete each statement.

EXAMPLE When I got to class today, _I gave the teacher my composition._

1. While I was in elementary school, _____
2. When I finished elementary school, _____
3. Until I came to this city / school, _____
4. When I arrived in the U.S., _____
5. Until I started this course, _____

EXERCISE 3 **ABOUT YOU** Finish the time expression to complete each statement.

EXAMPLE I stayed in my country until _I won the diversity lottery._

1. I found my apartment / house while _____
2. I enrolled in this English class when _____
3. I didn't understand English until _____
4. I got married / found a job / bought a car / came to this country
   (*choose one*) when _____

EXERCISE 4 **ABOUT YOU** If you are from another country, name something you never . . . until you came to the U.S.

EXAMPLE Name something you never had.
I never had a car until I came to the U.S.

1. Name something you never did.
2. Name something or someone you never heard of.
3. Name something you never saw.
4. Name something you never thought about.
5. Name something you never had.
6. Name something you never ate.
7. Name something you never knew.

7.2 When and Whenever

EXAMPLES	EXPLANATION
When I went to New York last year, I visited Ellis Island.	*When* means *at that time* or *after that time.*
Whenever I visit New York, I go to the theaters there.	*Whenever* means *any time* or *every time.*

EXERCISE 5   **ABOUT YOU** Add a main clause to complete each statement. Use the general present.

EXAMPLE   Whenever I take a test, __I feel nervous._____

1. Whenever I feel sad or lonely, _____
2. Whenever I get angry, _____
3. Whenever I need advice, _____
4. Whenever I receive a present, _____
5. Whenever I'm on an airplane, _____
6. Whenever I'm sick, _____
7. Whenever the weather is bad, _____
8. Whenever the teacher explains the grammar, _____
_____

EXERCISE 6   **ABOUT YOU** Finish each sentence with a time clause.

EXAMPLES   I feel nervous __when I take a test._____
I feel nervous __whenever I have to speak in class._____

1. I feel relaxed _____
2. I get angry _____
3. I get bored _____
4. I can't concentrate _____
5. I'm happy _____
6. I'm in a bad mood _____
7. I sometimes daydream[2] _____
8. Time passes quickly for me _____

[2]*To daydream* means to dream while you are awake. Your mind does not stay in the present moment.

7.3 Time Words

TIME WORD	EXAMPLES	EXPLANATION
on	We came to the U.S. **on** April 16, 2008. We came to the U.S. **on** a Monday.	Use *on* with a specific date or day.
in	Ellis Island closed **in** 1924. My cousins came to the U.S. **in** August.	Use *in* with a specific year or month.
in vs. after	a. My brother will come to the U.S. **in** two months. b. My brother will come to the U.S. **after** he gets his visa.	a. Use *in* to mean after a period of time. b. Use *after* with an activity. *Wrong:* My brother will come to the U.S. *after* two months.
during	a. Many immigrants came to America **during** the war. b. Ellis Island was open from 1892 to 1924. **During** that time, 12 million immigrants passed through there.	a. Use *during* with an event (*the war, the trip, the movie*, etc.). b. Use *during* with a period of time (*during that time, during the month of May, during the first week in August*, etc.).
for	**For** many years, Ellis Island was the main entrance for immigrants to America. My grandfather waited at Ellis Island **for** ten hours.	Use *for* with the quantity of years, months, weeks, days, etc. *Wrong:* They waited at Ellis Island *during* ten hours.
before vs. by	a. **Before 1990**, Ellis Island was closed. b. **By 1990**, restoration of Ellis Island was complete.	a. In the example to the left, if you use *before*, 1990 is not included. b. If you use *by*, 1990 is included.
before vs. ago	a. She got married **before** she came to the U.S. b. She got married three years **ago**.	a. Use *before* with a date, time, or event. b. Use *ago* to mean *before now*.
from . . . to till until	Ellis Island was open **from** 1892 **to** 1924. Ellis Island is open **from** 9:30 A.M. **till** 5:15 P.M. You can take a boat to Ellis Island **from** 9 A.M. **until** 4:30 P.M.	Use *from* with the starting time. Use *to, till,* or *until* with the ending time.

EXERCISE 7 Circle the correct time word to fill in the blanks.

EXAMPLE He lived with his parents (*during /* (until) */ by*) he was 19 years old.

1. (*When / During / Whenever*) he was a child, he lived with his grandparents.

2. (*During / For / While*) several years, he lived with his grandparents.

3. (*For / While / During*) his childhood, he lived with his grandparents.

4. (While / Until / When) he got married, he lived with his grandparents. Then he found an apartment with his wife.

5. (While / During / Whenever) he was in elementary school, he lived with his grandparents.

6. (Whenever / While / When) he was ten years old, his grandparents gave him a bike.

7. She worked for her father (during / while / whenever) she was in college.

8. She worked for her father (for / during / while) her free time.

9. She worked for her father (during / whenever / when) she was single.

10. She worked for her father (for / during / while) three years.

11. She worked for her father full-time (while / when / during) her summer vacation.

12. She worked for her father (when / until / while) she got married. Then she quit her job to take care of her husband and children.

13. She worked for her father 12 years (before / ago / after).

14. (Until / Whenever / During) her husband needs help in his business, she helps him out.

15. She can't help you now. She's busy. She'll help you (by / after / in) an hour.

16. Please finish this exercise (by / in / until) 8:30.

17. Please finish this exercise (by / before / until) you go home. The teacher wants it today.

18. Please finish this exercise (in / after / by) ten minutes.

19. He'll retire (after / in / by) two years.

20. He'll retire (when / while / until) he's 65 years old.

21. He'll work (when / while / until) he's 65 years old. Then he'll retire.

22. I'm not going to eat dinner (when / while / until) my wife gets home. Then we'll eat together.

23. The Ellis Island Museum is open every day (for / from / by) 9:30 A.M. (at / by / till) 5:15 P.M.

24. The Ellis Island Museum is not open (in / at / on) December 25.

7.4 The Past Continuous Tense—Forms

We use the past continuous tense to show that something was in progress at a particular moment in the past.

EXAMPLES	EXPLANATION

In 2007, I **was living** in the U.S.
In 2007, my parents **were living** in Ecuador.
	To form the past continuous tense, we use *was* or *were* + verb *-ing*[3].
	    I, he, she, it $\rightarrow$ *was*
	    you, we, they $\rightarrow$ *were*

In 2007, they **were living** in California. They **weren't living** in New York. **Were** they **living** in Los Angeles? No, they **weren't**. Where **were** they **living**? Why **weren't** they **living** in Los Angeles? Who **was living** in New York?	Compare the affirmative, negative, *yes/no* question, *wh-* question, negative question, and subject question with the past continuous tense.

Terence and Charlotte—Refugees

Before You Read

1. Do you know the difference between an immigrant and a refugee?

2. Do you know anyone who is a refugee?

CD 2, TR 26

Read the following magazine article. Pay special attention to sentences with the past continuous tense.

In addition to immigrants, the U.S. takes refugees from many countries. A refugee is a person who runs away from his country because his or her life is in danger. The U.S. takes in more refugees than any other country in the world.

Terence and Charlotte and their children are refugees from Burundi, Africa. Burundi has two major tribes: the Hutus and the Tutsis. Terence is a Hutu and his wife Charlotte is a Tutsi. Terence **was working** in a hospital when he **heard** the news: Someone killed the president of Burundi. When they heard the news, violence began. Members of the Hutu tribe started killing members of the Tutsi tribe. Because the family was in danger, they ran from their country. First they ran to Congo. But their lives were in danger there. Then they ran to Zambia. While they **were living** in a Zambian refugee camp, they didn't have enough food and their children didn't go to school. Life was very hard. They applied to the UNHCR (United Nations

[3]To review the spelling of the *-ing* form, see Appendix A.

High Commissioner for Refugees) for permission to come to the U.S. In 2006, when they heard that they got permission, they were so happy.

When they **arrived** in Chicago, a volunteer from a refugee agency **was waiting** to meet them at the airport. She took them to their new apartment and helped them get settled. Volunteers helped them learn about life in the U.S. They helped them enroll their children in school and get medical attention. At first everything was very strange for them, but little by little life became easier. Charlotte found a job cleaning hotel rooms. Terence found a job in a factory.

When they become American citizens, they want to go back to Burundi to search for their family.

7.5 The Past Continuous Tense—with Specific Times

EXAMPLE	EXPLANATION
Terence **was working** in a hospital in 1993. Charlotte and Terence **were living** in Zambia in 2003.	We use the past continuous tense to show what was in progress at a specific moment in the past.

EXERCISE 8 **ABOUT YOU** Tell if the following things were happening in January 2008.

EXAMPLE go to school
I was (not) going to school in January 2008.

1. work
2. go to school
3. study English
4. live in the U.S.
5. live with my parents
6. take a vacation

EXERCISE 9 **ABOUT YOU** Ask a question with *"What were you doing . . . ?"* at these times. Another student will answer.

EXAMPLE at six o'clock this morning

A: What were you doing at six o'clock this morning?

B: I was sleeping.

1. at ten o'clock last night
2. at four o'clock this morning
3. at five o'clock yesterday afternoon
4. at this time yesterday
5. at this time last year[4]

[4]*At this time last year* is very general; it does not refer to a specific hour.

Time Words and Time Clauses; The Past Continuous Tense **221**

7.6 The Past Continuous Tense + a *When* Clause

EXAMPLE	EXPLANATION
Terence **was working** in a hospital when he **heard** the news. They **were living** in Zambia when they **got** permission to come to the U.S.	We use the past continuous tense with the simple past to show the relationship of a longer past action to a shorter past action.

Language Notes:
1. If the main clause precedes the time clause, do not separate the two clauses with a comma.
   If the time clause precedes the main clause, separate the two clauses with a comma.
   > He was working in a hospital when he heard the news. (No comma)
   > When he heard the news, he was working in a hospital. (Comma)
2. To form a question with two clauses, only the verb in the main clause is in question form.
   > Where **was he living** when he got the news?

EXERCISE 10   **Decide which of the two verbs has the longer action (past continuous) and which has the shorter action (simple past). Fill in the blanks with the correct tense.**

EXAMPLES   She _____was taking_____ a shower when the telephone
(take)

_____rang_____.
(ring)

When it _____started_____ to rain, I _____was walking_____
(start)   (walk)

to school.

1. Mary _____ in a department store when she
(shop)

_____ her purse.
(lose)

2. I _____ my homework when my friend
(do)

_____ over.
(come)

3. When he _____ at the airport, his friends
(arrive)

_____ for him.
(wait)

4. When my neighbor _____ on the door,
(knock)

we _____ dinner.
(eat)

5. She _____ dinner when the smoke alarm
(cook)

_____ off.[5]
(go)

6. He _____ snow when he _____
(shovel)   (lose)

his glove.

7. She _____ when the baby _____
(sleep)   (start)

to cry.

8. When I _____ to class, the teacher
(get)

_____ out the tests.
(pass)

9. I _____ to a friend when the baby
(talk)

_____.
(interrupt)

Albert Einstein—Refugee from Germany

Before You Read

1. Can you name any famous immigrants or refugees to the U.S.?

2. Did anyone from your native culture become famous in the U.S.?

CD 2, TR 27

Read the textbook article on the next page. Pay special attention to the relationship of the simple past and the past continuous tenses.

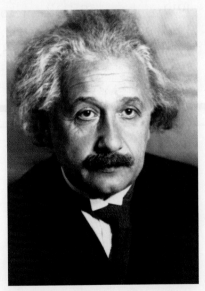

Albert Einstein, 1879–1955

[5]When an alarm *goes off*, it starts to sound.

Of the many refugees who came to the U.S., one will always be remembered throughout the world: Albert Einstein. Einstein changed our understanding of the universe.

Einstein was born in Germany in 1879 to Jewish parents. When he graduated from college in Switzerland in 1900, he was planning to become a teacher of physics and math but could not find a job in those fields. Instead, he went to work in a patent[6] office as a technical expert from 1902 to 1909. While he **was working** at this job, he **studied** and **wrote** in his spare time. In 1905, when he was only 26 years old, he published three papers that explained the basic structure of the universe. His theory of relativity explained the relationship of space and time. He returned to Germany to accept a research position at the University of Berlin. However, in 1920, while he **was lecturing** at the university, anti-Jewish groups often **interrupted** his lectures, saying they were "un-German."

In 1920, Einstein visited the United States for the first time. During his visits, he talked not only about his scientific theories, but also about world peace. While he **was visiting** the U.S. again in 1933, the Nazis **came** to power in Germany. They took his property, burned his books, and removed him from his university job. In 1933 Einstein helped establish the International Rescue Committee to assist anti-Nazi opponents of Hitler. The U.S. offered Einstein refugee status, and in 1940, he became a U.S. citizen. He received many job offers from all over the world, but he decided to accept a position at Princeton University in New Jersey. He lived and worked there until he died in 1955.

Einstein's Life	
1879	Born in Germany
1902–1909	Worked in a Swiss patent office
1905	Published his theory of relativity
1919	Scientists recognized his theory to be correct
1933	Visited the U.S.
1940	Became a U.S. citizen
1955	Died

[6]A *patent* is a document that identifies the owner of a new invention. Only the person or company who has the patent can sell the invention.

7.7 The Past Continuous Tense in a *While* Clause

EXAMPLE	EXPLANATION
While Einstein **was living** in Switzerland, he developed his theory of relativity. While Einstein **was visiting** the U.S., the Nazis took power in Germany.	Use *while* + the past continuous with the longer action.
Compare: Einstein was living in the U.S. **when** he **died**. **While** he **was living** in the U.S., he wrote many papers.	Use *when* + the simple past with the shorter action. Use *while* + the past continuous with the longer action.

Language Notes:
1. You can use *when* in place of *while* with a continuous action.
   While Einstein was living in Switzerland, he developed his theory.
   When Einstein was living in Switzerland, he developed his theory.
3. You cannot use *while* with an action that has no continuation.
   Wrong: I was running *while* I fell.
   Right: I was running *when* I fell.

EXERCISE 11 Decide which of the two verbs has the longer action (past continuous) and which has the shorter action (simple past). Fill in the blanks with the correct tense.

EXAMPLE It ____started____ to rain while I ____was walking____ to school.
(start) (walk)

1. While the teacher _____ on the blackboard, she
(write)

   _____ the chalk.
   (drop)

2. He _____ his arm while he _____
(break) (climb)

   a tree.

3. She _____ her husband while she
(meet)

   _____ college.
   (attend)

4. While I _____ to work, I _____ out
(drive) (run)

   of gas.[7]

5. While I _____ my bike, I _____ a
(ride) (get)

   flat tire.

[7]To *run out of* means to use something up completely.

(continued)

6. I _____ my tooth while I _____ a nut.
   (break)   (eat)

7. I _____ an old friend while I _____
   (meet)   (walk)

   in the park.

8. While he _____ dishes, he _____
      (wash)   (break)

   a plate.

EXERCISE **12** **Fill in the blanks with the simple past or the past continuous form of the verb in parentheses ( ) in the following conversations.**

CD 2, TR 28

Conversation 1, **between a wife (W) and husband (H)**

W: Look what I found today! Your favorite watch!

H: Where ___did you find___ it?
            (example: find)

W: In your top drawer. I _____ away your socks when
                              (1 put)

   I _____ it.
      (2 find)

H: I wonder how it got there.

W: Probably while you _____ something in that drawer,
                            (3 put)

   it _____ off your wrist.
       (4 fall)

Conversation 2, **between two students**

A: When did you come to the U.S.?

B: Two months ago.

A: Really? But you speak English so well.

B: While I _____ in a refugee camp in Kenya, I studied
                (1 live)

   English.

A: _____ to come to the U.S.?
       (2 you/plan)

B: Not really. I had no plans at all. I _____ in the
                                            (3 just/wait)

   refugee camp.

A: Are you from Kenya?

B: No. I'm from Sudan. But while I _____ in Sudan, a
                                       (4 live)

   war _____ there and I had to leave my country.
        (5 start)

A: Are you here with your family?

B: No. I'm alone. When the war _____ ,

(6 start)

I _____ far away from my family. I escaped to Kenya.

(7 live)

Conversation 3, between a granddaughter (GD) and grandmother (GM)

GD: I _____ through some old boxes when I

(1 look)

_____ this picture of you and Grandpa when you were

(2 find)

young. By the way, how _____ Grandpa?

(3 you/meet)

GM: One day I _____ in the park in my hometown

(4 walk)

when he _____ me to ask what time it was. We

(5 stop)

_____ to talk, and then he _____

(6 start) (7 ask)

me to go out with him.

GD: Did you date for a long time?

GM: We _____ for ten months. A few months after we

(8 date)

met, his family _____ for the green card lottery in the

(9 apply)

U.S. While we _____ , they _____ a

(10 date) (11 receive)

letter that gave them permission to immigrate to the U.S.

GD: What _____ ?

(12 happen)

GM: At first, I was worried that I'd never see your grandfather again. But he

_____ to me often and _____ me

(13 write) (14 call)

whenever he could. About a year later, he _____ back

(15 go)

to our country to visit me. While we _____ in a

(16 eat)

beautiful restaurant, he _____ me to marry him.

(17 ask)

GD: _____ him right away?

(18 you/marry)

GM: Yes, we got married a few weeks later and then he

_____ to the U.S. But I couldn't go to the U.S. with

(19 return)

him. I _____ to wait for permission.

(20 have)

Finally, I _____ permission to come.

(21 get)

7.8 Was/Were Going To

We use *was/were going to* + the base form to describe a plan that we didn't carry out. It means the same thing as *was/were planning to*.

EXAMPLES	EXPLANATION
a. Einstein **was going to** return to Germany, but the Nazis came to power.	a. Einstein was planning to return, but didn't.
b. I **was going to** call you, but I lost your phone number.	b. I was planning to call, but didn't.

EXERCISE 13 Fill in the blanks with *was going to* + one of the verbs from the box below.

use	write ✓	go
say	call	

CD 2, TR 29

A: What did you write for your composition today?

B: I ___was going to write___ about Einstein, but I couldn't find
       (example)
any information.

A: What? There's tons of [8] information. Did you go to the library?

B: I _____ to the library, but the library near my
       (1)
house is closed for construction.

A: How about the college library?

B: I didn't think of it.

A: Why didn't you use the Internet? You can find plenty of information there.

B: I _____ the Internet, but my computer crashed.
       (2)

A: Why didn't you call me? You're welcome to use my computer.

B: I _____ you, but I lost your phone number.
       (3)

A: I'm beginning to think you didn't really want to do your homework.

B: Maybe you're right. I'm kind of lazy.

A: I _____ that, but I didn't want to hurt your feelings.
       (4)

---

[8]*Tons of* means *a lot of.*

EXERCISE 14 Fill in the blanks to tell what prevented a plan from happening.

EXAMPLE He was going to return to his country, but ___he couldn't get permission.___

1. My cousin was going to come to the U.S., but _____

2. He was going to work in the U.S. for only three months, but _____

3. We were going to return to our country, but _____

4. I was going to call my grandparents last night, but _____

5. We were going to rent an apartment in this city, but _____

7.9 Simple Past vs. Past Continuous with *When*

Both the simple past and the past continuous can be used in a sentence that has a *when* clause. However, the time sequence is completely different.

EXAMPLES	EXPLANATION
a. *When* Einstein graduated from college, he **tried** to get a job as a teacher. b. *When* Einstein entered college, he **was living** in Switzerland.	In sentences (a), the simple past in the main clause shows what happened **after** an action.
a. Einstein **came** to live in the U.S. *when* he lost his German citizenship. b. Einstein **was living** in the U.S. *when* he died.	In sentences (b), the past continuous in the main clause shows what was happening **at the same time** a shorter action occurred.
a. *When* Terence got permission, he **came** to the U.S. b. *When* Terence got permission, he **was living** in Zambia.	

EXERCISE 15 Fill in the blanks with the simple past or the past continuous of the verb in parentheses ( ).

EXAMPLES Terence ___was living___ in a refugee camp when he got his visa.
   (live)

When he got to the U.S., he ___needed___ to find a job.
   (need)

1. When he _____ permission, he left Zambia.
   (get)

He _____ in a hospital when he heard the news.
   (work)

(continued)

2. When they arrived in the U.S., volunteers _____ them.
   (help)

   When they arrived in the U.S., a volunteer _____ for them at the
   (wait)

   airport.

3. They _____ in the U.S. when their fourth child was born.
   (live)

   When their fourth child was born, they _____ to a bigger apartment.
   (move)

4. When Charlotte learned English well enough, she _____ to
   (start)

   work in a hotel.

   She _____ in a hotel when her daughter was born.
   (work)

5. Terence _____ morning English classes when he found a job.
   (take)

   Terence _____ to night classes when he found a job.
   (change)

6. When Einstein entered college, he _____ to become a teacher.
   (want)

   When Einstein entered college, he _____ in Switzerland.
   (live)

7. Einstein _____ a resident of the U.S. when he lost his German
   (become)

   citizenship.

   Einstein _____ in the U.S. when he died.
   (live)

7.10 Simple Past vs. Past Continuous

EXAMPLES	EXPLANATION
While they **lived** in the refugee camp, they **studied** English. **While** Einstein **worked** at a patent office, he **studied** and **wrote**.	We can connect two past actions that happened in the same time period with *while* and use the simple past tense in both clauses.
While I **was reading** the story about Terence and Charlotte, I **was underlining** the verbs. **While** we **were doing** the last exercise, the teacher **was helping** us.	We can connect two past actions that happened in the **exact** same time period with *while* and use the past continuous tense in both clauses.
When they **got** permission, they came to the U.S. **When** they **came** to the U.S., they started to study English.	Use *when* to mean *at a specific time*. Use the simple past tense.

EXERCISE 16 Fill in the blanks with *when* for an action at a specific time or *while* for an action that continues over time.

EXAMPLE ___While___ Terence was working in a factory, he practiced English with his coworkers.

1. _____ Terence left his country, he went to Congo.

2. _____ I was reading the story, I was paying attention to the verbs.

3. _____ Charlotte cleaned hotel rooms, she listened to music.

4. _____ their youngest daughter was born, Charlotte stopped working.

5. Charlotte started to work again _____ her daughter was a year old.

6. _____ Charlotte worked, her baby was in day care.

7. Terence worked in a factory _____ Charlotte worked in a hotel.

7.11 Using the *-ing* Form After Time Words

When the main clause and the time clause have the same subject, we can delete the subject of the time clause and use a present participle (verb + *-ing*) after the time word.

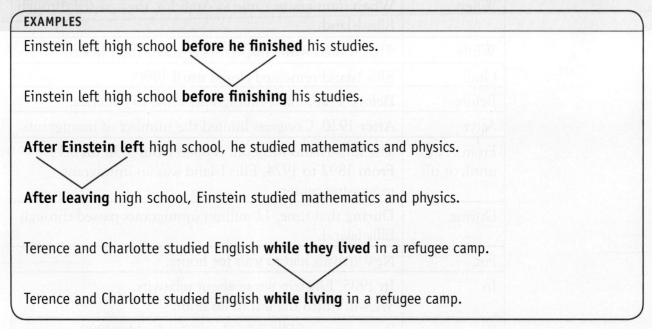

EXAMPLES
Einstein left high school **before he finished** his studies.
Einstein left high school **before finishing** his studies.
After Einstein left high school, he studied mathematics and physics.
After leaving high school, Einstein studied mathematics and physics.
Terence and Charlotte studied English **while they lived** in a refugee camp.
Terence and Charlotte studied English **while living** in a refugee camp.

EXERCISE 17 **Change these sentences. Use a present participle after the time word. Make any necessary changes.**

EXAMPLE After ~~Einstein entered~~ the university, ~~he~~ developed his theory.
(entering above "Einstein entered", Einstein above "he")

1. Einstein passed an exam before he entered the university.

2. He left high school before he received his diploma.

3. After Einstein developed his theory of relativity, he became famous.

4. He became interested in physics after he received books on science.

5. After Einstein came to the U.S., he got a job at Princeton.

6. Before they came to the U.S., Terence and Charlotte lived in Zambia.

7. While they lived in the refugee camp, the children didn't go to school.

8. Charlotte listened to music while she cleaned hotel rooms.

9. The parents were working and going to school while they were raising a family.

Summary of Lesson 7

1. Time Words

Time Word	Examples
When	**When** immigrants came to America, they passed through Ellis Island.
While	They waited **while** inspectors checked their health.
Until	Ellis Island remained closed **until** 1990.
Before	**Before** 1920, many immigrants came to America.
After	**After** 1920, Congress limited the number of immigrants.
From . . . to, until, or till	The Ellis Island Museum is open **from** 9:30 **till** 5:15. **From** 1892 **to** 1924, Ellis Island was an immigrant processing center.
During	**During** that time, 12 million immigrants passed through Ellis Island.
For	New arrivals had to wait **for** hours.
In	**In** 1905, Einstein wrote about relativity. We will finish the test **in** an hour.
By	Restoration of Ellis Island was finished **by** 1990.
Ago	One hundred years **ago**, new arrivals passed through Ellis Island.
On	We came to the U.S. **on** Wednesday.

2. Uses of the past continuous tense:

    A. To describe a past action that was in progress at a specific moment:
    He **was sleeping** at six o'clock this morning.
    Where **were** you **living** in December 2001?

    B. With the past tense, to show the relationship of a longer past action to a shorter past action:
    Terence **was living** in Zambia when he **got** permission to come to the U.S.
    Einstein **was living** in New Jersey when he **died**.
    While I **was reading** the story, I **had** to use my dictionary.

    C. To show past intentions:
    I **was going to call** you, but I lost your phone number.
    She **was going to cook** dinner, but she didn't have time.

Editing Advice

1. Put the subject before the verb in all clauses.

    the teacher entered
    When ~~entered the teacher~~, the students stood up.

2. Use *when*, not *while*, if the action has no duration.

    When
    ~~While~~ she spilled the milk, she started to cry.

3. Don't confuse *during* and *for*.

    for
    He watched TV ~~during~~ three hours.

4. Don't confuse *until* and *when*.

    when
    She will eat dinner ~~until~~ her husband comes home.

5. Don't confuse *before* and *ago*.

    ago
    They came to the U.S. three years ~~before~~.

6. After a time word, use an *-ing* form, not a base form.

    finding
    After ~~find~~ a job, he bought a car.

Editing Quiz

Some of the shaded words and phrases have mistakes. Find the mistakes and correct them. If the shaded words are correct, write C.

                                    C
I left my country three years ago. But my husband didn't come with me.
                    (example)
                               for
He wanted to stay in our country ~~during~~ two more years until he
                                 (example)   *(1)*

finished college. While I got here, I started to study English right away.
                     (2)

While I was going to school, I was work in the school library.
(3)   *(4)*   *(5)*

   My husband was going to get a degree in engineering when a war broke
                    (6)   *(7)*   *(8)*

out in our country. When started the war, he fled the country quickly
                          (9)

and went to a neighboring country. He was in a refugee camp during one
                                                              (10)

year. While he was in the camp, he started to study English. He applied
      (11)

for permission to come to the U.S. After wait for one year, he finally got
                                         (12)

permission. When he was getting here, we were so excited to see each other
            (13)   *(14)*

again.

   He's learning English quickly. After he learns English well enough, he's

going to enter an engineering program. I know he'll be happy until he gets
                                                              (15)

his engineering degree.

Lesson 7 Test/Review

PART ❶ Fill in the blanks with the simple past or the past continuous form of the verb in parentheses ( ).

EXAMPLE   He ___was walking___ to his car when he ___lost___ his glove.
                    (walk)   *(lose)*

1. What _____ at 4 P.M. yesterday afternoon? I tried
            (you/do)

   to call you, but you weren't home.

2. She _____ to be an engineer when the war
            (study)

   _____.
    (start)

3. I _____ your necklace while I _____ for
      (find)   *(look)*

   my watch.

4. She _____ a house three years ago.
   (buy)

5. He _____ his wife while he _____ in a
   (meet)   (work)

   restaurant.

6. When my grandfather _____ to America, he
                              (come)

   _____ a job in a factory.
         (find)

7. When he _____ at Ellis Island, his uncle
              (arrive)

   _____ for him.
         (wait)

8. While she _____ the computer, it _____.
                    (use)   (crash)

9. He _____ dinner when the fire _____.
           (cook)   (start)

10. I _____ my car and _____
          (drive)   (listen)

    to the radio when I _____ about the plane crash.
                              (hear)

PART 2 **Fill in the blanks with an appropriate time word. Choose *when*,
whenever, *while*, *until*, *before*, *after*, *by*, *ago*, *in*, *for*, *on*, *from*, *till*, *to*,
or *during*. In some cases, more than one answer is possible.**

EXAMPLE   I will continue to work ____until____ I am 65 years old. Then I will retire.

1. _____ it snows, there are a lot of traffic accidents.

2. I was walking to my friend's house _____ it started to rain. I was
   glad I had my umbrella with me.

3. The teacher was watching the students _____ the test.

4. _____ I finished my homework last night, I watched the news
   on TV.

5. I got my visa _____ coming to the U.S.

6. He must stay in his country _____ he gets permission to come to
   the U.S.

7. _____ he dropped his glasses, they broke.

8. We have to finish this lesson _____ ten o'clock.

9. He found a job two months _____.

10. He found a job three weeks _____ coming to the U.S.

11. He found a job _____ April.

(continued)

12. It's 7:50. The movie will begin _____ ten minutes, at 8:00.

13. _____ the movie began, everyone became quiet.

14. _____ she was watching the sad movie, she started to cry.

15. Einstein was 61 years old _____ he became a U.S. citizen.

16. Einstein lived in the U.S. _____ 22 years.

17. I had a doctor's appointment _____ Monday.

18. I work every day _____ 9:00 A.M. _____ 5:00 P.M.

19. _____ the summer, many teenagers get jobs.

Expansion

Classroom
Activities

❶ Pick an important event in your life (*immigrating to a new country, moving to a new town, going to a new school, getting married,* etc.) **and make a list of things you did before, during, and after the event. Discuss your sentences with a small group.**

Event: _____

Before	
During	
After	

❷ Form a small group. Turn to the person next to you and say a year or a specific time of the year. The person next to you tells what was happening in his or her life at that time.

EXAMPLES 1996

I was living with my parents.

January 2004

I was studying to be a nurse.

Talk
About It

❶ Read these quotes by Einstein. Discuss their meaning.

- "Imagination is more important than knowledge."
- "The only real valuable thing is intuition."
- "A person starts to live when he can live outside himself."
- "I never think of the future. It comes soon enough."
- "Anyone who has never made a mistake has never tried anything new."
- "Science is a wonderful thing if one does not have to earn one's living at it."
- "Peace cannot be kept by force. It can only be achieved by understanding."
- "Education is what remains after one has forgotten everything he learned in school."
- "Not everything that counts can be counted, and not everything that can be counted counts." (Sign hanging in Einstein's office at Princeton)

❷ Einstein is often called a genius. Can you think of any other famous people who are geniuses?

❸ In a small group or with the entire class, discuss your experience of immigration. Was the process difficult? How did you feel during the process?

Write

About It

1 Write a paragraph about the changes that took place after a major historical event in your country or elsewhere in the world.

2 Write about the reasons people leave your country or the reasons you left your country.

3 Write about your arrival in the U.S.

EXAMPLE

My Arrival in the U.S.

My family and I arrived in the U.S. in September 2008. When we arrived, our cousins were waiting for us at the airport. They took us to their house and gave us something to eat. But we were tired and we just wanted to sleep for a while...

 For more practice using grammar in context, please visit our Web site.

Appendices

Appendix A

Spelling and Pronunciation of Verbs

Spelling of the -s Form of Verbs

Rule	Base Form	-s Form
Add -s to most verbs to make the -s form.	hope eat	hopes eats
When the base form ends in ss, zz, sh, ch, or x, add -es and pronounce an extra syllable, /əz/.	miss buzz wash catch fix	misses buzzes washes catches fixes
When the base form ends in a consonant + y, change the y to i and add -es.	carry worry	carries worries
When the base form ends in a vowel + y, do not change the y.	pay obey	pays obeys
Add -es to go and do.	go do	goes does

Three Pronunciations of the -s Form		
We pronounce /s/ if the verb ends in these voiceless sounds: /p t k f/.	hope—hopes eat—eats	pick—picks laugh—laughs
We pronounce /z/ if the verb ends in most voiced sounds.	live—lives grab—grabs read—reads	run—runs sing—sings borrow—borrows
When the base form ends in ss, zz, sh, ch, x, se, ge, or ce, we pronounce an extra syllable, /əz/.	miss—misses buzz—buzzes wash—washes watch—watches	fix—fixes use—uses change—changes dance—dances
These verbs have a change in the vowel sound.	do/**du**/—does/d**ʌz**/	say/**sei**/—says/**sez**/

Spelling of the *-ing* Form of Verbs

Rule	Base Form	*-ing* Form
Add *-ing* to most verbs. **Note:** Do not remove the *y* for the *-ing* form.	eat go study carry	eating going studying carrying
For a one-syllable verb that ends in a consonant + vowel + consonant (CVC), double the final consonant and add *-ing*.	p l a n | | | C V C s t o p | | | C V C s i t | | | C V C g r a b | | | C V C	planning stopping sitting grabbing
Do not double the final *w*, *x*, or *y*.	show mix stay	showing mixing staying
For a two-syllable word that ends in CVC, double the final consonant only if the last syllable is stressed.	refér admít begín rebél	referring admitting beginning rebelling
When the last syllable of a multi-syllable word is not stressed, do not double the final consonant.	lísten ópen óffer límit devélop	listening opening offering limiting developing
If the word ends in a consonant + *e*, drop the *e* before adding *-ing*.	live take write arrive	living taking writing arriving

Spelling of the Past Tense of Regular Verbs

Rule	Base Form	-ed Form
Add -ed to the base form to make the past tense of most regular verbs.	start kick	started kicked
When the base form ends in e, add -d only.	die live	died lived
When the base form ends in a consonant + y, change the y to i and add -ed.	carry worry	carried worried
When the base form ends in a vowel + y, do not change the y.	destroy stay	destroyed stayed
For a one-syllable word that ends in a consonant + vowel + consonant (CVC), double the final consonant and add -ed.	s t o p | | | C V C p l u g | | | C V C	stopped plugged
Do not double the final w or x.	sew fix	sewed fixed
For a two-syllable word that ends in CVC, double the final consonant only if the last syllable is stressed.	occúr permít	occurred permitted
When the last syllable of a multi-syllable word is not stressed, do not double the final consonant.	ópen háppen devélop	opened happened developed

Pronunciation of Past Forms that End in -ed

The past tense with -ed has three pronunciations.			
We pronounce a /t/ if the base form ends in these voiceless sounds: /p, k, f, s, š, č/.	jump—jumped cook—cooked	cough—coughed kiss—kissed	wash—washed watch—watched
We pronounce a /d/ if the base form ends in most voiced sounds.	rub—rubbed drag—dragged love—loved bathe—bathed use—used	charge—charged glue—glued massage—massaged name—named learn—learned	bang—banged call—called fear—feared free—freed stay—stayed
We pronounce an extra syllable /əd/ if the base form ends in a /t/ or /d/ sound.	wait—waited hate—hated	want—wanted add—added	need—needed decide—decided

Appendix B

Irregular Noun Plurals

Singular	Plural	Explanation
man woman tooth foot goose	men women teeth feet geese	Vowel change (**Note:** The first vowel in *women* is pronounced /I/.)
sheep fish deer	sheep fish deer	No change
child person mouse	children people (OR persons) mice	Different word form
	(eye)glasses belongings clothes goods groceries jeans pajamas pants/slacks scissors shorts	No singular form
alumnus cactus radius stimulus syllabus	alumni cacti (OR cactuses) radii stimuli syllabi (OR syllabuses)	*us → i*
analysis crisis hypothesis oasis parenthesis thesis	analyses crises hypotheses oases parentheses theses	*is → es*
appendix index	appendices (OR appendixes) indices (OR indexes)	*ix → ices* OR *→ ixes* *ex → ices* OR *→ exes*

Singular	Plural	Explanation
bacterium	bacteria	*um* → *a*
curriculum	curricula	
datum	data	
medium	media	
memorandum	memoranda	
criterion	criteria	*ion* → *a*
phenomenon	phenomena	*on* → *a*
alga	algae	*a* → *ae*
formula	formulae (OR formulas)	
vertebra	vertebrae	

Appendix C

Spelling Rules for Adverbs Ending in *-ly*

Adjective Ending	Examples	Adverb Ending	Adverb
Most endings	careful quiet serious	Add *-ly*.	carefully quietly seriously
y	easy happy lucky	Change *y* to *i* and add *-ly*.	easily happily luckily
e	nice free	Keep the *e* and add *-ly*.*	nicely freely
consonant + *le*	simple comfortable double	Drop the *e* and add *-ly*.	simply comfortably doubly
ic	basic enthusiastic	Add *-ally*.**	basically enthusiastically
Exceptions: *true—truly **public—publicly			

Appendix D

Metric Conversion Chart

Length

When You Know	Symbol	Multiply by	To Find	Symbol
inches	in	2.54	centimeters	cm
feet	ft	30.5	centimeters	cm
feet	ft	0.3	meters	m
yards	yd	0.91	meters	m
miles	mi	1.6	kilometers	km
Metric:				
centimeters	cm	0.39	inches	in
centimeters	cm	0.03	feet	ft
meters	m	3.28	feet	ft
meters	m	1.09	yards	yd
kilometers	km	0.62	miles	mi

Note:
12 inches = 1 foot
3 feet / 36 inches = 1 yard

Area

When You Know	Symbol	Multiply by	To Find	Symbol
square inches	in²	6.5	square centimeters	cm²
square feet	ft²	0.09	square meters	m²
square yards	yd²	0.8	square meters	m²
square miles	mi²	2.6	square kilometers	km²
Metric:				
square centimeters	cm²	0.16	square inches	in²
square meters	m²	10.76	square feet	ft²
square meters	m²	1.2	square yards	yd²
square kilometers	km²	0.39	square miles	mi²

Weight (Mass)

When You Know	Symbol	Multiply by	To Find	Symbol
ounces	oz	28.35	grams	g
pounds	lb	0.45	kilograms	kg
Metric:				
grams	g	0.04	ounces	oz
kilograms	kg	2.2	pounds	lb

Note:
1 pound = 16 ounces

Volume

When You Know	Symbol	Multiply by	To Find	Symbol
fluid ounces	fl oz	30.0	milliliters	mL
pints	pt	0.47	liters	L
quarts	qt	0.95	liters	L
gallons	gal	3.8	liters	L
Metric:				
milliliters	mL	0.03	fluid ounces	fl oz
liters	L	2.11	pints	pt
liters	L	1.05	quarts	qt
liters	L	0.26	gallons	gal

Temperature

When You Know	Symbol	Do this	To Find	Symbol
degrees Fahrenheit	°F	Subtract 32, then multiply by $\frac{5}{9}$	degrees Celsius	°C
Metric:				
degrees Celsius	°C	Multiply by $\frac{9}{5}$, then add 32	degrees Fahrenheit	°F

(continued)

Sample temperatures

Fahrenheit	Celsius
0	− 18
10	−12
20	−7
32	0
40	4
50	10
60	16
70	21
80	27
90	32
100	38
212	100

Appendix E

The Verb *GET*

***Get* has many meanings. Here is a list of the most common ones:**

- get something = receive
  I got a letter from my father.

- get + (to) place = arrive
  I got home at six. What time do you get to school?

- get + object + infinitive = persuade
  She got him to wash the dishes.

- get + past participle = become

get acquainted	get worried	get hurt	get engaged
get lost	get bored	get married	get accustomed to
get confused	get divorced	get used to	get scared
get tired	get dressed		

  They got married in 1989.

- get + adjective = become

get hungry	get sleepy	get rich	get dark	get nervous
get angry	get well	get old	get upset	get fat

  It gets dark at 6:30.

- get an illness = catch
  While she was traveling, she got malaria.

- get a joke or an idea = understand
  Everybody except Tom laughed at the joke. He didn't get it.
  The boss explained the project to us, but I didn't get it.

- get ahead = advance
  He works very hard because he wants to get ahead in his job.

- get along (well) (with someone) = have a good relationship
  She doesn't get along with her mother-in-law.
  Do you and your roommate get along well?

- get around to something = find the time to do something
  I wanted to write my brother a letter yesterday, but I didn't get around to it.

- get away = escape
  The police chased the thief, but he got away.

- get away with something = escape punishment
  He cheated on his taxes and got away with it.

- get back = return
  He got back from his vacation last Saturday.

- get back at someone = get revenge
  My brother wants to get back at me for stealing his girlfriend.

- get back to someone = communicate with someone at a later time
  The boss can't talk to you today. Can she get back to you tomorrow?

- get by = have just enough but nothing more
  On her salary, she's just getting by. She can't afford a car or a vacation.

- get in trouble = be caught and punished for doing something wrong
  They got in trouble for cheating on the test.

- get in(to) = enter a car
  She got in the car and drove away quickly.

- get out (of) = leave a car
  When the taxi arrived at the theater, everyone got out.

- get on = seat yourself on a bicycle, motorcycle, horse
  She got on the motorcycle and left.

- get on = enter a train, bus, airplane
  She got on the bus and took a seat in the back.

- get off = leave a bicycle, motorcycle, horse, train, bus, airplane
  They will get off the train at the next stop.

- get out of something = escape responsibility
  My boss wants me to help him on Saturday, but I'm going to try to get out of it.

(continued)

- get over something = recover from an illness or disappointment
  She has the flu this week. I hope she gets over it soon.

- get rid of someone or something = free oneself of someone or something undesirable
  My apartment has roaches, and I can't get rid of them.

- get through (to someone) = communicate, often by telephone
  I tried to call my mother many times, but her line was busy. I couldn't get through.

- get through (with something) = finish
  I can meet you after I get through with my homework.

- get together = meet with another person
  I'd like to see you again. When can we get together?

- get up = arise from bed
  He woke up at six o'clock, but he didn't get up until 6:30.

Appendix F

MAKE and *DO*

Some expressions use *make*. Others use *do*.

Make	Do
make a date/an appointment	do (the) homework
make a plan	do an exercise
make a decision	do the cleaning, laundry, dishes, washing, etc.
make a telephone call	do the shopping
make a meal (breakfast, lunch, dinner)	do one's best
make a mistake	do a favor
make an effort	do the right/wrong thing
make an improvement	do a job
make a promise	do business
make money	What do you do for a living? (asks about a job)
make noise	How do you do? (said when you
make the bed	meet someone for the first time)

Prepositions of Time

- **in** the morning: He takes a shower *in* the morning.
- **in** the afternoon: He takes a shower *in* the afternoon.
- **in** the evening: He takes a shower *in* the evening.
- **at** night: He takes a shower *at* night.
- **in** the summer, fall, winter, spring: He takes classes *in* the summer.
- **on** that/this day: May 4 is my birthday. I became a citizen *on* that day.
- **on** the weekend: He studies *on* the weekend.
- **on** a specific day: His birthday is *on* March 5.
- **in** a month: His birthday is *in* March.
- **in** a year: He was born *in* 1978.
- **in** a century: People didn't use cars *in* the 19th century.
- **on** a day: I don't have class *on* Monday.
- **at** a specific time: My class begins *at* 12:30.
- **from** a time **to** (OR **till** OR **until**) another time: My class is *from* 12:30 *to* (OR *till* OR *until*) 3:30.
- **in** a number of hours, days, weeks, months, years: She will graduate *in* three weeks. (This means "after" three weeks.)
- **for** a number of hours, days, weeks, months, years: She was in Mexico *for* three weeks. (This means during the period of three weeks.)
- **by** a time: Please finish your test *by* six o'clock. (This means "no later than" six o'clock.)
- **until** a time: I lived with my parents *until* I came to the U.S. (This means "all the time before.")
- **during** the movie, class, meeting: He slept *during* the meeting.
- **about/around** six o'clock: The movie will begin *about* six o'clock. People will arrive *around* 5:45.
- **in** the past/future: *In* the past, she never exercised.
- **at** present: *At* present, the days are getting longer.
- **in** the beginning/end: *In* the beginning, she didn't understand the teacher at all.
- **at** the beginning/end of something: The semester begins *at* the beginning of September. My birthday is *at* the end of June.
- **before/after** a time: You should finish the job *before* Friday. The library will be closed *after* six o'clock.
- **before/after** an action takes place: Turn off the lights *before* you leave. Wash the dishes *after* you finish dinner.

Verbs and Adjectives Followed by a Preposition

Many verbs and adjectives are followed by a preposition.

accuse someone of	(be) familiar with	(be) prepared for/to
(be) accustomed to	(be) famous for	prevent (someone) from
adjust to	feel like	prohibit (someone) from
(be) afraid of	(be) fond of	protect (someone) from
agree with	forget about	(be) proud of
(be) amazed at/by	forgive someone for	recover from
(be) angry about	(be) glad about	(be) related to
(be) angry at/with	(be) good at	rely on/upon
apologize for	(be) grateful to someone for	(be) responsible for
approve of	(be) guilty of	(be) sad about
argue about	(be) happy about	(be) satisfied with
argue with	hear about	(be) scared of
(be) ashamed of	hear of	(be) sick of
(be) aware of	hope for	(be) sorry about
believe in	(be) incapable of	(be) sorry for
blame someone for	insist on/upon	speak about
(be) bored with/by	(be) interested in	speak to/with
(be) capable of	(be) involved in	succeed in
care about	(be) jealous of	(be) sure of/about
care for	(be) known for	(be) surprised at
compare to/with	(be) lazy about	take care of
complain about	listen to	talk about
(be) concerned about	look at	talk to/with
concentrate on	look for	thank (someone) for
consist of	look forward to	(be) thankful (to someone) for
count on	(be) mad about	think about/of
deal with	(be) mad at	(be) tired of
decide on	(be) made from/of	(be) upset about
depend on/upon	(be) married to	(be) upset with
(be) different from	object to	(be) used to
disapprove of	(be) opposed to	wait for
(be) divorced from	participate in	warn (someone) about
dream about/of	plan on	(be) worried about
(be) engaged to	pray to	worry about
(be) excited about	pray for	

Appendix I

Direct and Indirect Objects

The order of direct and indirect objects depends on the verb you use. It also can depend on whether you use a noun or a pronoun as the object.

Group 1 Pronouns affect word order. The preposition used is *to*.

Patterns: He gave a present to his wife. (DO to IO)
He gave his wife a present. (IO/DO)
He gave it to his wife. (DO to IO)
He gave her a present. (IO/DO)
He gave it to her. (DO to IO)

Verbs:
bring	lend	pass	sell	show	teach
give	offer	pay	send	sing	tell
hand	owe	read	serve	take	write

Group 2 Pronouns affect word order. The preposition used is *for*.

Patterns: He bought a car for his daughter. (DO for IO)
He bought his daughter a car. (IO/DO)
He bought it for his daughter. (DO for IO)
He bought her a car. (IO/DO)
He bought it for her. (DO for IO)

Verbs:
bake	buy	draw	get	make
build	do	find	knit	reserve

Group 3 Pronouns don't affect word order. The preposition used is *to*.

Patterns: He explained the problem to his friend. (DO to IO)
He explained it to her. (DO to IO)

Verbs:
admit	introduce	recommend	say
announce	mention	repeat	speak
describe	prove	report	suggest
explain			

Group 4 Pronouns don't affect word order. The preposition used is *for*.

Patterns: He cashed a check for his friend. (DO for IO)
He cashed it for her. (DO for IO)

Verbs:
answer	change	design	open	prescribe
cash	close	fix	prepare	pronounce

Group 5 Pronouns don't affect word order. No preposition is used.

Patterns: She asked the teacher a question. (IO/DO)
She asked him a question. (IO/DO)

Verbs:
ask	charge	cost	wish	take (with time)

Capitalization Rules

- The first word in a sentence: My friends are helpful.

- The word "I": My sister and I took a trip together.

- Names of people: Julia Roberts; George Washington

- Titles preceding names of people: Doctor (Dr.) Smith; President Lincoln; Queen Elizabeth; Mr. Rogers; Mrs. Carter

- Geographic names: the United States; Lake Superior; California; the Rocky Mountains; the Mississippi River

  NOTE: The word "the" in a geographic name is not capitalized.

- Street names: Pennsylvania Avenue (Ave.); Wall Street (St.); Abbey Road (Rd.)

- Names of organizations, companies, colleges, buildings, stores, hotels: the Republican Party; Heinle Cengage; Dartmouth College; the University of Wisconsin; the White House; Bloomingdale's; the Hilton Hotel

- Nationalities and ethnic groups: Mexicans; Canadians; Spaniards; Americans; Jews; Kurds; Eskimos

- Languages: English; Spanish; Polish; Vietnamese; Russian

- Months: January; February

- Days: Sunday; Monday

- Holidays: Christmas; Independence Day

- Important words in a title: *Grammar in Context*; *The Old Man and the Sea*; *Romeo and Juliet*; *The Sound of Music*

  NOTE: Capitalize "the" as the first word of a title.

Glossary of Grammatical Terms

- **Adjective** An adjective gives a description of a noun.

  It's a *tall* tree.   He's an *old* man.   My neighbors are *nice*.

- **Adverb** An adverb describes the action of a sentence or an adjective or another adverb.

  She speaks English *fluently*.   I drive *carefully*.
  She speaks English *extremely* well.   She is *very* intelligent.

- **Adverb of Frequency** An adverb of frequency tells how often the action happens.

  I *never* drink coffee.   They *usually* take the bus.

- **Affirmative** means *yes*.

- **Apostrophe '** We use the apostrophe for possession and contractions.

  My *sister's* friend is beautiful.   Today *isn't* Sunday.

- **Article** The definite article is *the*. The indefinite articles are *a* and *an*.

  I have *a* cat.   I ate *an* apple.   *The* teacher came late.

- **Auxiliary Verb** Some verbs have two parts: an auxiliary verb and a main verb.

  He *can't* study.   We *will* return.

- **Base Form** The base form, sometimes called the "simple" form, of the verb has no tense. It has no ending (*-s* or *-ed*): *be, go, eat, take, write*.

  I didn't *go* out.   We don't *know* you.   He can't *drive*.

- **Capital Letter** A B C D E F G . . .

- **Clause** A clause is a group of words that has a subject and a verb. Some sentences have only one clause.

  She speaks Spanish.

  Some sentences have **a main clause** and a **dependent clause**.

MAIN CLAUSE	DEPENDENT CLAUSE **(reason clause)**
She found a good job	because she has computer skills.

MAIN CLAUSE	DEPENDENT CLAUSE **(time clause)**
She'll turn off the light	before she goes to bed.

MAIN CLAUSE	DEPENDENT CLAUSE **(if clause)**
I'll take you to the doctor	if you don't have your car on Saturday.

(continued)

- **Colon** :

- **Comma** ,

- **Comparative Form** A comparative form of an adjective or adverb is used to compare two things.

  My house is *bigger* than your house.
  Her husband drives *faster* than she does.

- **Complement** The complement of the sentence is the information after the verb. It completes the verb phrase.

  He works *hard*.   I slept *for five hours*.   They are *late*.

- **Consonant** The following letters are consonants: *b, c, d, f, g, h, j, k, l, m, n, p, q, r, s, t, v, w, x, y, z.*

  NOTE: *y* is sometimes considered a vowel, as in the world *syllable*.

- **Contraction** A contraction is made up of two words put together with an apostrophe.

  He's my brother.   *You're* late.   They *won't* talk to me.
  (*He's = he is*)   (*You're = you are*)   (*won't = will not*)

- **Count Noun** Count nouns are nouns that we can count. They have a singular and a plural form.

  1 pen – 3 pens   1 table – 4 tables

- **Dependent Clause** See **Clause**.

- **Direct Object** A direct object is a noun (phrase) or pronoun that receives the action of the verb.

  We saw *the movie*.   You have *a nice car*.   I love *you*.

- **Exclamation Mark** !

- **Frequency Words** Frequency words are *always, usually, generally, often, sometimes, rarely, seldom, hardly ever, never.*

  I *never* drink coffee.   We *always* do our homework.

- **Hyphen** –

- **Imperative** An imperative sentence gives a command or instructions. An imperative sentence omits the word *you*.

  Come here.   *Don't be* late.   Please *sit* down.

- **Infinitive** An infinitive is *to* + base form.

  I want *to leave*.   You need *to be* here on time.

- **Linking Verb** A linking verb is a verb that links the subject to the noun or adjective after it. Linking verbs include *be, seem, feel, smell, sound, look, appear, taste.*

  She *is* a doctor.   She *seems* very intelligent.   She *looks* tired.

- **Modal** The modal verbs are *can*, *could*, *shall*, *should*, *will*, *would*, *may*, *might*, *must*.

    They *should* leave.   I *must* go.

- **Negative** means no.

- **Nonaction Verb** A nonaction verb has no action. We do not use a continuous tense (*be* + verb *-ing*) with a nonaction verb. The nonaction verbs are: *believe, cost, care, have, hear, know, like, love, matter, mean, need, own, prefer, remember, see, seem, think, understand, want*, and sense-perception verbs.

    She *has* a laptop.   We *love* our mother.   You *look* great.

- **Noncount Noun** A noncount noun is a noun that we don't count. It has no plural form.

    She drank some *water*.   He prepared some *rice*.
    Do you need any *money*?   We had a lot of *homework*.

- **Noun** A noun is a person (*brother*), a place (*kitchen*), or a thing (*table*). Nouns can be either count (*1 table, 2 tables*) or noncount (*money, water*).

    My *brother* lives in California.   My *sisters* live in New York.
    I get *advice* from them.   I drink *coffee* every day.

- **Noun Modifier** A noun modifier makes a noun more specific.

    fire department   *Independence* Day   *can* opener

- **Noun Phrase** A noun phrase is a group of words that form the subject or object of the sentence.

    A *very nice woman* helped me at registration.
    I bought *a big box of cereal*.

- **Object** The object of the sentence follows the verb. It receives the action of the verb.

    He bought *a car*.   I saw *a movie*.   I met *your brother*.

- **Object Pronoun** Use object pronouns (*me, you, him, her, it, us, them*) after the verb or preposition.

    He likes *her*.   I saw the movie. Let's talk about *it*.

- **Parentheses** ( )

- **Paragraph** A paragraph is a group of sentences about one topic.

- **Participle, Present** The present participle is verb + *-ing*.

    She is *sleeping*.   They were *laughing*.

- **Period** .

- **Phrase** A group of words that go together.

    Last month my sister came to visit.
    There is a strange car *in front of my house*.

(continued)

- **Plural** Plural means more than one. A plural noun usually ends with *-s*.

    She has beautiful *eyes*.   My *feet* are big.

- **Possessive Form** Possessive forms show ownership or relationship.

    Mary's coat is in the closet.   *My brother* lives in Miami.

- **Preposition** A preposition is a short connecting word: *about, above, across, after, around, as, at, away, back, before, behind, below, by, down, for, from, in, into, like, of, off, on, out, over, to, under, up, with.*

    The book is *on* the table.   She studies *with* her friends.

- **Pronoun** A pronoun takes the place of a noun.

    I have a new car. I bought *it* last week.
    John likes Mary, but *she* doesn't like *him*.

- **Punctuation** Period . Comma , Colon : Semicolon ; Question Mark ? Exclamation Mark !

- **Question Mark** ?

- **Quotation Marks** " "

- **Regular Verb** A regular verb forms its past tense with *-ed*.

    He *worked* yesterday.   I *laughed* at the joke.

- **-s Form** A present tense verb that ends in *-s* or *-es*.

    He *lives* in New York.   She *watches* TV a lot.

- **Sense-Perception Verb** A sense-perception verb has no action. It describes a sense. The sense perception verbs are: *look, feel, taste, sound, smell.*

    She *feels* fine.   The coffee *smells* fresh.   The milk *tastes* sour.

- **Sentence** A sentence is a group of words that contains a subject[1] and a verb (at least) and gives a complete thought.

    SENTENCE: She came home.
    NOT A SENTENCE: When she came home

- **Simple Form of Verb** The simple form of the verb, also called the base form, has no tense; it never has an *-s*, *-ed*, or *-ing* ending.

    Did you *see* the movie?   I couldn't *find* your phone number.

- **Singular** Singular means one.

    She ate a *sandwich*.   I have one *television*.

- **Subject** The subject of the sentence tells who or what the sentence is about.

    My *sister* got married last April. *The wedding* was beautiful.

---

[1]In an imperative sentence, the subject *you* is omitted: *Sit down. Come here.*

- **Subject Pronouns** Use subject pronouns (*I, you, he, she, it, we, you, they*) before a verb.

  They speak Japanese.　　*We* speak Spanish.

- **Superlative Form** A superlative form of an adjective or adverb shows the number one item in a group of three or more.

  January is the *coldest* month of the year.
  My brother speaks English the *best* in my family.

- **Syllable** A syllable is a part of a word that has only one vowel sound. (Some words have only one syllable.)

  change (one syllable)　　after (af·ter = two syllables)
  look (one syllable)　　responsible (re·spon·si·ble = four syllables)

- **Tag Question** A tag question is a short question at the end of a sentence. It is used in conversation.

  You speak Spanish, *don't you?*　　He's not happy, *is he?*

- **Tense** A verb has tense. Tense shows when the action of the sentence happened.

  SIMPLE PRESENT: She usually *works* hard.
  FUTURE: She *will work* tomorrow.
  PRESENT CONTINUOUS: She *is working* now.
  SIMPLE PAST: She *worked* yesterday.

- **Verb** A verb is the action of the sentence.

  He *runs* fast.　　I *speak* English.

  Some verbs have no action. They are linking verbs. They connect the subject to the rest of the sentence.

  He *is* tall.　　She *looks* beautiful.　　You *seem* tired.

- **Vowel** The following letters are vowels: *a, e, i, o, u.* Y is sometimes considered a vowel (for example, in the word *mystery*).

Appendix L

Special Uses of Articles

No Article	Article

Personal names:
    John Kennedy
    Michael Jordan
	The whole family:
	    the Kennedys
	    the Jordans

Title and name:
    Queen Elizabeth
    Pope Benedict
	Title without name:
	    the Queen
	    the Pope

Cities, states, countries, continents:
    Cleveland
    Ohio
    Mexico
    South America
	Places that are considered a union:
	    the United States
	    the former Soviet Union
	    the United Kingdom
	Place names: the _____ of _____
	    the Republic of China
	    the District of Columbia

Mountains:
    Mount Everest
    Mount McKinley
	Mountain ranges:
	    the Himalayas
	    the Rocky Mountains

Islands:
    Coney Island
    Staten Island
	Collectives of islands:
	    the Hawaiian Islands
	    the Virgin Islands
	    the Philippines

Lakes:
    Lake Superior
    Lake Michigan
	Collectives of lakes:
	    the Great Lakes
	    the Finger Lakes

Beaches:
    Palm Beach
    Pebble Beach
	Rivers, oceans, seas, canals:
	    the Mississippi River
	    the Atlantic Ocean
	    the Dead Sea
	    the Panama Canal

Streets and avenues:
    Madison Avenue
    Wall Street
	Well-known buildings:
	    the Willis Tower
	    the Empire State Building

Parks:
    Central Park
    Hyde Park
	Zoos:
	    the San Diego Zoo
	    the Milwaukee Zoo

No Article	Article

Seasons:
    summer   fall
    spring   winter
    Summer is my favorite season.
NOTE: After a preposition, *the* may be used.
    In (the) winter, my car runs badly.
	Deserts:
	    the Mojave Desert
	    the Sahara Desert

Directions:
    north   south
    east   west
	Sections of a piece of land:
	    the Southwest (of the U.S.)
	    the West Side (of New York)

School subjects:
    history
    math
	Unique geographical points:
	    the North Pole
	    the Vatican

Name + *college* or *university*:
    Northwestern University
    Bradford College
	The University/College of _____:
	    the University of Michigan
	    the College of DuPage County

Magazines:
    Time
    Sports Illustrated
	Newspapers:
	    the *Tribune*
	    the *Wall Street Journal*

Months and days:
    September
    Monday
	Ships:
	    the *Titanic*
	    the *Queen Elizabeth*

Holidays and dates
    Thanksgiving
    Mother's Day
    July 4 (month + day)
	The day of the month:
	    the Fourth of July
	    the fifth of May

Diseases:
    cancer   AIDS
    polio   malaria
	Ailments:
	    a cold a toothache
	    a headache the flu

Games and sports:
    poker
    soccer
	Musical instruments, after *play*:
	    the drums
	    the piano
	NOTE: Sometimes *the* is omitted.
	    She plays (the) drums.

Languages:
    French
    English
	The _____ language:
	    the French language
	    the English language

Last month, year, week, etc. = the one before this one:
    I forgot to pay my rent last month.
    The teacher gave us a test last week.
	The last month, the last year, the last week, etc. = the last in a series:
	    December is the last month of the year.
	    Summer vacation begins the last week in May.

(continued)

No Article	Article
In office = in an elected position: The president is in office for four years.	In the office = in a specific room: The teacher is in the office.
In back/front: She's in back of the car.	In the back/the front: He's in the back of the bus.

Appendix M

Alphabetical List of Irregular Verb Forms

Base Form	Past Form	Past Participle	Base Form	Past Form	Past Participle
be	was/were	been	drink	drank	drunk
bear	bore	born/borne	drive	drove	driven
beat	beat	beaten	eat	ate	eaten
become	became	become	fall	fell	fallen
begin	began	begun	feed	fed	fed
bend	bent	bent	feel	felt	felt
bet	bet	bet	fight	fought	fought
bid	bid	bid	find	found	found
bind	bound	bound	fit	fit	fit
bite	bit	bitten	flee	fled	fled
bleed	bled	bled	fly	flew	flown
blow	blew	blown	forbid	forbade	forbidden
break	broke	broken	forget	forgot	forgotten
breed	bred	bred	forgive	forgave	forgiven
bring	brought	brought	freeze	froze	frozen
broadcast	broadcast	broadcast	get	got	gotten
build	built	built	give	gave	given
burst	burst	burst	go	went	gone
buy	bought	bought	grind	ground	ground
cast	cast	cast	grow	grew	grown
catch	caught	caught	hang	hung	hung[2]
choose	chose	chosen	have	had	had
cling	clung	clung	hear	heard	heard
come	came	come	hide	hid	hidden
cost	cost	cost	hit	hit	hit
creep	crept	crept	hold	held	held
cut	cut	cut	hurt	hurt	hurt
deal	dealt	dealt	keep	kept	kept
dig	dug	dug	know	knew	known
dive	dove/dived	dove/dived	lay	laid	laid
do	did	done	lead	led	led
draw	drew	drawn	leave	left	left

[2]*Hanged* is used as the past form to refer to punishment by death. *Hung* is used in other situations: She *hung* the picture on the wall.

Base Form	Past Form	Past Participle	Base Form	Past Form	Past Participle
lend	lent	lent	spit	spit/spat	spit/spat
let	let	let	split	split	split
lie[1]	lay	lain	spread	spread	spread
light	lit/lighted	lit/lighted	spring	sprang/sprung	sprung
lose	lost	lost	stand	stood	stood
make	made	made	steal	stole	stolen
mean	meant	meant	stick	stuck	stuck
meet	met	met	sting	stung	stung
mistake	mistook	mistaken	stink	stank/stunk	stunk
overcome	overcame	overcome	strike	struck	struck/stricken
overdo	overdid	overdone	strive	strove/strived	striven
overtake	overtook	overtaken	swear	swore	sworn
overthrow	overthrew	overthrown	sweep	swept	swept
pay	paid	paid	swell	swelled	swelled/swollen
plead	pled/pleaded	pled/pleaded	swim	swam	swum
prove	proved	proven/proved	swing	swung	swung
put	put	put	take	took	taken
quit	quit	quit	teach	taught	taught
read	read	read	tear	tore	torn
ride	rode	ridden	tell	told	told
ring	rang	rung	think	thought	thought
rise	rose	risen	throw	threw	thrown
run	ran	run	understand	understood	understood
say	said	said	uphold	upheld	upheld
see	saw	seen	upset	upset	upset
seek	sought	sought	wake	woke	woken
sell	sold	sold	wear	wore	worn
send	sent	sent	weave	wove	woven
set	set	set	wed	wedded/wed	wedded/wed
sew	sewed	sewed/sewn	weep	wept	wept
shake	shook	shaken	win	won	won
shed	shed	shed	wind	wound	wound
shine	shone/shined	shone/shined	withhold	withheld	withheld
shoot	shot	shot	withdraw	withdrew	withdrawn
show	showed	shown/showed	withstand	withstood	withstood
shrink	shrank/shrunk	shrunk/shrunken	wring	wrung	wrung
shut	shut	shut	write	wrote	written
sing	sang	sung			
sink	sank	sunk			
sit	sat	sat			
sleep	slept	slept			
slide	slid	slid			
slit	slit	slit			
speak	spoke	spoken			
speed	sped	sped			
spend	spent	spent			
spin	spun	spun			

Note: The past and past participle of some verbs can end in -ed or -t.

burn	burned or burnt
dream	dreamed or dreamt
kneel	kneeled or knelt
learn	learned or learnt
leap	leaped or leapt
spill	spilled or spilt
spoil	spoiled or spoilt

[1]When *lie* means to place, the forms are *lie, lay, lain*. When *lie* means to speak an untruth, the forms are *lie, lied, lied*.

Map of the United States of America

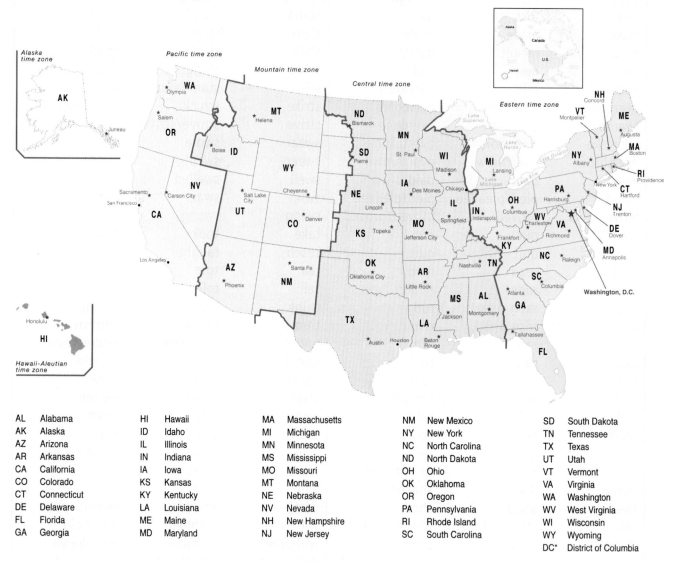

AL	Alabama	HI	Hawaii	MA	Massachusetts	NM	New Mexico	SD	South Dakota
AK	Alaska	ID	Idaho	MI	Michigan	NY	New York	TN	Tennessee
AZ	Arizona	IL	Illinois	MN	Minnesota	NC	North Carolina	TX	Texas
AR	Arkansas	IN	Indiana	MS	Mississippi	ND	North Dakota	UT	Utah
CA	California	IA	Iowa	MO	Missouri	OH	Ohio	VT	Vermont
CO	Colorado	KS	Kansas	MT	Montana	OK	Oklahoma	VA	Virginia
CT	Connecticut	KY	Kentucky	NE	Nebraska	OR	Oregon	WA	Washington
DE	Delaware	LA	Louisiana	NV	Nevada	PA	Pennsylvania	WV	West Virginia
FL	Florida	ME	Maine	NH	New Hampshire	RI	Rhode Island	WI	Wisconsin
GA	Georgia	MD	Maryland	NJ	New Jersey	SC	South Carolina	WY	Wyoming
								DC*	District of Columbia

*The District of Columbia is not a state. Washington, D.C., is the capital of the United States.
Note: Washington, D.C., and Washington state are not the same.

Index

Photo Credits